SEGREGATION IN THE NEW SOUTH

SEGREGATION
in the NEW SOUTH

Birmingham, Alabama, 1871–1901

CARL V. HARRIS

Completed and Edited by W. ELLIOT BROWNLEE

LOUISIANA STATE UNIVERSITY PRESS

BATON ROUGE

Published by Louisiana State University Press
lsupress.org

DESIGNER: Barbara Neely Bourgoyne
TYPEFACE: Fournier MT Pro

COVER PHOTOGRAPH:
Mardi Gras spectators in downtown Birmingham, ca. 1897.
Courtesy of Birmingham, Ala. Public Library Archives.

The maps and figure were created by Mary Lee Eggart.

LIBRARY OF CONGRESS CATALOGING-IN-PUBLICATION DATA
Names: Harris, Carl V., author. | Brownlee, W. Elliot, 1941– author, editor.
Title: Segregation in the new South : Birmingham, Alabama, 1871–1901 / Carl V.
  Harris ; completed and edited by W. Elliot Brownlee.
Description: Baton Rouge : Louisiana State University Press, [2022] | Includes
  bibliographical references and index.
Identifiers: LCCN 2022014264 (print) | LCCN 2022014265 (ebook) | ISBN
  978-0-8071-7837-9 (cloth) | ISBN 978-0-8071-7890-4 (pdf) | ISBN
  978-0-8071-7889-8 (epub)
Subjects: LCSH: African Americans—Segregation—Alabama—Birmingham—
  History—19th century. | African Americans—Alabama—Birmingham—Social
  conditions—19th century. | Birmingham (Ala.)—Race relations—History—
  19th century.
Classification: LCC E185.61 .H254 2022 (print) | LCC E185.61 (ebook) |
  DDC 305.896/0730761781—dc23/eng/20220614
LC record available at https://lccn.loc.gov/2022014264
LC ebook record available at https://lccn.loc.gov/2022014265

CONTENTS

EDITOR'S PREFACE

Carl V. Harris (1937–2018) received his PhD degree from the University of Wisconsin, Madison, in 1968 and was a professor in the Department of History at the University of California, Santa Barbara, for over forty years. His scholarly career combined in-depth research in primary sources with innovative social science methods of studying politics and political power during the late nineteenth and early twentieth centuries.

Carl's book *Political Power in Birmingham, 1871–1921*, together with an article, "Reforms in Governmental Control of Negroes in Birmingham, Alabama, 1890–1920," published in the *Journal of Southern History*, provided an intricate examination of the political economy of a city that in important ways was both similar to, and different from, other rapidly industrializing cities during the period. This work enriched the history of the postbellum South. It also contributed to US urban history because Harris questioned two leading paradigms (Floyd Hunter's "power elite" and Robert A. Dahl's "pluralist") regarding the distribution of political power in modern American cities. Carl received the Genevieve Gorst Herfurth Award for the best book published in the social sciences in 1978 by a former student at the University of Wisconsin.[1]

Carl turned next to the analysis of central economic and sectional issues of national political power in the late nineteenth century. He published an essay, "Right Fork or Left Fork? The Section-Party Alignments of Southern Democrats in Congress, 1873–1897," in the *Journal of Southern History*. This article, which drew heavily on empirical methods from political science, provided meticulous analysis of Congressional voting behavior. The article challenged the prevailing view (that of historian C. Vann Woodward) of the congressional voting strategies and outcomes associated with the return the former Confederate states to the Union. It received the Charles W. Ramsdell Award from the Southern Historical Association for the best article in the *Journal of Southern History* during 1975–76.[2]

In later essays Carl returned to the urban South, and to Birmingham. In this scholarship he focused on the intersection of issues of race and class, particularly as they played out in education and the political initiatives of African Americans. An article from this research, "Stability and Change in Discrimination against Black Public Schools: Birmingham, Alabama, 1871– 1931," appeared in the *Journal of Southern History*.[3] Subsequently, he deepened his investigation of segregation through further research in the Birmingham archives and immersion in the analysis of racial prejudice by social psychologists as well as historians. For many years he worked on a major manuscript on segregation in the New South in the late nineteenth century, using the Birmingham experience as a case study. Extended illnesses prevented him from completing the book you hold in your hands.

After Carl's death, his children, David and Susan Harris, invited me to complete and edit his book manuscript for publication. I found that Carl had drafted versions of all the chapters that appear in this book. He had also outlined its general organization and accumulated copious notes in which he discussed his evidence, interpretations, and plans for completion. Moreover, over the years he and I had extensive conversations regarding the book. I decided that I would have clear guidance in completing and editing it. I accepted the invitation.

I know that Carl would want to thank the individuals who read and commented on the manuscript during its development. Those I am able to identify include Paul Barba, Jay Carlander, Sarah Case, Patricia Cohen, Charles Corman, Douglas Daniels, Douglas Dodd, Erin Edmonds, George Fredrickson, Laura Kalman, Robert Kelley, Robert Kenzer, Morgan Kousser, John Majewski, Henry McKiven, Alicia Rodriquez, and J. Mills Thornton. Other people, including former students and scholars cited in the notes, also influenced Carl's thinking about the history of social segregation, but I will not try to list them here for fear of inadvertent omissions. David Harris and Susan Harris read the revised drafts and provided superb editorial advice and technical assistance, just as they had to their father. They helped him design the maps for the book, and Mary Lee Eggart, a cartographic designer, expertly created the final versions.

Carl received major institutional support for this project. Noteworthy was the funding by the University of California, Santa Barbara, Division of the Academic Senate for trips to Birmingham; by the National Endowment of the Humanities for a fellowship year; and by the University of California for sabbaticals. Vital as well was the assistance of librarians and other specialists at the UC Santa Barbara Library, the University of Alabama Library, the Birmingham Public Library, the Alabama Department of Archives and History, and various agencies of the City of Birmingham and Jefferson County, Alabama, particularly the Tax Assessor's Office.

Carl would be grateful, as I am, to Rand Dotson, editor-in-chief of Louisiana State University Press, for his support and editorial professionalism. I am glad that I accepted the invitation David Harris and Susan Harris offered and had the opportunity to continue the intellectual relationship that Carl and I began in Richard Current's seminar at the University of Wisconsin.

W. ELLIOT BROWNLEE
Santa Barbara, California

SEGREGATION IN THE NEW SOUTH

THE SOCIAL HISTORY OF
JIM CROW

In 1903 the sociologist and historian W. E. B. Du Bois began his book *The Souls of Black Folk* by declaring: "Herein lie buried many things which if read with patience may show the strange meaning of being Black here in the dawning of the Twentieth Century. This meaning is not without interest to you, Gentle Reader; for the problem of the Twentieth Century is the problem of the color line." That line had been drawn by slavery and then by Jim Crow, the system of segregation and degradation of African Americans that replaced slavery in the American South. It spread throughout most of the nation during the twentieth century, as Du Bois predicted. He also foresaw no resolution for "several generations." If thirty years constitute a generation, nearly four generations have passed since Du Bois made his prediction.[1]

Segregation in the New South: Birmingham, Alabama, 1871–1901 joins the many books written by historians working to understand the origins of the Jim Crow color line and system, the intellectual and institutional forms and emotional components of Jim Crow, and the possibilities for eradication of its legacies. It asks questions such as how and why white Americans created this system of racism, what the effects of it were on both white and Black Americans, how African Americans resisted its imposition, and how and why the system survived into the twenty-first century. The premise of this book is that a deep historical understanding of Jim Crow is required for American society to address the persistent legacy of slavery in the twenty-first century.

Like many other historical studies of Jim Crow, *Segregation in the New South* focuses on the history of a specific community. This focus can be a productive way to acquire an in-depth and fine-grained understanding of how Jim Crow originated and operated as a system of social control. Birmingham, Alabama, was chosen for this study in part because it was one of the most urban and industrial settings in the South after the Civil War. The historian C. Vann Woodward influenced the choice by calling out, in 1988, the potential significance of cities like Birmingham. He speculated that segregation did not appear first in the eastern seaboard cities of the Old South, where many "white and black families" had "known each other for generations." The cities that "took the lead" in constructing Jim Crow, and thus the cities where study could reveal most about its origins, he said, were the "interior cities of the newer South" in which "large numbers of whites and blacks were newcomers and where long experience of racial cohabitation was lacking."[2]

Birmingham was just such a city. It sprang to life in 1871 at a spot where two new railroad lines had intersected near the vast deposits of coal and iron ore in the hill country of northern Alabama. African American workers and whites of all classes, most of them initially strangers to each other, all of them newcomers, migrated to the booming industrial town dubbed the "Magic City," all hoping for a better life.[3]

In Birmingham during the 1870s, African Americans were eager to exploit the disarray of slavery's old racial lines, to assert their autonomy, and to advance toward full equality. But most southern whites, elite and non-elite alike, hoped to restore the restrictive racial lines of the slave South or to invent new ones that would guarantee the subordination of African Americans. From its founding, color lines divided Birmingham, and as people strove to erase or to fortify those lines, they shaped their futures in fateful ways.

Segregation in the New South narrates the Birmingham story of the origins of Jim Crow in a way that attempts to open avenues to a deeper and broader understanding of the history of Jim Crow throughout the South and the nation as a whole. This book does so by developing an interpretation of the early history of Jim Crow that places social segregation at the center of the story. From the beginning of Reconstruction, southern whites engaged in a comprehensive program of assigning social dishonor to African Americans—the same kind of dishonor that whites of the Old South had imposed on African American people while enslaving them. The interpretation emphasizes the importance, even in early Reconstruction, of the white doctrine that African Americans were inherently inferior, had inherited the low social status of slaves, and had to be rigorously excluded from social fellowship and social institutions.

To move toward a comprehensive social history of Jim Crow, this study draws on an extensive body of theoretical and empirical research in social psychology undertaken by scholars in a variety of disciplines but very rarely utilized by historians. A key approach in this research is the study of the creation of "boundaries" that demarcate an "in-group" from an "out-group," and thus of how categories called races or ethnic groups are "socially constructed." This approach sees insiders and outsiders defining and constructing groups by generating "interaction boundaries" between them. Such boundaries consist of criteria and expectations—or "protocols"—of proper behavior which govern and organize everyday interactions with people in "other" groups. These expectations include stereotypes—images or judgmental sets of beliefs about the personal attributes, the personality traits, and the typical behaviors of members of both the out-group and the in-group.

Segregation in the New South supplements this kind of boundary analysis with the insights developed during the American civil rights movement by sociologist Herbert Blumer. He argued that the southern color line should not be conceived as a single line. Instead, he described it as a set of lines, and referred to it metaphorically as "a series of ramparts, like the 'Maginot Line,' extending from outer breastworks to inner bastions." The smallest inner bastion was one of social exclusion. It was surrounded by a slightly larger bastion, one of economic disadvantage. A larger bastion was on the outside—the "outer" color line of political discrimination. Within this series of concentric bastions, said Blumer, "Outer portions . . . may . . . be given up only to hold steadfast to inner citadels."

In Blumer's model, whites defended the inner social color line more fiercely than the two outer color lines. Their defense of the "inner citadel," which constituted the social core of segregation, was motivated by an intense emotional "feeling that the Negro is alien and different." Accordingly, within the "inner citadel" whites rigorously excluded Blacks from fellowship with whites in any familial or close social setting, especially courtship and marriage. The intermediate economic color line restricted Black economic opportunity and enforced economic subordination. The outer political color line denied Blacks basic civic and political rights and segregated them in public accommodations.

3

Blumer sorted the prejudices responsible for the three color lines into two fundamental categories or components. One was "instrumental." It operated on the outer political and the intermediate economic color lines. The instrumental component drew upon white motivations to achieve material and political power or advantage, and it involved rules, actions, and discriminations that subordinated Blacks. The second component of prejudice was emotional and often moralistic in tone, operating on the inner color line to enforce the social exclusion of Blacks. It featured negative stereotypes that made Blacks seem alien, and it fostered a deep sense that Blacks were inferior in personality traits, capabilities, and inner disposition. This form of prejudice, Blumer argued, arose from emotionally intense identification with the in-group and emotionally intense dishonoring of the out-group. He referred to this form of prejudice as "socio-emotional." This book takes up as a central issue the interplay between these two components of prejudice—the instrumental and the socio-emotional. This formulation provides a powerful way of delineating the changing patterns of social relations and power relations between the races in Birmingham.[4]

Segregation in the New South stresses the swiftness and rigidity with which the color line was drawn in Birmingham after the Civil War. This is by no means a novel description of the timing of Jim Crow. It was one proposed by Du Bois in *The Souls of Black Folk*. Latent conflicts, Du Bois argues, had been deeply embedded in slavery. These boiled over in the heat of war and emancipation and brought bitterness and hatred, rather than cooperation, into Black-white interaction during the precious first years of freedom—the era of Reconstruction. In a key chapter, "Of the Sons of Master and Man," Du Bois argues that from the moment of emancipation onward it had become more and more difficult to sustain viable contact and cooperation between the children of slaves and the children of masters. Since 1865 the South had suffered a relentless trajectory of racial separation, and the result was a polarization so sharp that the "best element of the whites" and elite Blacks seldom even saw each other and had "little or no intellectual commerce."[5]

In contrast, C. Vann Woodward, as first expressed in his book *The Strange Career of Jim Crow*, concluded that the New South did not immediately replace slavery with a new set of tightly constructed, and rigidly consistent, racial boundaries. Rather, between 1865 and the 1890s, "there transpired an era of experiment and variety in race relations of the South in which segregation

4

was not the invariable rule," an era in which whites and Blacks experienced instability, inconsistency, fluidity, crosscurrents, and contradictions in race relations. Woodward argued that, only after southern whites had disfranchised African Americans around 1900, were they able to construct the new system of segregation, one that extended into the social and economic spheres of life. Thus, he placed political discrimination and disfranchisement at the center of the story of the creation of the full Jim Crow system, and placed less emphasis on the socio-emotional component of Jim Crow than does the present study.[6]

My strategy is to extend the path that Du Bois pioneered by posing two central and interrelated hypotheses. The first is that the socio-emotional sources of racism, rather than transactional or instrumental factors, were the most powerful in shaping segregation in the cities of the New South. The second is that, while the timing of segregation might vary across New South cities because of differences in transactional or instrumental factors associated with the variations in economic structure and political institutions, socio-emotional factors produced a sharp drawing of Jim Crow lines very early in the postbellum era in Birmingham, and quite likely elsewhere.

There is relatively little historical literature that examines the role the psychological functions of Jim Crow and the related social construction of racism. An important example of such scholarship is that of Grace Elizabeth Hale, whose broad study of segregation stresses the socio-emotional component of prejudice. But she does not pay close attention to the interplay between the socio-emotional and instrumental components of racial prejudice, especially in the late-nineteenth century.[7] The presumption of *Segregation in the New South* is that the interactions between the two factors are probably best studied first intensively within particular locations and then comparatively across the cities of the New South. Rigorous comparisons of the timing and severity of segregation across New South cities might well reveal strong similarities between Birmingham and other rapidly industrializing cities of the New South. For example, the development of racial lines in Birmingham and industrializing Durham, North Carolina, which historian Leslie Brown studied, might be usefully compared.[8] Historian Glenda Elizabeth Gilmore found that in North Carolina after 1896 the efforts of African Americans to achieve equality significantly shaped the hardening of Jim Crow. It might be fruitful to extend a comparison between Birmingham and North Carolina cities into the twentieth century, beyond the scope of this study.[9] This book concludes that the same was the case in Birmingham, although it finds that the hardening within the political sphere began earlier, during the 1880s. Comparisons that included Roanoke, Virginia, whose railroad industries drove rapid industrialization during the late nineteenth century, might also reveal similarities in both the timing of segregation and the significance of Black antidiscrimination activism. Historian Rand Dotson suggests that Roanoke and Birmingham had a similar "employment paradigm."[10]

Comparisons across the landscape of southern cities must include and take account of Howard Rabinowitz's 1978 book, *Race Relations in the Urban South, 1865–1890*.[11] His book led C. Vann Woodward to recognize the urban setting of Jim Crow, and influenced John W. Cell, a historian who emphasized urban origins in a comparative history of segregation in South Africa and the American South.[12] Rabinowitz's book remains the most ambitious comparative study of the urban origins of Jim Crow. He regarded the five cities he studied—Atlanta, Montgomery, Nashville, Raleigh, and Richmond—as representing a "cross section of Southern urban experience," and some of the five experienced significant industrial growth. In these cities he found segregation well established by 1890, as does this book in Birmingham, and he too suggested that Black activism during the 1880s "prompted the final step in the longstanding effort of whites to control the region's black population."[13]

In contrast to Rabinowitz's study, *Segregation in the New South* pushes the exploration of segregation into its "inner citadel," or "social core," probes the motivations of southern whites who devised Jim Crow, identifies and assesses the relative importance of transactional versus socio-emotional factors in the origins of Jim Crow, and discusses the reasons for the prolonged survival of Jim Crow. It is my hope that, by undertaking this kind of analysis, *Segregation in the New South* will create a foundation for future comparative analysis.

The following chapters trace racial interactions across the social, economic, and political realms of life in Birmingham from its founding in 1871 through the next three decades. The book concludes with the formal disfranchisement adopted by the state of Alabama in 1901. The first three chapters describe and analyze how whites in Birmingham adapted to postwar emancipation and Reconstruction by justifying the continuing subordination of the formerly enslaved men and women. The southern whites of Birmingham developed an elaborate set of criteria, rules, and images to sustain strict racial separation within the "inner citadel" of the social realm. The next four chapters detail the history of school segregation, residential segregation, and segregation of economic life in Birmingham over the last three decades of the nineteenth century. These chapters explore the experience of segregation as Blacks confronted the barriers that whites established. The two chapters which follow tell the story of how African American political leaders attempted, from the formation of Birmingham in 1871 to disfranchisement in 1901, to expand their influence over civic life in the city, and how Birmingham's white community reacted to Black initiatives. In the process, chapters 8 and 9 explore how social segregation affected development of the political system and the ultimate exclusion of Blacks from any role in that system in 1901. A coda places the interpretations of this book in the context of classic studies of the interplay of class, race, and caste in the New South.

The case study of Birmingham reveals the emotional intensity, persistence, and broad scope of the Jim Crow system that emerged in the wake of the Civil War. This approach helps explain the continuing power of racist ideas, practices, and policies in the United States during the twentieth and twenty-first centuries.

CHAPTER I

CITY OF OPPORTUNITIES
AND BOUNDARIES

In 1871, real estate promoters and railroad developers founded Birmingham at the site where two major new railroads intersected in the center of a northern Alabama valley. Iron ore and coal in the surrounding hills had portended propulsive industrial prosperity, and hundreds of speculators, industrialists, gamblers, engineers, shysters, shopkeepers, and laborers had swarmed into town. They had stomped around in muddy streets, buying, selling, renting, hiring, laboring, building, scheming, and concocting visions of industrial preeminence.

For more than two whirlwind years the new town boomed. But in 1873 a cholera epidemic and a national economic downturn hit Birmingham hard, and six years of dreary depression followed. In 1879 boom times returned when the Pratt Coal and Coke Company discovered and dug high-quality coking coal in Pratt Mines, six miles northwest of Birmingham. Straightaway industrialists built two iron furnaces, a rolling mill, and numerous major ironwork shops. By 1883 Birmingham was a sight to behold. Nearly eleven thousand people, 60 percent white and 40 percent Black, lived and worked in four square miles that twelve years earlier had been open farmland.

Birmingham had become the fastest-growing industrial center in the South. For that reason, in 1883 US Senator Henry W. Blair, chair of the Committee on Education and Labor, selected it as one of five southern locales for the committee's hearings on the relations between labor and capital.[1]

SOCIAL SEPARATION:
HENRY W. BLAIR V. ISAIAH H. WELCH

Senator Blair's committee had a broad mandate that included proposing "legislation calculated to promote harmonious relations between capitalists and laborers, and the interests of both, by the improvement of the conditions of the industrial classes of the United States."[2] In the committee's investigations in the South, Blair, a Republican from New Hampshire, was most interested in three intertwined topics: the social condition of Black citizens, the condition of public education, and the need for greater federal participation in the funding of education.

One central issue regarding federal involvement in southern education had already been resolved to the satisfaction of the Congress. During Reconstruction, Massachusetts Republican Senator Charles Sumner had proposed including in the Civil Rights Bill of 1875 a clause prohibiting racial segregation of schools. Southern white Democrats, who had been requiring and implementing school segregation since emancipation, opposed Sumner's mixed-school clause. Republican congressmen had never rallied to it, and excluded it from the Civil Rights Act of 1875, leaving the matter to the states. Subsequently during the late nineteenth century all southern states, with the exception of Louisiana during Reconstruction, segregated public schools by race.[3]

Henry Blair had not been in Congress when the Civil Rights Act passed and was not interested in rehashing the issues of 1875. However, Blair did want the federal government to help strengthen Black education in the South. To that end, in 1883 he was sponsoring a federal education bill that would annually allocate large sums of federal aid to schools. Under his legislation, the funds would be divided among states in proportion to illiteracy, so that three-fourths of the money would go to southern states. The bill would allow states to continue to segregate schools by race, but it would require the states to divide both federal money and matching state money equally between Black and white children.[4]

When organizing the hearings in Birmingham, Blair relied on Birmingham Congressman Goldsmith W. Hewitt, a Democrat, and Alabama Senator James L. Pugh, also a Democrat, who was a member of the Senate Committee on Education and Labor. Hewitt was in charge of lining up witnesses and had given Black community leaders the "unpleasant impression" that they could not get on his list. However, a clergyman, Isaiah H. Welch, appealed to Blair directly, and he agreed to include Welch, and eight other Blacks, on the list of witnesses. The Black witnesses knew all about the Blair bill, and they come to the hearings primed to endorse it.

Immediately after Birmingham's Democratic mayor, Alexander O. Lane, completed his testimony, Blair called on Isaiah Welch. The two men, Lane and Welch, faced each other in the main courtroom of the Birmingham courthouse. Both were Union Army veterans, both scarred from Civil War wounds. Blair began by questioning Welch about churches in Birmingham. After Welch testified that whites and Blacks were organized in distinct churches, Blair responded with the assertive query: "The tendency of both races is to organize separately where they exist in sufficient numbers, is it not?"[5]

The question put Welch in a bind. Blair was clearly urging the pastor, as the leading spokesman for the entire Birmingham Black community, to affirm before the assembled white politicians and Black leaders that African Americans, just like whites, tended toward racial separation and actually preferred it, particularly in social institutions like churches. Welch had been in many tight spots in his life, and he was famous for his coolness, dignity, and eloquence under pressure. But in response to the senator's discomforting question he managed only a flat "Yes, sir."

The laconic affirmation did not satisfy Blair. He persisted. "Is it not generally the preference of both races to do that"—to organize separately? Welch was determined to avoid direct endorsement of the implication that it was the "preference" of Blacks to be separate in social institutions. He tried to slip by with a noncommittal: "It appears to be so." Blair wanted a clearer Black endorsement: "You find it so on the part of the colored people, do you not?" Welch tried to dodge, slipping into the passive voice: "Yes sir; there is a strong tendency to be separate." Blair explicitly expanded the scope of separation, leading the witness: "In school and in church and in social gatherings?" Again Welch responded with a terse "Yes, sir."

The pastor could not have been comfortable with the shift in the conversation from separation in churches, which were private institutions, to separation in schools, which were government institutions presumably subject to political principles of equality. Nor could he have been entirely happy with the senator's obvious presumption that "yes" was the correct answer. During the early 1870s, when Congress had debated whether to require racial integration of public schools, Welch had given a speech at a Black political convention that helped persuade the convention to endorse Sumner's proposed prohibition of racial segregation in schools.[6] Blair was now asking him to contradict a public stand he had taken during a more hopeful time, and to contradict himself in a highly public setting, in the presence of a number of Black leaders. But Welch was politically sophisticated and understood that Blair was now embracing social separation and hoping for Black agreement as he struggled to win crucial southern white support for his education bill. Welch understood that, to get the votes of southern leaders like Congressman Hewitt and Senator Pugh, Blair had to silence all fear that federal money might bring federal pressure to integrate classrooms by race.[7] Nonetheless, Welch felt cross-pressured. Hence his skillful evasions and finally his reluctant but unqualified "Yes, sirs."[8]

The flat "Yes sirs" did not satisfy Senator Blair. He pressed further: "There is a social line of demarkation [sic] distinctly drawn between the races in accordance with the wishes of both races?" he asked. Welch again responded "Yes, sir." Blair wanted even more. "That does not lead to any ill feeling between the races, I suppose, because it is a thing that each desires for itself; a separation that is meant for their mutual pleasure and their mutual good."

Pastor Welch knew very well that, if he went further by embracing Blair's formulation about "a social line of demarkation" for "mutual pleasure" and "mutual good," the white politicians would be pleased, but his Black friends would be dismayed. Blacks would regard his acceptance of Blair's mutually desired "social line of demarkation" as acquiescence to a demeaning southern white principle: the dictum that separation was good and necessary for whites because African ancestry and slave heritage had rendered African Americans inherently dishonorable and thus unworthy for close social fellowship with whites.

Welch was known to be diplomatic, but he was not willing to accept or to seem to acquiesce in the southern white doctrine that Blacks were inherently unworthy. Many events in his life had affirmed his commitment to equality and excellence. Born a free Black in eastern Maryland in 1845, he had worked several years in the free state of Pennsylvania. In 1861 he had enrolled in Wilberforce University in Ohio, an African American college named after the British abolitionist William Wilberforce. In 1863, the year of the Emancipation Proclamation, Welch had decided that the battle for freedom took precedence over academic pursuits, and had left Wilberforce to enlist in an African American unit in the Union Army—first in the Fifty-Fourth Massachusetts Volunteers, from which he transferred to Company C Fifty-Fifth Regiment. He had gone into battle in South Carolina, been wounded, and then reassigned to the Freedman's Bureau to write and supervise contracts between freedmen and planters. In 1870, after he returned to Wilberforce, he had become valedictorian in the university's first graduating theology class, earning a doctor of divinity degree.[9]

The African Methodist Episcopal Church immediately ordained Doctor Welch and assigned him to major pastorates in large churches, first in Mobile, Alabama, and then in Selma, Alabama. In those early years Welch attained a reputation for eloquence, and in 1874 the Conservative Democratic Montgomery *Advertiser* identified him as one of "the most cultivated" of his race and one of the "grand orators" at the Alabama Black political convention that had endorsed Senator Sumner's civil rights bill and its school integration clause.[10]

Welch, when facing Senator Blair's request that he agree that strictly demarcated social separation was for the mutual good of the races, resorted to a standard formulation employed by many Black leaders who found themselves in similar situations: "Yes sir, we think it is better not to thrust ourselves upon the other race, and to avoid race-clashing as much as possible; we prefer that way both in worship and in social gatherings." The formulation explicitly but narrowly denied any intention by Blacks to force their way impolitely into private white social gatherings—a possibility that whites often viewed with alarm—but it carefully avoided any affirmation of the fundamental underlying white dictum that whites should exclude Blacks from all social fellowship because Blacks were inherently unworthy and lacking in honor.

Welch's gambit did not satisfy Blair, and he continued, raising the issue of the trend in Black opinion: "Is that feeling increasing or lessening among your people?" "Well," said Welch cautiously, affirming the direction but not the pace that Blair wanted: "I think it is increasing slowly." Blair wanted more explicit confirmation of Black endorsement of separation to maintain good will: "Along with that, is good nature preserved, or is there a tendency toward acrimony and hostility of feeling between the races?" It was clear that Blair wanted to hear about good nature, and Welch embraced it, albeit vaguely: "Good nature and good feeling seem to be cherished quite generally." Blair returned to the central issue: "And you think that is the way to preserve good feeling; to keep the races separate?" Welch retreated to "Yes sir; I think so."

Blair, perhaps deciding that he had achieved as direct an acceptance of the white principle of social separation as he was likely to get from this witness, finally offered Welch the chance he had been waiting for, asking him to state "in your own way, such things as you would like to say about your own race and the white race in this part of the country." Welch was ready, and he skillfully articulated past discouragements and present aspirations, including Black hope for passage of the Blair federal education bill.[11]

The episode was revealing. Blair's salvo of questions demonstrated that even he, an unusually sympathetic northern white Republican leader, considered it necessary to embrace the southern white contention that in the social realm, particularly within institutions that involved close interaction, it was right and proper that whites should continue to separate themselves from people of African ancestry and slave heritage. The senator was dramatizing for southern whites his view that good will and progress in race relations depended upon Black acceptance of social separation.

ARRIVAL OF A DYNAMIC NEW PASTOR

When Pastor Welch testified in the courthouse at the US Senate hearings in November of 1883, he himself was still getting acquainted with Birmingham. In the spring he and his family had moved to the city to take up the pastorate of the young but rapidly growing African Methodist Episcopal congregation. In April of 1883 they packed their belongings, said goodbye to their friends in the Black Belt city of Selma, and loaded their baggage and their four boys, ages two through nine, on the train for Montgomery. They would have changed trains in Montgomery to the Louisville & Nashville (L&N) Railroad and then traveled one hundred miles through the cotton fields of southern Alabama and into the northern Hill Country.[12]

The Welch family was part of a steady stream of Black people moving from the plantation cotton country to Birmingham.[13] The migrants approached the unknown industrial city with apprehension, but also anticipation, hoping that within it Black people would find greater opportunity and more flexible racial boundaries.

When Welch's train approached Birmingham, it would have climbed around a long hill and descended into the city from the southwest. Map 1 delineates the outlines of the city Welch entered. On the left loomed the Alice Iron Furnace, on the right the Birmingham Rolling Mill, and between them curved the entering L&N tracks. Once past the rolling mill, the L&N straightened and ran parallel beside the Alabama Great Southern Railroad, which entered the town from the west. A broad railroad reservation, lying like a wide belt across the waist of the city, accommodated the tracks, sheds, switching yards, and repair shops of the two railways and divided Birmingham into Northside and Southside. Together the iron furnace and the rolling mill formed an imposing gateway to the industrial city, but wooden cabins neighbored the mills.[14]

In 1871 a group of railroad promoters, surveyors, and developers—all white—had chosen the site of the railroad intersection and the town. Using inside information, they had formed the Elyton Land Company, quietly bought up the surrounding farmland, and laid out a street plan that configured the new town around the railroad reservation. The furnaces, foundries, warehouses, tracks, depots, and sheds offered many and varied jobs for young men with strong backs and sturdy endurance. But the vast industrial structures were owned and operated entirely by whites, and the pastor would have known that invisible boundaries excluded Blacks from any controlling position and consigned most of them to the subordinate role of unskilled industrial workers.[15]

The broad outline of residential areas was also visible from a train entering the city. On its western edge many small cabins clustered near the railroads and the smokiest industries. The central business district was on the left, already filled with impressive three- and four-story brick commercial structures. A few blocks further north, a bit removed from the smoke and noise of railroads and industries, lay the prime white residential area, filled with substantial two-story homes belonging to the town's prospering business class. Homes of white workers spread along the edges of the white residential area and also across the less-developed Southside. Also on the Southside were several Black residential clusters. To the right, on the far southern edge of town, just beyond the 1883 southern city limits, lay the "South Highlands"—the rolling foothills of Red Mountain, where developers were just beginning to lay out and build a new elite white residential area.[16]

In Union Station, Welch's impressions might have been similar to those recorded by a reporter for the Huntsville *Gazette* who had arrived in Birming-

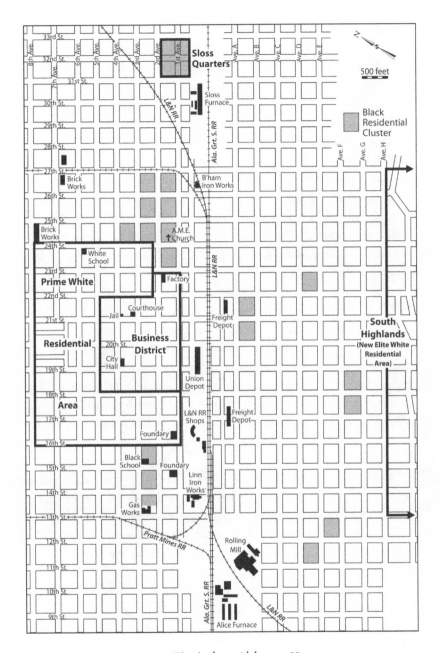

MAP 1. Birmingham, Alabama, 1883

ham a few months earlier. "I found all confusion," he had written. "Trains coming, trains leaving, whistles blowing, bells ringing, men and women pushing and hurrying to and fro." As passengers gathered their belongings and moved out of the depot, they saw a lurid glow on the horizon, a clank of steam hammers, a distant roar of the iron furnaces, and had a sense of general "Pandemonium."[17]

Outside the station the main downtown business street ran north and south at right angles to the railroad tracks. The Elyton Land Company had named it Twentieth Street to assert confidence in rapid expansion of the surrounding town. The street was broad and straight, and usually packed with the hurly-burly of pedestrians and horse-drawn carriages. It was "paved" with several inches of reddish-brown slag—the crushed cinders of burnt-out iron ore from the furnaces. When hot wind kicked up red cinder dust, it hung thick in the air.[18]

The AME church where Welch would preach was on the east side of town, out toward the Sloss Furnace, whose towers stood as an eastern "gateway" into Birmingham. To get there a carriage probably would have turned east off of Twentieth Street and bounced over three blocks of unpaved dirt avenue before arriving at Twenty-Fourth Street, where the AME church stood on the edge of a congested "Negro Quarter" of small rented cabins. Welch and his family stayed, at least for a time, in the nearby boardinghouse of William Froner, whose boarders included a painter, two masons, and a machinist—skilled workers who could afford higher rent than could unskilled day laborers.[19]

In the evening the Welch family would have almost certainly become aware of a fiery orange glow that filled the sky and made the whole landscape shimmer. It was, in the words of a Black reporter, "a brilliant Aurora Boreallis [sic] from the lights and fierce fires of the rolling mills and furnaces." The Froner house was just a few short blocks from the Sloss towers.[20]

SEGREGATED CHURCHES

Welch plunged into his activities as an elder of the AME congregation of six hundred. His church, like every other Black church in the city, was a center of both religion and social life. Each church sponsored elaborate programs that included many social activities designed to appeal to people of all ages. On

Sundays many devout members spent most of the day at church. At Welch's church the Sabbath School began at 9:00 in the morning, with classes for all ages. Welch preached his main sermon at 3:00 in the afternoon and another at 8:00 in the evening. Between classes and services, potluck meals fostered social fellowship. On Monday evenings Welch conducted class meetings and on Wednesday evenings prayer meetings. On other evenings he held special meetings, and sometimes the church was bustling until after 10 p.m. The other Black churches had similar Sunday schedules, and almost every weekday at least one of the churches was holding prayer meetings or class meetings.[21]

By the time Pastor Welch took up his post, organized religion was very much a segregated activity in Birmingham. In fact, by the time the city was founded, six years after emancipation, religious separation was already well advanced, and every church in the new city was established as exclusively white or exclusively Black.[22] By 1883 the first Birmingham *City Directory* listed churches under two separate boldface subheadings: "White Churches" and "Colored Churches."[23] But the patterns of exclusion were asymmetrical, and the asymmetry indicated an ongoing white denigration of people of African ancestry. Black churches typically welcomed white visitors and treated them with great deference, but nearly every white church quickly became exclusively white and made it abundantly clear that no Black should cross its doorstep.[24]

Early in Reconstruction, rigid racial segregation had become the rule in southern churches, and southern whites had little reason to worry about northern Republican or federal interference with the racial segregation of churches. Most northern white Republicans would not support legislation that would require churches to grant equal access to all races. Most members of Congress believed such legislation would infringe upon the principle of free exercise of religion guaranteed by the First Amendment to the Constitution.[25]

The segregated churches became powerful cultural and moral institutions in both the Black and the white communities during Reconstruction. Segregated churches developed divergent worship styles and fostered separate friendship circles, building upon and intensifying white exclusion of Blacks from close social fellowship. The rigid separation of cultural institutions produced separate cultural styles, experiences, and activities, further estranging the two races from each other.

The cultural separation spilled over into politics. People who became trusted friends in congregational fellowship could extend that trust into political alliances and patterns of support. But the racial grouping of such friendships strengthened political trust and cooperation within the races, while fostering distrust and competition between the races. The racial separation of churches fostered separate political leadership, divergent political attitudes, conflicting political goals, and separate political organization. Often, Black pastors like Isaiah Welch became important political leaders, but a Black pastor would have no sway over white churchgoers. One of the leading newspapers, the *Iron Age,* frequently appealed to the moral concerns of white churchgoers to influence them to vote for the local Democratic faction. When it did, it often lumped the denizens of saloons and Blacks together as unworthy groups whose influence in politics should be minimized.

THE DOWNTOWN BUSINESS DISTRICT

The main downtown business district was a short walk from Pastor Welch's church. It and several of the other larger Black churches had built substantial houses of worship that stood facing the central business district. The only African Americans who operated shops in the two- to four-story structures in the business district between Nineteenth and Twenty-First streets were a few barbers, all of whose clients were white. Off in one marginal corner of the business district at the intersection of Nineteenth Street and Third Avenue stood a modest row of one-story shacks that housed small businesses owned by and serving African Americans.[26] Most of the white business buildings around this block were two stories, but most of the Black businesses were in simple one-story structures. But for many Black people the fledgling Black business center symbolized opportunity even as it also displayed the limitations imposed by restrictive boundaries.[27]

BLACK NEWSPAPERS

Another Black business, established in the summer of 1883, soon after Welch's arrival, was the Birmingham *Weekly Pilot.* Its founder and editor was John Henry Thomason, who became an assertive voice for the Black community. He was a star graduate of Trinity Hall, a private school established in the northern Alabama town of Athens in 1865 for the education of the children of former slaves. He was also a well-connected Republican Party activist. Every issue of the *Pilot* carried the front-page slogan: "DEVOTED TO THE INTERESTS OF THE COLORED PEOPLE OF ALABAMA," and Pastor Welch eagerly embraced the editor and paper as allies in rallying communal effort.[28]

Black readers received the *Pilot* every Saturday. It was actually a single sheet, folded from left to right to make a small four-page paper, about twelve inches wide and eighteen inches high, with five columns across each page. Though smaller and thinner than the several white newspapers, it was well written, accurately edited, neatly composed, and attractively printed by a professional press.

Thomason wrote and edited only the front and back pages. The two inside pages were boilerplate printed elsewhere and filled with feature articles, home and garden hints, fiction, humor, light verse, and advertisements for assorted paraphernalia and patent medicines. The advertising, plus a probable subsidy from some level of the Republican Party organization, helped Thomason finance the paper.[29]

Thomason packed the front and back pages with editorials, national news items, brief essays on issues of concern to the race, comments clipped from other Black newspapers, columns of three-line notices of the personal comings and goings of the Black citizens of Birmingham, announcements of events and meetings, a directory of churches and fraternal societies, a complete local railroad schedule, and, tucked into corners, numerous pithy editorial squibs denouncing such abominations as the convict labor system and the exclusion of Blacks from jury lists.[30]

The *Pilot* dealt primarily with the activities of Black people in business, the professions, and the skilled trades—approximately the top 10 percent of the adult Black male population. The focus was reflected in its board of officers, including a brickmason, a barber, a carpenter, two grocers, and a saloonkeeper, in addition to Thomason himself, the only professional man on the board. But Thomason dealt also with issues of concern to workingmen, and he gained a wide readership, generating a subscription list of four hundred, equal to 20 percent of the adult Black males in Birmingham.[31]

Also widely read in Birmingham was an out-of-town Black newspaper, the Huntsville *Gazette*, published starting in 1879 by an able editor, Charles Hendley Jr., in the older town of Huntsville, seventy-five miles north of Birmingham. In the 1880s several young Huntsville businessmen moved to booming Birmingham. They kept close ties with their Huntsville relatives and eagerly promoted the *Gazette* in Birmingham. The enterprising *Gazette* editor expanded his readership in both towns by establishing a "Gazette Bureau" consisting of two fluent Huntsville migrants who entertained readers with tongue-in-cheek comparisons of Birmingham and Huntsville.[32]

"BUZZARD ROOST," "SCRATCH ANKLE," AND THE CHURCHES

One of the concerns of the leaders of Pastor Welch's church was a shantytown of saloons, dance halls, gambling houses, and brothels. The neighborhood stretched along Twenty-Seventh Street between First Avenue and Second Avenue, and along the north side of Second Avenue and an alley behind Second Avenue. Partly hidden by trees, the shanty-town shacks and cabins were collectively nicknamed "Buzzard Roost." All of the owners were white.[33]

The pioneer in creating Buzzard Roost had been grocer John Polis, who boosted his profits and property value impressively when he turned his grocery store into a disreputable saloon. Soon other white owners followed suit, building more drinking and dancing establishments. Among the white owners of the Buzzard Roost land were, at different times, the Elyton Land Company, a former mayor, a future governor, a former Democratic Party county chairman, a city associate judge, a wholesale grocer, a utility company president, and several wholesale liquor dealers. Like most white owners of property occupied by Blacks, they collected substantial rent.[34]

A white journalist described the "low unsightly cabins" of the Buzzard Roost as "eye sores by day, scenes of drunken revelry and bloody crimes by night." There was "not a street light within three blocks of the place" (because the city had not installed any streetlights in the "Quarters"), and "pine trees just back of the cabins added their shadows to the general darkness." From cabin windows gleamed "small lamps or tallow candles" that cast "a feebly sickly light about the small rooms, which only seemed to heighten the hideousness of the scene, while outside all was darkness." According to rumor, the name "Buzzard Roost" had originated when an out-of-town white visitor looked in on a dance. He found the sight of "over 100 negroes . . . shouting, cursing, and dancing" to be "weird and startling," and in amazement he asked "Where do all these buzzards roost?"[35]

A similar but smaller shantytown, called "Scratch Ankle," sprang up on the far western edge of town, in the shadow of foundries and ironworks where Fourteenth Street met Second Avenue. By 1885 it would include a restaurant, an ambiguously labeled "Liquor Storage" structure, and a saloon with billiard hall that was prospering so dynamically that soon it would add a large "Dance Shed" in back.[36]

A white journalist penned the following description.

> The time, midnight. The place, the "Rialto," the leading saloon of the Ankle, with a dance hall in the rear, lighted by a single gasoline lamp, which, struggling with the midnight darkness, adds an additional hideousness to the wild scene below.
>
> The "hall" is probably twenty feet square, with a band stand in one corner, on which a string band grinds out weird and unearthly music. A dozen negro women, sometimes more sometimes less, are present and probably fifty negro men, all of the worst character. There are no wall flowers among the women, no strangers among the men; they are all on the floor together, in one confused mass, dancing, shouting and swearing. . . . There is no "between sets" unless the band breaks down. The dance goes on incessantly until the morning is far advanced. Drinks are served to the dancers between "swings," and nothing but the sudden appearance of a bluecoated officer is allowed to check the mad revelry. . . . Night after night these dances go on at the "Ankle," and in the "Roost." After pay-day at the furnace the crowd is larger, there is more drinking, and the dancing is harder and faster, but there is always a fair crowd at every dance.[37]

The reporter highlighted gambling and violence. "Crap shooting went on all night," and "No ball is considered a complete success unless there is a fight. Blood is the spice of life in Scratch Ankle, and the flash of the razor, as it descends upon the throat of some dusky victim, adds brilliancy to the scene."[38]

Black leaders like Welch shuddered at the sensationalistic reports. They complained that the reports were biased and that the white newspapers completely ignored the quiet lives and steady constructive activities of pious Black churchgoers. Welch did not deny that Black workers patronized the saloons. However, when asked to estimate the "damage" drink did to Black people, he broadened the damage beyond Blacks, replying that "Eternity alone can disclose its appalling effects upon humanity." He led in rallying the Black churches to temperance reform, and on occasion they intruded into the shantytowns with revival campaigns designed to "reform the Roost."[39]

The churches and the saloon–dance halls were competing social centers. Many church members would never be seen in the saloon shantytowns, except at reform revivals, and many regulars at the dance halls were not churchgoers. But the two constituencies did overlap, and some swayed between the two. Reports had it that many workingmen frequented saloons regularly despite a lack of enthusiasm on the part of their churchgoing wives. Welch noted that temperance reform efforts needed to focus first upon church members themselves, and in early 1884 he pointed out that "my church" had "commenced a reformatory work, which I pray will be continued until the last tippler is reformed or expelled."[40]

RESIDENTIAL PATTERNS

In 1883 Pastor Welch could have begun the exploration of Black residential neighborhoods by simply stepping outside his AME Church, which stood on Twenty-Fourth Street, half a block from First Avenue. (See map 1.) Stretching from Twenty-Fourth Street to the city limits at Twenty-Seventh Street were two blocks packed full of cabins and boardinghouses. On the edges of the blocks, several white-owned stores or saloons catered to Black families. On narrow yards and alleys were two-room cabins, each of which housed at least two families. People were moving into town so fast that there were not enough houses to go around, and rent took a hefty chunk out of a weekly paycheck. Families moving into town almost always had to start out either in a large boardinghouse or sharing a cabin with a settled family that was willing to coinhabit in order to help pay the rent.[41]

Beyond Pastor Welch's neighborhood there were other residential areas within Birmingham's Black community. Chapter 5 explores in detail the complexities of these areas' patterns and concludes that they amounted to a rigid system of segregation. There was stark segregation within the iron furnaces, the machine shops, railroad yards, mines, and other places where African Americans labored. These are discussed in chapter 6.

RACIAL BOUNDARIES AND CLASS DIFFERENCES

The boundaries that separated Black households from white households were examples of the many restrictive boundaries that Welch encountered confining him and his people. Some of the boundaries, like the invisible lines that encapsulated the separate Black residential clusters, seemed physical, and an observer could easily see their consequences. Other boundaries, like the inflexible rule that excluded all Black children from the "Free White School," seemed partly physical, since they prohibited Blacks from entering specific buildings. But school boundaries were also social, economic, and political in their intentions and their consequences. Still other boundaries, like the invisible but nearly impermeable boundary that held most Blacks down in unskilled occupations, were not physical, but were rather interactional barriers created by white perceptions, strategies, intentions, and rules and by Black handicaps and disadvantages.

In the antebellum South, whites had created tight racial boundaries and strict antiblack social norms to subordinate Black slaves, allowing them no economic autonomy, no social honor, and no political standing. But Civil War, invasion, emancipation, and Reconstruction had thrown the old slave boundaries into disarray. In the new industrial town of Birmingham an ambitious and perceptive African American leader like Pastor Welch would have encountered a confusing maze of informal and shifting boundaries which restricted his behavior and structured his interaction with whites. And Welch, assertively seeking to maximize the meaning of the new freedom of his people, would push to undermine or to redefine the maze of post-emancipation racial boundaries.

In 1883 Birmingham and the entire South still grappled with the disarray into which war and Reconstruction had thrown racial boundaries. For Pastor Welch and his fellow Blacks, the new boomtown of Birmingham, far removed from the old slave plantation regime, seemed one of the most promising places in the entire post-emancipation South for the further dismantling and divergence of old racial boundaries. The town of Birmingham had literally been laid out in one fell swoop in an old cornfield at the intersection of two new railroad lines, and its physical structures and residential arrangements symbolized a sharp break from old patterns of interaction between Black slave families and those of their owners.

Every building was brand new, and no house had an old enclosed slave quarter or some other physical remnant of slave residential patterns. No sumptuous townhouses of wealthy planters adorned Birmingham's best white residential sections. Birmingham's elite social life did not revolve around the prestige and traditions and values of an antebellum plantation aristocracy. Jefferson County's few former slave-owning plantation families continued to play influential roles out in the rural valleys on either side of Birmingham, but Birmingham's bustling urban life and dynamic politics were dominated by businesspeople, industrialists, and workers.[42]

Northerners were far more powerful and visible in the offices and stores and industries and mines of Birmingham than were relics of the old southern planter aristocracy. The industrial promise of the new boomtown had attracted many engineers, technicians, managers, shopkeepers, workers, and miners from northern industrial and commercial centers. A substantial share of the workers and miners were foreign-born, and by the 1890s first- and second-generation immigrants accounted for over 13 percent of Birmingham's total population, and almost 25 percent of the white population. Initially the largest foreign groups were the German and Irish immigrants. After 1890 Italians dominated foreign immigration to Birmingham and by 1910 became the largest foreign-born group. The transplanted northerners and foreigners were by no means egalitarian integrationists, but they had not grown up practicing and enforcing the many customary boundary rules that were habitual to most southern-born whites. Sometimes it was noticed that in their homes, in places of work, in conversations, and in street encounters the northerners and foreigners were less fastidious in insisting upon and enforcing racial boundary practices. The presence of such imperfectly initiated newcomers helped to make Birmingham one of the southern places most likely to tolerate further boundary breakdown and divergence.[43]

Birmingham had been built entirely in the new southern era of free wage labor. Gone was the antebellum plantation system of ownership of labor by capital, and gone, also, was the traditional pattern of daily control of the Black slave by the white plantation master. Although severe handicaps—illiteracy, underdevelopment of skills, and lack of wealth and land—continued to limit the opportunities of Blacks, Black unskilled laborers enjoyed a new independence that became a major topic of white complaint.[44]

The historical record is skewed toward the top echelon of Blacks. In the *Pilot*, for example, editor Thomason paid far more attention to "the best of our colored people" and provided a great deal more information about their activities and aspirations and frustrations than about the lives and actions of the vast army of Black laborers and domestic servants. But, in facing most color lines and racial boundaries, the experiences of the top 10 percent of Blacks were quite similar to the experiences of the lower 90 percent. Since the prosperity of Black business and professional people was so modest, the disparities of wealth and income and lifestyle within the Black community were much smaller than within the white community. A step up into the ranks of skilled artisans, small business operators, and professionals would serve to place a Black person among the "best" Black people. But the "best" Black families did not stand out far above the families of unskilled common workers. By contrast, in the white community, the "best" families, headed by the owners of Birmingham's major industries, banks, and downtown businesses, towered above both the common white and the Black level in their affluence and lifestyle.

All members of the thin top layer of Blacks encountered the same restrictive racial barriers by which whites subordinated all Blacks, lower- and middle-class. No Black person, no matter how successful economically, could enter a white church or white restaurant, or could approach the front door of a white home, or could eat at a table with white folks, or could send his children to the white school, or could avoid being addressed by untitled first name when he encountered whites. But the top 10 percent did have some capacity to place into the historical record vivid accounts and discussions and complaints about their boundary encounters, and their encounters reveal much about the constraints faced by all Blacks.

The thin top-tier of Black middle-class people knew very well that their relative economic success had come by providing basic services to Birmingham's growing throng of Black workers, and they sought to maintain close ties with those workers. Black employers courted the loyal patronage of Black workers, and Black professional people sympathized eloquently with the problems of Black workers, even as they sought to sustain social and cultural refinements that distinguished them from the workers. Although editor Thomason of the *Pilot* did not feature the personal comings and goings of Black workers as prominently as he did those of the Black elite, Thomason did pay close attention to the constraints and dangers faced by ordinary Blacks, and he continually advocated changes that would improve their situation.

Blacks of all classes had seen emancipation and urbanization as offering the promise of greater independence, opportunity, and freedom. They perceived accurately that city life had undermined old slavery boundaries and had provided significant improvement. But all Blacks of all classes quickly discovered that whites were determined to rehabilitate and reinforce as many of the old color-line boundaries as possible, even in the new free-labor city of Birmingham. Consequently, all Blacks who cast their lot with the industrial boomtown, even those who climbed into the small Black middle class, found they continually had to cope with boundaries that excluded them socially, circumscribed their movements, restricted their behavior, limited their economic opportunity, abridged their education, narrowed their life chances, and undermined their political power.

CHAPTER 2

TRANSITION TO THE NEW SOUTH

Reconstructing Boundaries

In the Old South, whites had created racial criteria and rules that were congruent in all three realms of life: political, economic, and social. The convergent boundaries produced a rigorously hierarchical and polarized system that excluded Blacks from the political order, turned them into dependent property in the economic sphere, and deprived them of any respectable standing in the social realm. To reinforce the boundaries, whites employed a complicated stereotype of Blacks that conveyed the image of a "child-savage duality," to use the phrasing of historian George Fredrickson. On one extreme of the duality, the image of the Black slave as a "murderous savage" justified the "brute force" that the slave system often employed. On the other extreme, the image of Black slaves as "contented and naturally servile" could help soothe white consciences, rationalize paternalism, and recruit support from whites outside the South.[1]

Whites intended for the earlier white/Black boundaries imposed by slavery to be impermeable and permanent. But the racial boundaries proved not to be permanent. War, invasion, defeat, emancipation, radical Reconstruction, and Black enfranchisement shattered the Old South and deranged its system of Black/white boundaries. Southern whites faced a sequence of what sociologist Herbert Blumer called "big events" in the development of race prejudice. Such events are crucial, Blumer proposed, "in developing a conception of the subordinate racial group." Each "big event" threatens the position of a dominant racial group in a way that "seems momentous, that touches deep sentiments, that seems to raise fundamental questions about relations, and that awakens strong feelings of identification with [the] racial group."[2] In response to the string of "big events" of the 1860s and 1870s, southern whites sought to reconstruct and strengthen racial boundaries and stereotypes.

THREE UNEARNED GIFTS

In March of 1875 an influential assessment and reformulation of racial boundaries appeared in an editorial in the Mobile *Register,* a leading mouthpiece of the Alabama Conservative Democratic Party, which in November 1874 had won an electoral victory that essentially ended Reconstruction in Alabama. The editorial attacked the federal Civil Rights Act, which the Republican Congress passed and President Ulysses S. Grant signed into law on March 1, 1875. The editorial denounced the act as abominable, and futile. Congress had attempted an impossible feat, the *Register* declared. It had sought to lift the vastly inferior Black former slaves to make them socially acceptable to the supposedly vastly superior southern white people. The *Register* editorial had wrapped its anti–civil rights argument in the broad claim that all the Civil War and Reconstruction-era advancements in the status of African Americans had been fake, and all still stood as counterfeit "gifts" from the Radical Republicans. The *Register* embellished arguments that had appeared widely in the Alabama Democratic press, including the Birmingham *Iron Age,* during campaigns against Congressional Reconstruction. The bold sweep of the *Register*'s formulation gave it wide circulation beyond Mobile and Birmingham. The *Register*'s editorial caught the eye of the most fervid antiblack polemicist in the state—former Ku Klux Klan leader Ryland Randolph—and he reprinted it in his newspaper, the *Tuskaloosa Blade,* on March 11, 1875.

The Civil Rights Law, said the *Register,* was the last in a sequence of three dubious "Radical gifts" to African Americans—the gifts of *freedom, suffrage,* and *social equality.* The *Register* identified three realms of life—economic, political, and social—as it defined the three "gifts." Blacks had neither sought nor earned the gifts, said the *Register,* and the gifts had entailed "far more trouble and harm than benefit to [African American] interests." Any notion of "benefit to the negro has always been a secondary consideration" to the Radical Republicans. "All the legislation of the Radical party on the colored question has been shaped with a single eye to the advantage of the Radical party."

In the *economic realm*, the Radical Republicans had thrown the Black freedmen "into the deep waters of life and told to swim for their existence, when they knew not how to make a single stroke of the art."[3] In the *political realm* the Radicals had granted suffrage "before the negro was prepared for it, either for his own or the country's good," said the *Register.* The suffrage had been "just such another fatal and intensely selfish Radical gift" and made "the negro . . . and his vote the slaves of the Radical party. With [under] the name of freedom the black people have simply exchanged masters; with this difference, that the old master used to feed and clothe and house and doctor them, while their new ones leave them to make their hard fight for life by themselves, except when elections come around." The *Register* editorial went on to declare that "The last selfish gift to the negro" was the 1875 federal Civil Rights Law which sought to breach boundaries in the *social realm.* The *Register,* echoing the platform of the Alabama Democratic Party, asserted instead that, while the Civil Rights Law granted Blacks equal access to the social milieu of such public accommodations, its long-run, covert goal was to extend to Blacks full social equality in private fellowship, home, and fireside.[4]

The most significant point, asserted the *Register,* was that the intended "gift" of "social equality" simply was not within the power of the Republican Congress to give. It was "an attempt by Congress to work an impossibility. Congress can as easily change the color of the skin of a human being, by statute, as it can create social equality. It is nothing more than an attempt to change the laws of nature and to eradicate from the minds and souls of men feelings and instinct that are as vital in his [*sic*] experience as the veins and arteries, the nerves and bones, and the tissues of his anatomy."[5]

The *Register* acknowledged that in the *economic realm* triumphant battalions and a ruling political party could remove legal boundaries between slaves and free men and could transform human chattel into free economic actors. The *Register* further acknowledged that in the *political realm* a victorious federal administration and a dominant political party could alter the Constitution, transform noncitizen into citizen, grant the right to vote, and eliminate political boundaries between white and Black. But the *Register* confidently asserted that in the *social realm* neither honor nor social equality could be given to Blacks as a gift by an outside force, no matter how powerful. Honor and social equality depended entirely upon southern whites' judgment about Blacks. Only southern whites, the *Register* declared, had the power to determine what people were worthy of social fellowship among them, and southern whites had rejected Blacks as socially unworthy. "Neither President, Congress or Army have the power to secure to [Blacks] what they are led to hope from this [Civil Rights] law," said the *Register*, "for mortal power cannot undo what God has decreed"—namely the "instinct" deeply embedded in the "minds and souls" of whites not to mingle intimately with people of African ancestry and slave heritage.[6]

Whites, the *Register* implied, had succeeded in resisting any boundary change in the *social realm*. By the mid-1870s many southern whites and their newspapers said they would accept northern Republican insistence upon Black economic liberty and political suffrage, so long as the North in turn would acquiesce in the white South's determination to continue to deny Blacks equality in the *social realm*. In September 1874, the weekly *Iron Age*, the leading Democratic newspaper in Birmingham, endorsed an assertion in the white Democratic Selma *Argus* that "no man in Alabama proposes to deprive negroes of any civil or political right, but all are determined to protect them in all the privileges and immunities of freemen." However, the *Iron Age* made it clear that, when Blacks went too far and began to "demand that the social equality of the races be enforced by stringent laws and hard penalties," then "the whites have united to guard from pollution their homes and firesides."[7]

RYLAND RANDOLPH

In the immediate aftermath of the Civil War the white voice in northern Alabama most effective in reshaping the images of formerly enslaved Blacks was the vicious wordsmith Ryland Randolph, who had widely circulated the editorial from the Mobile *Register*. In the Tuscaloosa *Independent Monitor* and then the *Blade*, Ryland Randolph staked out the extreme end of the spectrum of stereotype architects in northern Alabama.[8]

Randolph had arrived in Tuscaloosa in October of 1867, during Radical Reconstruction and four years before the founding of Birmingham. He was outraged to find Republicans controlling local politics and the University of Alabama, located in Tuscaloosa. In his view, "The leading negroes of the place had become quite insolent in their demeanor to white-folks," and whites had "grown timid." In the *Monitor*, which was Randolph's first newspaper in Tuscaloosa, he launched a personal crusade to rally the demoralized white

Democrats against Reconstruction. During the Civil War, Randolph had served under General Nathan Bedford Forrest, who after the war became the first "grand wizard" of the Ku Klux Klan. Inspired by Forrest, Randolph organized the Ku Klux Klan in Tuscaloosa and became its "grand cyclops." He explained that he rallied the Klan "for the purpose of punishing those negroes who had become notoriously and offensively insolent to white people, and, in some cases, to chastise those white-skinned men who, at that particular time, showed a disposition to affiliate socially with negroes."[9]

Randolph's *Monitor* flaunted the motto: "White Man—Right or Wrong— Still the White Man!" The newspaper bristled with sinister Klan notices and orders, many of them clear threats to specific Black political leaders, who had made themselves "odious to the superior race." Among the notices in one issue was a denunciation of "an incendiary buck-nigger" of Tuscaloosa and a threat that he "is certainly a candidate before the Ku Klux Klan for *grave* honors." Soon the *Monitor* boasted that "the very night of the day on which said notices made their appearance, three notably offensive negro men were dragged out of their beds, escorted to the old boneyard (¾ mile from Tuscaloosa) and thrashed in the regular ante-bellum style, until their unnatural nigger pride had a tumble, and humbleness to the white man reigned supreme."[10]

The language that Randolph injected into postwar Alabama politics reeked of anger and resentment against an "insolent," "odious," and "offensive" Black challenge to the supremacy of whites. Allen Trelease, the leading historian of the Ku Klux Klan, observed that Randolph "had a quick wit, a sharp tongue and facile pen, a passion for controversy, and an instinct for identifying with and mobilizing the basest instincts of his constituency."[11] Randolph spewed out angry, abusive images, and in 1869 he ran successfully for the state House of Representatives, where he ridiculed the fifteen Black members as "niggers," as "variegated animals" and as "colored monkeys." He contemptuously referred to the "lower house of the Menagerie." Such extreme language deeply offended not only Blacks, but also their white Republican allies. The Republican majority, in a rare action, formally expelled Randolph from the legislature.[12]

Randolph was a "fighting editor" who ostentatiously displayed guns and knives on his desk and who engaged in frequent personal fights and street brawls. On one occasion he encountered two Black men beating a white man in front of twenty passive whites who were intimidated by an angry mob of two hundred Blacks. Randolph stabbed one of the attacking Blacks repeatedly, breaking off an inch of the blade in the man's back. Leaving the stabbed Black man for dead, Randolph then "coolly and very deliberately" wiped the bloody knife on his shoe "in the presence of the large body of dumbfounded negroes who stood nearby."[13] Black anger mounted, and Randolph returned to his office and grabbed a double-barreled shotgun and a repeating rifle. Rejecting advice that he flee on horseback, he resolved "to settle the matter of race supremacy right there and then." He confronted the angry crowd of Blacks, leveled a gun at them, and, according to his account, caused them to "skeedaddle." Randolph believed "this event made me a hero."

In the *Monitor,* Randolph announced that the stabbing was "a caution to those many insolent Negroes who essay to fight the ruling race of the land." He exulted that it had intimidated all of "niggerdom" so that "they now feel their inferiority, in every particular to the white man." The stabbed Black man survived, and authorities arrested Randolph and charged him with assault and battery. In the end he beat the charges and rejoiced that the event caused many timid whites to get "off the fence" and stand up for their race. For Randolph, terror and violence were proper methods for intimidating freedmen and forcing them to behave according to what he considered to be the essential nature of Black people.[14]

In September 1868, Randolph overreached. He created a woodcut cartoon and published it in the *Monitor.* Two men, one holding a carpetbag labeled "OHIO," hung by ropes from a tree limb while a mule labeled "KKK" walked out from under them. An editorial explained, "The above cut represents the fate in store for those great pests of southern society—the carpet-bagger and scalawag," and it added that "there is room left on the limb for the suspension of any bad Grant negro who may be found at the propitious moment."[15] A nationwide uproar greeted the cartoon. Republicans saw that such a public southern Democratic endorsement of violence could become valuable Republican campaign material in the 1868 presidential contest, and their newspapers reprinted it. Alabama Democratic newspapers quickly denounced Randolph and disavowed the cartoon, fearing that it would cause the Democrats to lose the pivotal state of Ohio, and the state's Democratic executive committee publicly read Randolph and the *Monitor* out of the Democratic Party.[16]

Most Alabama Democratic politicians and editors found Randolph's stereotypes, his woodcut, and his violence to be counterproductive in a national context. Consequently his images did not receive public endorsement from Democratic politicians and editors, and his language remained outside the public mainstream. Nonetheless, Randolph's extremism would converge with other less angry stereotypes. In the end both the harshest and softest extremes would fade, and the southern white in-group would achieve consensus on an image that featured a central set of negative Black personality traits—an image that was juxtaposed with a stereotype of "whiteness."

THE GRANGER MOVEMENT AND THE WHITENESS STEREOTYPE

Randolph was a persistent man. In 1873 and 1874, two years after the founding of Birmingham, he whipped up white opposition to Radical Reconstruction as part of the white Democratic Party "redemption" campaign that recaptured political control of Alabama. To energize rural whites for redemption, Randolph launched a new newspaper, the *Tuskaloosa Blade*, in Tuscaloosa, located in the county adjacent to Birmingham's Jefferson County. With his newspaper Randolph mobilized rural support for a new agricultural organization—the Grange, or Patrons of Husbandry. Randolph continued his white-supremacist themes, rejoicing that the Grange "has been composed strictly of whites." The white South, he predicted, would "like a drowning man" avidly seize the Grange "life boat" and would "endeavor to make of it a powerful political lever to prize the white race out of the 'bottom-rail' predicament in which she has been placed by Black Republicanism."[17]

As Randolph helped build the Grange, he gradually dropped his early Reconstruction image of Blacks as "insolent," and instead took up the theme of Blacks as "indolent." Black freedmen, he argued, were hopelessly inadequate as a postwar southern agricultural labor force. To remedy the negative effects of "negro indolence," Randolph trumpeted the idea that the white South, led by the Grange, should mount a campaign to attract immigration of intelligent and industrious whites and to foster an "exodus" of "inefficient and "intolerable" Black labor.[18]

Soon W. H. Chambers, the "worthy master," or president, of the Alabama state Grange, endorsed Randolph's immigration ideas. Chambers proposed that the organizational apparatus of the nationwide Grange be used to advertise the advantages of the South in order to attract white immigrants to replace a large Black "pauper population of hireling laborers." In contrast to Blacks, white immigrants "would bring with them the means of buying small farms, their implements of improved husbandry, and habits of industry and economy already formed in the school of the farm."[19] The Grange vision of attracting white immigrants would turn out to be unrealistic. But the Grange campaign did help to reveal key aspects of white farmers' concept of a good society, and of their own white self-stereotype, which they implicitly contrasted with their stereotype of Black farmers.

As Randolph mobilized the Grange politically on behalf of the Democratic "redemption" campaign, he sponsored a Grange recruiting agent who spread the Grange organization into Jefferson County and Birmingham. Soon a Birmingham farmer and attorney, Peyton G. King, the chairman of the Jefferson County Democratic executive committee, emerged as Birmingham's primary leader of the Grange movement.[20] Under King, the County Democratic Committee unanimously adopted resolutions proclaiming that "The ascendancy of the white race in this county is *endangered.*" The committee resolved that "the white people . . . will never cease to battle on that issue until the supremacy of the white race is completely established and the corrupt and incendiary leaders of negro radicalism are driven in disgrace from office and power."[21] Colonel King was a well-educated and eloquent lawyer who was from a prominent county family and had married into a similar family. He brought into the construction of stereotypes a more urbane and genteel voice than that of Randolph, but King reiterated many of Randolph's themes and settled on a similar postwar image of Black character.[22]

In April 1874, King delivered a Grange lecture that addressed the events of war and Reconstruction which had fundamentally altered relations between African Americans and whites. "The revolutions of the last fifteen years," he declared, have swept away many cherished ideas and institutions," and "we make slow progress in accommodating our habits and opinions to the new order of things." Crucial among the undigested "revolutions" had been the abolition of slavery, and upon that revolution King, in words less flamboyant that those of Ryland Randolph, placed much of the blame for agricultural decline. Since the war, "Agriculture is in a low, depressed condition; labor is thriftless and unproductive, demoralized and discontented." Since 1860 county cotton and corn production had plummeted, and in 1874 King lamented: "A valley, once beautiful almost beyond description, and productive beyond present be-

lief, now presents an almost unvaried spectacle of dilapidation and decay."
Worse yet, he said, had been an accompanying sense of rural community
malaise, a withering and deterioration of rural community spirit and life.[23]

Jefferson County had not been a major slave plantation area, but in 1860
its farmers had owned 2,649 slaves who had comprised nearly one-fourth of
the county population. Their coerced labor had made the valleys of the county
into what King remembered as a "vast garden as far as the eye could reach."
In the 1870s most of the former slaves and their offspring continued to live in
small shacks in the long valley surrounding Birmingham. They worked either
as farm laborers or sharecroppers on the nearby farms owned by whites. One
factor in the decline in production had been a substantial decline in the hours
of labor per person supplied by African Americans. When they became free,
Blacks reduced their hours of labor to bring their work time more in line
with the typical work patterns of the free white population, and to reserve
more time for family activities, schooling, and leisure. The best estimate is
that throughout the South the supply of labor provided by the emancipated
postbellum Black population was approximately one-fourth to one-third less
than the supply of labor that had been extracted from Blacks through the
coercions of slavery.[24]

Black people considered the reduction of their work time to the standard
of free white labor to be a proper response to the new rules of freedom. But
Peyton King, like most southern whites, interpreted the reduction not as a
reasonable response to a new Black status or to altered external rules and
controls. Instead he saw it as evidence of an inherent and persistent racial
propensity for laziness and demoralization.

Therefore, King said, for whites to restore prosperity under the new order, they must develop an intense new work ethic among all white farm-family
members, young and old, male and female, and they should stop relying upon
Black labor. King proposed to "treat with contempt the dissipated and ener-
vated idlers who regard labor as disgraceful." Farm wives should "practice
economy in their household affairs and dress, dispense with servants as far
as possible, and instruct their daughters to perform all domestic duties with
neatness and dispatch. By such means they can do much to revive industry,
and put to shame our disgraceful dependence upon the negro for labor."[25]
The *Iron Age* endorsed the need for a new white work ethic. Whites should
"lay off your linen, your kids, your beavers, and put on homespun, and what

you find to do, that do with your might." These were words of white self-stereotyping—words aimed at differentiating whites from Blacks.[26]

The Grange offered significant organizational and social roles to white husbands, wives, sons, and daughters, and Grange social gatherings fostered social unity and equality and hearty community fellowship among neighboring white farm families of all economic levels. White Grangers not only deployed positive self-stereotypes to distinguish themselves from Blacks, they fortified their political and economic solidarity by emphasizing the importance of the familial social core. "The Grange is a social institution," proclaimed one Grange report. "It makes every neighborhood one kind affectionate family." It "unite[s] in bonds of brotherly love all who take shelter under its arches." Consistent with the familial spirit of unity and equality, Grangers referred to one another and addressed one another with the titles "Brother" and "Sister," even in reports to the newspapers. Resolutions of one local Grange affirmed that, "as society is organized in this section of the country," it "embrac[es] all honest, honorable citizens in the same circle without any regard to their pecuniary endowments, enjoying each other's society as equals in every respect."[27]

One way for Grange leaders to reinforce a sense of an egalitarian family community was to exclude Blacks from community gatherings in the same breath that they heartily included all whites. In 1876, for example, the County Grange and the Ruhama Horti-Agricultural Society published a joint notice:

> To any and all classes of citizens we respectfully insist that you come out with lunch baskets, (FILLED WITH DINNER!!!) and let us have a regular social picnic.
> To any and all white citizens, we say come, COME, and join us in our festivities.
> Parties who live at a convenient distance are *expected* and *requested* to bring out a sufficient amount of dinner for *themselves* and a few others. COME, WITHOUT MONEY. Come, COME, COME.

For less wealthy white farmers such a hearty invitation without regard to ability to pay could provide comforting status assurance. All white families merited inclusion because, within the stereotype of whiteness, they all stood far above Blacks culturally and socially. At the same time, the explicit exclusion of Blacks located them outside the white "circle" of "honest, honorable citizens."[28]

Colonel King's Grange themes were all eloquently seconded by another son of a Jefferson County pioneer family—forty-two-year-old Francis M. Grace, a highly educated Methodist preacher, college professor, farmer, editor, and Grange chaplain.[29] In April 1874 Grace wrote a companion essay to Peyton King's Grange lecture. He reinforced King's complaint about the postwar decline of Jefferson County agriculture, asserting that most of the county's old plantation lands, which "originally" had been "the best in the county," were "lying idle," creating a general "desert appearance." They had been "cultivated by slave labor" and hence "were the worst worn, and soon abandoned after freedom."

By contrast, in the small farm valley northeast of Birmingham, "houses are thick, generally new, and many of them present an attractive appearance." The farms were "fresh and productive" and "give evidence of careful cultivation. Orchards abound, fine cattle have been introduced, clover and the grasses are being successfully tried, and every different crop adapted to our climate seems to yield abundantly." There "Intelligent white people, doing their own labor, are converting these smiling valleys into the abodes of peace and plenty. If the same spirit of improvement prevailed over the entire county . . . , there would be no more scarcity of provisions or of money within a few years." And the way to transform the backward old plantation lands would be for the Grange to foster white immigration.[30]

Many Jefferson County whites found Grace's image compelling. In 1875 the Grange and the closely associated Ruhama Horti-Agricultural Society, believing that an infusion of progressive white families would be "one grand stride toward building up our languishing agricultural interests," launched a campaign to identify land that would be offered at good prices to attract immigrant families that were white and industrious. "We are taking steps to open our section of the country to immigration," reported the Ruhama Society to the *Iron Age.* "We say to all who may come to our lovely valley, WELCOME. We will make homes for all; and when we say *homes,* Mr. Editor, we mean all that that word implies" (emphasis in original).[31]

The desire to attract white settlers who would create *homes* worthy of "all that that word implies," invoked an ideal articulated by state Grange president W. H. Chambers. During a visit to Jefferson County, Chambers said, "Let us make the farm a *home,* with such surroundings as to make it attractive, a comfortable dwelling, good orchard, well kept yards, neat fences, handsome shades, gardens filled with vegetables, snug farm houses, green pastures, fat live-stock, well arranged stables, etc." The Ruhama Horti-Agricultural Society fostered a similar ideal. Its reports praised homesteads with "better gardens, young orchards and vineyards, fences kept in repair, gates hanging square upon their hinges, clean stables and well kept barnyards."[32]

The Grange and the Ruhama Society, in other words, created a distinctive and attractive self-stereotype of whiteness. The Ruhama Society promoted the inference that from the well-groomed appearance of white farm homes the observer could conclude that inside them were progressive, disciplined families living in accord with a work ethic, receiving economic effort from all their members, and contributing to the improvement of the surrounding community.

The Grangers' self-stereotype of the dynamic white family inside the tidy white farm *home* contrasted sharply with their negative image of the typical Black family inside its "shack." They visualized the common Black dwelling as a shabby log cabin or primitive shanty of rough unpainted boards, with topsy-turvy surroundings and no fences, destitute of improvements, exhibiting signs of indifference, indolence, neglect, and poverty inside. Whites saw the unkempt appearance of the ubiquitous Black cabin not as evidence of the economic difficulties of a newly freed people with underdeveloped skills and no capital. Rather, they saw it as evidence of a flawed disposition, a deficient work-ethic, and profound defects in the Black family.[33]

Some visiting northern journalists saw similar meaning in the appearance of Black dwelling places. The Montgomery *Advertiser* reprinted as "only too true" a report from a special correspondent to the New York *Tribune*, who had written, "With a strong desire to discover evidence that he ["the Negro"] is making some substantial advances in intelligence, independence and physical comfort, I am forced to say that I have not been able to find them." As evidence the correspondent presented his impression of the typical Black place of habitation: "The ordinary negro cabin, such as one sees all over the Southern States, is a small hut of pine logs or rough boards, roofed with shingles split out with an ax. It contains only one room with a rude fire-place that terminates in a stick-and-mud chimney, a door in front, and another in the rear, and one or two square holes for windows, closed at night and in cold weather with wooden shutters. A cheaper, uglier, or poorer dwelling cannot be found in any civilized country. The hovels of the Irish peasantry are luxurious compared with it." Such evidence led the northern correspondent to the verdict that "the great mass of the black people appear to be at a standstill." The correspondent went even further, adding that "it is not easy to resist the conclusion that the negroes on the large cotton plantations have actually retrograded toward barbarism."[34]

For many white southerners and Grangers the familiar dilapidated Black cabin served as a standard to define a defective lifestyle at the bottom social level in the countryside, a standard above which all white farmers should hold themselves. Of course, many white farm families had lived in similar cabins, and some still did. But the Grange spirit encouraged aspiring progressive farmers to rise above that level, and farmers who did build improved residences could refer to the unimproved cabin as a standard against which to measure their own tidy homes and their own upward course of advancement. Such a view was implicit in an 1876 Grange report on visits to local Granges by County Deputy Henry J. Sharit. "I was particularly struck with the spirit of improvement everywhere manifested along my route," wrote Sharit. "Many new and handsome residences have been built in place of the log cabins, and frugality, industry, and economy are everywhere presented to the eye of the traveler."[35]

Contributing crucially to white farmers' conviction that more improvement-oriented white families were needed to foster rural community progress was a widespread white belief that Black family discipline was deplorable. Many whites asserted that Black homelife was as disorderly as the dilapidated appearance of typical Black cabins. The result, these whites claimed, was that the younger generation of Blacks, raised since the war with discipline provided only by their own parents, were totally unreliable, with no sense of the need for work and self-improvement.

During the reconstruction of images of Black people after the Civil War, many white commentators remarked in a positive way about enslaved Blacks. Only the older generation of Blacks, raised before the war, worked well, they said. The "orderly, sober, well behaved colored men and women to be found throughout the Southern States," said an editorial reprinted in the *Iron Age* in 1874, were "invariably the men and women trained to frugal and industrious habits by kind, intelligent and humane masters in pure and honorable Southern homes; invariably ex-slaves, raised to maturity in slavery, and exemplifying by their daily conduct the virtues of the homes where they were raised." By contrast, "ninety per cent of the lawbreakers are young men and young women who have reached maturity *since* 1864. They are those who have grown to manhood and womanhood under the teachings of Radicalism, and who have early rotted [*sic*] in the too warm sun of Radical freedom."[36]

TESTIMONY FOR THE COMMITTEE
ON LABOR AND CAPITAL

Almost a decade later, in 1883, the outcomes of the reconstruction of the stereotyping of African Americans were on display in Alabama at the courthouse hearings of Senator Henry Blair's regarding labor and capital in the postwar South.[37] The hearings functioned as a major arena for a variety of white spokesmen to articulate images of Black people. There were disagreements on the details of the various images. But all of the southern whites who posed as experts on Alabama agriculture and industry agreed that the central problematic trait of Black people in the postwar era was an internal disposition that was deficient in discipline, initiative, reliability, and work ethic. Many also agreed that inadequate family discipline was the primary culprit in fostering the deficient Black disposition.

Among the witnesses who advanced such an interpretation was Robert M. Patton, an antebellum Whig planter-industrialist who had in 1865, under Presidential Reconstruction, become Alabama's first postwar governor. Patton told the Senate committee that "The black labor is demoralized, and is not so reliable as it was in former times." To emphasize the change, he added: "The negroes raised and educated before the war are much more capable, learn better, and work better than those that are now growing up." In slavery times, "the young negroes were raised under discipline and government, and the consequence was that they were better trained to industry and better able to do any kind of work with advantage to themselves as well as to their owners." But since emancipation, "the father of the black boy has not the capacity to inculcate the necessity of regular habits of industry, and of complying with the obligations of contracts."[38]

Patton interrupted himself to explain that "I want to say again, that in making these criticisms, I must not be understood to be saying anything unfriendly to the black people. I have always taken a peculiar interest in our negroes here. . . . I, of course, was raised among the colored people and have been familiar with them all my life, and I know a great deal about their natural disposition and capacity," and "I am not disparaging the poor negro at all."[39] Patton was no Ryland Randolph Ku-Kluxer trying to extinguish Black "insolence." And yet, when it came to assessing the central character traits of postwar Blacks with whom he avowed friendship, Patton was in essential agreement with Randolph.

After declaring his alleged friendship, Patton added that "the negroes in their present demoralized condition do not like to be controlled or guided to any sort of regular habits." In fact, "a colored boy growing up is apt to feel that if he is controlled by his employer he is a slave. . . . They are not controlled by their parents as the white children are, and they are not willing to be controlled or guided by their employers, because they have an idea that that is submitting to slavery again." Indeed, "sometimes they feel that any kind of discipline or government, anything that is compulsory, is slavery." In short, "they do not realize the nature of freedom." Only if whites were able to "educate the negroes so as to teach them the nature of freedom, and the necessity of regular industry," would whites and Blacks "get along very well together." That had not happened yet, and "The black boys and girls in my part of the State are not controlled or trained as they used to be. . . . now they are running about night and day, and if you go out here on a Saturday evening, you can hardly get along the pavement on account of the crowd of those young people. They have left their plows and their hoes and their cotton picking, and have rushed into Birmingham to see what they can see." In short, "The negro population in the neighborhood of the towns and cities is untrained and demoralized, and cannot be depended upon. . . . You cannot get negroes now to work steadily for regular pay. They work a few days until they get a little money, and then they go off to the towns and spend it. That was not the case in old times, although they had plenty of indulgence then from their owners."[40]

Patton was actually more positive about Blacks than were most southern white witnesses. He insisted, for example, that Blacks possessed plenty of capacity to become skilled mechanics. In fact, he asserted, "In relation to this question of the relative capacities of the white and black people, the difference is not so great as you may suppose. . . . They may not be able to plan as well as white men, but they can execute just as well."[41]

Despite his positive assessment of Black capacity, Patton joined the more negative witnesses in asserting that young postwar Black workers were far less reliable than had been well-disciplined slaves. In his mind the central dispositional traits of enslaved Blacks were alive inside young postwar Blacks, but, under the conditions of freedom, the discipline that had controlled those traits had faded.

A Huntsville cotton planter, R. Barnwell Rhett Jr., the son of South Carolina's "fire-eating" secessionist senator, agreed about the post-emancipation "deterioration of the character of the labor," and the alleged Black deficiency in initiative and ambition. But Rhett ventured beyond a dispositional lack of ambition. He came closer than any other witness to articulating a doctrine of inherent biological inferiority. But Rhett advanced it inconclusively, vaguely invoking "the Darwinian theory—the survival of the fittest" to argue that within a few generations white competition would push Blacks out and down to "extinction."[42]

Such talk about distant Black destiny was absent at Senator Blair's hearings on capital and labor, and most witnesses focused upon images of white relations with Blacks in the immediate present. A typical example was Colonel James W. Sloss, founder and president of Birmingham's Sloss Iron Furnace. He relied entirely upon Blacks for his unskilled labor, and he conceded that they made good common laborers while they worked, but he complained that they were "in the main unreliable." "It is seldom that one of them is found disposed to settle down to regular, systematic work," he said. "They are migratory by nature; love to change; to-day at work, and to-morrow away or idle." They were "a moving, restless, migratory class, quite different from the farm or plantation negroes. . . . it is no terror to them to be discharged, none in the world," because they knew they could find a new job as soon as they wanted it. And "As long as they have a dollar in their pockets they feel independent and indisposed to work."[43]

"Is there no way to correct that evil?" asked Senator Blair. Answered Sloss: "I have not found any way, and I have studied the subject very closely." The main problem, said Sloss, affirming the main point of agriculturalists Patton and Rhett, was the lack of internal motivation. According to Sloss, Black laborers found it easy to live on their wages, even on part-time wages. Lacking any desire to save money, they had no motivation for steady work. Sloss said he had gone to some pains to devise incentives. Once he had proposed that any man who worked regularly for twelve months would be able to invest earnings at 8 percent interest. If they had something invested, he thought, perhaps "they might be more careful and thoughtful." But the response had been discouraging: "some of them shook their heads and laughed, but it didn't seem to strike them favorably." Another time, said Sloss, "I thought . . . that I would offer them some inducement to settle down, a silver watch for each man or something of that sort," but the results had not been encouraging, and Sloss had concluded that "the evil is one that has got to work its own cure."[44]

The prospect of a cure seemed remote to Sloss. His ideas revolved mainly around inducing a desire to save and accumulate possessions. He employed only whites for skilled labor, and he offered Blacks no prospect of upward mobility to skilled positions. But he apparently had not considered the possibility that irregular Black work habits might stem not from inherent internal flaws, but rather from a realistic realization that, under Sloss's management, no amount of diligent labor would bring Black occupational advancement.

Two other successful industrialists—Truman Aldrich and Willard Warner—disputed the image of Blacks as by disposition unmotivated and unreliable. Both Aldrich and Warner had been born and educated in the North and were active Republicans. Even though they could be categorized as members of a group of southern white iron and coal industrialists who employed Black labor, they themselves had not identified strongly with the southern white racial in-group or with the in-group's typical affiliation with the white Democratic Party.

Truman Aldrich had credentials as one of three "captains of the Old Guard" who had started Birmingham's industrial boom. Aldrich was a mining engineer who in 1872 had joined the other two "captains," Henry DeBardeleben and James Sloss, in forming the Pratt Coal and Coke Company. Aldrich's stunning engineering expertise had enabled the company to find and to mine the high-quality coking coal that soon fueled the DeBardeleben Alice Furnace and the Sloss Furnace.[45] He had subsequently become president and treasurer of the million-dollar Cahaba Coal Mining Company. In this corporation Blacks had advanced to skilled positions, and Aldrich praised them as, "without exception, the best labor I have ever handled." He briefly affirmed two aspects of the southern white stereotype—Blacks had little opportunity or desire to save money, and they drank too much whisky. But unlike other industrialists, Aldrich did not belabor these points. He did not complain of Black irregularity or unreliability, but rather declared Blacks "much more faithful" than whites. Aldrich asserted that education would lead to significant

Black progress, and he, unlike some industrialists, enthusiastically endorsed Senator Blair's plan for federal aid to Black and white education in the South, calling it essential for industrial development.[46]

The other transplanted northern Republican industrialist, Willard Warner, also contradicted the common stereotype of Black labor by white southerners. He had grown up in Ohio as an antislavery Whig and then "an original Republican—what you may call . . . a Salmon P. Chase Republican." His father had owned slaves in Louisiana, and when Warner had inherited them he had emancipated them "as a matter of conscience." Before the Civil War, Warner had managed a large Cincinnati machine shop and foundry, and during the war he become a major general in the Union Army. At the end of hostilities, he had successfully operated an Alabama cotton plantation, employing freedmen. During Reconstruction, Warner had been a leading "carpetbag" Republican politician, representing Alabama for three years in the US Senate. In 1873 Warner had organized the Tecumseh Iron Company, which produced forty tons of pig iron a day in a charcoal furnace in the village of Tecumseh, seventy-five miles east of Birmingham.[47]

Warner's iron company provided schools, churches, and housing for its African American workers, although these facilities were separate, cheaper, and inferior.[48] Warner had never shared the common southern white view that a Black person would not work as well as a freedman as he had as a slave. While running his first Alabama plantation, his white neighbors had warned him that he could not expect reliable labor from freed slaves. But he had replied, "I have been used to a different system and I have faith that a man will do more work for himself than for anybody else, and that when a man owns himself he is of more value to himself and to the State than when anybody else owns him, and I am going to bet my money on that proposition." He said he had made firm, straightforward agreements with his Black workers regarding work, pay, and accommodations. He had entrusted them with responsibilities and supplies, and had carefully avoided the cheating that was common on the part of many southern planters. As a result, he reported, "these men did more work for me than they had ever done for their old masters, a great deal more," and they had been "a faithful, honest, good set of laborers." In fact, "I never saw a superior set of laborers in my life."[49]

Within Reconstruction-era Alabama, Warner had approached Black plantation workers from an ideological antislavery position, believing that "when a man owns himself he is of more value . . . than when anybody else owns him." Such images had caused him to expect Black energy and industry, and to demonstrate, in his behavior toward Blacks, his confidence in their competence and responsibility. His Black workers had recognized the vast difference between his approach and the approach they customarily experienced from whites who held images of Black indolence and incompetence. Black recognition had in turn shaped Black behavior. Warner's Black plantation workers had responded with appreciation, energy, and industry and had demonstrated to Warner that they were "a superior set of laborers."[50]

Warner seemed quite aware that his beliefs and images of Blacks and his resulting behavior toward them had influenced Black behavior toward him. But the typical southern white witnesses indicated no such awareness. It never seemed to occur to them that much of the Black behavior about which they complained might have been stimulated by white stereotypes about Blacks and by the resulting white expectations of and behavior toward them. Warner's white plantation neighbors had expected unreliable labor from Blacks, and unreliability is exactly what they got.

Warner's favorable assessment of Blacks as laborers had been reaffirmed, he reported, by his experience at his iron furnace. Unlike James Sloss, Warner had found his Black furnace operators to be "permanent" and "faithful, steady laborers." Many had stayed with him for ten years, some serving in responsible skilled positions, and he reported, "I know of no better laborer than the colored laborer."

Warner believed his experience demonstrated that irregularity and irresponsibility were not inherent traits of the Black race. He mentioned specific Blacks who were "superior" skilled workmen, and he believed that, if the two races were given equal opportunity and training, there would be little difference in their performance in all grades of iron labor. "I find," he said, "that whilst I have not as yet known of a colored man whom I wanted to trust as a founder, that is, a man to take charge of the furnace and control of all the men, yet as keepers, who are the next grade of employees, I find colored men just as good as white men. One colored man that we have now employed as a keeper is one of the best. I do not know of any white man that I could employ for equal wages that I would prefer."[51]

Thus two northern-born Republican industrialists painted an image of Black responsibility, reliability, talent, skill, discipline, initiative, and energy—

an image quite the opposite of the one commonly held by southern whites. Their regional and political perspectives had led them to expect such behavior from their Black employees, and their expectations had probably been rewarded, in part, because the positive expectation had fostered the positive behavior.

THE CORE IMAGE: DEFECTIVE INNER DISPOSITION

During the 1883 Senate hearings most southern white witnesses expressed little worry about the Black vote. Nonetheless, all embraced the central core of the postwar white stereotype of the defective inner disposition of the Black freedman. The fullest exposition of the core image came from W. H. Gardiner, an expert on Alabama agriculture who had been in the cotton commission business in Mobile for thirty years. He was well-versed in technical subjects such as cotton productivity trends, and he was somewhat scholarly in approach and demeanor.[52]

Among the southern white witnesses, Gardiner was one of the most favorably disposed toward Black labor. He praised his own "faithful and efficient" Black servants, about whom he "had no cause to complain . . . at all." But Gardiner believed also that, to obtain good service from Black labor, it was necessary to impose firmer discipline than was needed with white labor.[53]

Gardiner had a vision for reforming Alabama agriculture through diversification, and he, like the Jefferson County Grangers of the early 1870s, advocated white immigration. He articulated a highly idealistic stereotype of white farmers—"men of industrial frugal habits," men "who are thoroughly acquainted with every possible phase of economy, who have reduced the art of living down to the minimum of expenditure, and who know how to place every impulse of effort so as to make it yield a tangible and substantial result."[54]

That energetic image stood in stark contrast with Gardiner's image of postwar Blacks. He had observed Black character closely, he claimed, and "The negro is essentially an emotional being." Sensing that such words might seem uncharitable, he hastened to add, "I wish you gentlemen to understand that when I say this, I do not speak with any view to depreciate [*sic*] the negro character, because I have the warmest and most earnest sympathy with the negro race, and I know many of them for whom I would do a great deal. I am simply speaking of their character as a race as I know it."[55]

Gardiner appeared polite, considerate, and thoughtful, displaying none of the animosity of a Ryland Randolph. But he did share Randolph's view that African Americans lacked inner discipline, will, and initiative, and he had developed an elaborate explanation of the psychological sources of their character.

Gardiner took pains to be fair, carefully acknowledging exceptional Blacks who had "bought land and improved it," and who were "doing very well," living in substantial homes. But he saw trouble typically starting "When the young negro gets to be sixteen or seventeen years of age." At that time "he will probably run away from his parents, and go strolling around the country," drifting from job to job, earning just enough to get by, quitting whenever the fancy struck him, taking no thought for the morrow, indulging his immediate whims and emotions, never saving money. "The Negro," he said, "is generally improvident. He will not save. Whatever he gets into his hands, he spends at once; it 'burns a hole in his pocket.' If he sees anything that happens to touch his fancy, and he has the money to buy it, he buys it at once ... even with the last 50 cents that he has in his pocket. That is a general characteristic of the race."[56]

From such conclusions about Black behavior and conditions, Gardiner generated another set of adverse dispositional attributions. Because Black parents associated hard labor with slavery, he said, they wished their children to escape everything associated with slavery, and they usually allowed license and were "weakly indulgent." But then at times they became "harsh and almost brutal," thus creating an inconsistent and ineffective home environment. The crucial consequence, Gardiner declared, was that the young Black "finds in his own passions and impulses the law of his conduct. . . . His character is such that he is very likely to yield to the class of influences which are strongest in their bearing upon him at the moment."

Even Black religion fostered Black indulgence, Gardner maintained. At revival meetings Blacks experienced deep excitement from "the Holy spirit," and "they are conscientious when they tell you so." But, Gardner said, "remove him from the influence of those surroundings, and put the temptation of hunger strongly upon him, and if there is anything that does not belong to him upon which he can lay his hands, he will have no scruples about taking it."

Gardiner, like most southern whites, was prepared to testify to his personal observation of poor Black lifestyle, undeveloped Black skills, low-level

Black jobs, marginally productive Black farms, low Black income, and shabby Black housing. He could logically have attributed such negative conditions to major legacies of slavery (lack of capital and skills), to the structural disadvantages suffered by Blacks, and to white discrimination. Instead, Gardiner, like most southern whites, blamed the negative conditions upon a flawed Black character.

The image of the intrinsically defective Black character served many useful functions for southern whites. Fundamentally, it served to justify both the antebellum and the postbellum southern social, economic, and political systems. When whites claimed that freedom had undermined Black productivity and discipline, they were indirectly vindicating the old slave system and implicitly defending the creation of a new post-emancipation system of Black subordination.

By invoking the image of Blacks as dependent, irresponsible, and lacking in honorable autonomy, whites accentuated a contrasting stereotype of themselves. They used an image of whiteness to distinguish themselves positively from Blacks. Any white could assert his good standing in the white community by dramatizing his contempt for irresponsible Black character and his admiration for contrasting white responsibility and honor. Any white who feared that his own standing had descended to a level close to that of Blacks could reassure himself with the notion that degraded Black status was a product of an inherently degraded Black disposition. He could rally his spirit with the idea that he, as a white person, had inherited a noble character that made him immune from true degradation. White language indicates that whites seldom felt any guilt about the inequality in the economic well-being of Blacks as a group, in comparison with whites as a group.

The reconstructed stereotype of African Americans helped whites to detach themselves emotionally from Blacks, to ignore the economic plight of Blacks, to blame Blacks themselves for their depressed economic condition, and to affirm that the world in which whites fared much better than Blacks was fundamentally just and fair. In all these ways the ubiquitous stereotype about the deep and persisting internal character deficiencies of Blacks fostered positive white morale and white solidarity, and helped whites achieve a positive self-identity.

The stereotype of African Americans as inherently irresponsible, lazy, and improvident became a crucial component of the interaction boundaries that distinguished white from Black and that governed interactions between whites and Blacks in all realms of life. The stereotype of the deficient Black psyche could be invoked to explain and justify discrimination in the economic realm, to legitimate the limitation of Black power, and most of all, to justify the exclusion of Blacks from fellowship with whites in the social realm.

Even though the stereotype performed all these valuable functions for whites and white society, most whites perceived it to be a product of nature and of genuine Black character. They could embrace it, with a sense that it accurately portrayed racial reality. Exhibit A for this point was the testimony at the 1883 Senate hearings by W. H. Gardiner. To his white audience, he appeared to be a perceptive, well-informed, thoughtful man of good will, positive outlook, and gentle disposition. He believed that he knew Blacks well and that he was a genuine friend and supporter who stood ready to defend them against unfair criticism by hostile whites. He seemed to bear no malice toward Blacks, and he nuanced his psychological portrait of their character with details that that seemed to imply somewhat friendly intentions.

In the final analysis, Gardiner nonetheless embraced a stereotype of Black disposition and character that was fully congruent with the less sympathetic accounts of many other whites. When it came time to pronounce a summary formulation of his assessment of Black character, Gardiner declared that the key character trait of "the Negro" was simply this: "Place around him the temptation to the indulgence of any passion, and the means of that indulgence, and he is almost certain to avail himself of it. That is his natural tendency, and he has no counterbalancing elements of character. He is a slave of the influence which predominates around him for the moment."[57]

CHAPTER 3

PROTOCOLS, SANCTIONS, AND
MOB TERROR

To sustain strict racial separation in the "inner citadel" of the social realm, whites of Birmingham employed an elaborate set of criteria and rules. They justified these strong expectations, which social psychologists often refer as "protocols," as necessary to maintain their most fundamental social exclusions. Protocols applied to the most routine of daily interactions between whites and Blacks. The expectations prescribed in a comprehensive way the behavior and language that affirmed white privilege and Black deference. They forbade "social equality" and meticulously excluded Blacks from honorable standing in any occasion of social fellowship among whites. In a tight circular way such rules for Black/white interaction intensified the negative stereotypes that had justified the exclusion, heightened the white sense of sharp difference from Blacks, and fostered among elite and non-elite whites alike a congenial sense of similarity and solidarity.[1]

The everyday Black/white protocols of exclusion and deference inflicted upon Blacks a wide array of pressures. At the milder end of the scale, they experienced daily inconveniences, such as always having to go deferentially to the back door of any white house, and humiliations, such as having to hear themselves always addressed by their first names or diminutive nicknames. Toward the middle of the scale, Blacks experienced discriminatory boundaries that shut them out of public places such as white restaurants and consigned their children to separate and inferior schools.

The protocols were most rigid and fearsome in the realm of interracial sexual relationships. In 1865 Alabama made engaging in those relationships, including marriage, a felony.[2] In addition, the taboo prohibiting any sexual approach by a Black man to a white woman was absolute. Whites defended the miscegenation law and the taboo on suggestive behavior as necessary to maintain the purity of the white race. Whenever a Black man stood accused of violating the sexual taboo, the Black community faced, on the extreme end of the scale, the sanction of sheer terror inflicted by an outraged white mob hellbent on capturing and summarily putting him to death. In Birmingham such white terror erupted infrequently, but when it did it scarred memories and left a painful, recurring awareness that it could happen again at any moment. Such awareness caused all the color barriers to loom ominously over Black life.

Between the founding of Birmingham in 1871 and Alabama disfranchisement in 1901, lynch mobs struck three times in the city—twice in 1883 and once in 1889. In all three cases the Black male target stood accused of sexual assault on a white woman. In many parts of the post-Reconstruction South whites employed lynching also as punishment for other crimes, particularly murder of a white person. But as historian Edward Ayers has phrased it, most of the white rhetoric and justification of lynching "focused intently on the so-called 'one crime' or 'usual crime': the sexual assault of white women by blacks," and in nineteenth-century Birmingham only the accusation of sexual assault provoked documented mob violence against Blacks.[3]

LEWIS HOUSTON

The horror of lynching first descended upon Birmingham exactly one week after the November 1883 US Senate hearing in the courthouse. During most afternoons Black shoppers and businesspeople gravitated toward the group of shops and offices that clustered at Twentieth Street and Second Avenue, just north of the main downtown white business district, one block west of the courthouse. In that compact area Blacks talked among themselves as they worked and shopped and relaxed. During the week following the Senate hearing, conversations probably touched upon the frustrations, reassurances, and even hopes stimulated by the testimony before Senator Blair.[4]

On Friday afternoon, November 23, dreadful rumors banished such talk. Word had it that police had arrested a young Black man, Lewis Houston, at his work at the Louisville & Nashville Railroad roundhouse and had accused him of entering the bedroom of a white widow the night before and attempting to outrage her—to violate her sexually. Black shoppers discussed the rumors with great agitation and carried them back to the Black settlements.[5]

Reports soon circulated that Houston had denied any knowledge of the white widow or her bedroom, but that the police had taken him to her house, and that she had immediately identified him as the man who had awakened her the night before by his movements around her bed. She alleged that, when she had attempted to scream, he had gripped her, pressed his hand over her mouth, and forced her down on the bed, making a noise that awakened others in the house. He had then jumped out the window and fled. She claimed to have recognized him and, after delaying until late the next afternoon, she had called the police and told them his name, and where he lived—in a boardinghouse near her residence. When she confirmed that Houston was the man, the police took him to the courthouse—the same building where the Senate hearings had just adjourned—and imprisoned him in the county jail.

There was worried talk on Friday night and Saturday morning as Blacks who visited their business block began to hear frightening rumors. Angry whites were planning to raid the courthouse—just one block to the east— take Lewis Houston out, and hang him. Blacks generally believed Houston to be innocent. Everyone who lived with him at Annie Davis's boardinghouse reported emphatically that they were certain he had slept in his room all the previous night, and the next day Houston had gone to work as usual, showing no sign of fear and making no attempt to flee. He had been perfectly calm when approached by the policemen. Further, he had been working at the L&N roundhouse for more than a year, was known as an apt worker, and had never been in any trouble.

On Saturday evening Blacks who ventured into the Black businesses heard reports of mysterious comings and goings of groups of whites near the courthouse. Around 10 p.m. came the word that a mob of about 150 white men had entered the courthouse, threatened the county jailer with pistols, obtained the jail keys, taken Houston out, and carried him away up Twenty-First Street. Later that night came the horrifying confirmation. Lewis Houston's body had been found hanging by a clothesline rope from a pine tree in Capital Park, between Twentieth and Twenty-First streets, near Eighth Avenue.

Early Sunday morning hundreds of Blacks walked the few blocks to Capital Park to gaze in horror at the body, which was not cut down until the coroner arrived. They talked angrily among themselves, often loudly enough that a white newspaperman overheard them and reported their words. They believed Houston innocent. They protested the swift action of the mob. They asserted that, since the lynching had been talked about all day Saturday, the mayor should have called out troops to protect the prisoner. They avowed that the mob could easily have been frustrated had the city authorities acted promptly, and they charged that the jailer had been in sympathy with the mob and had willingly surrendered Houston.

Blacks had seen the rights of a fellow Black man disintegrate in the face of a dubious accusation by a white woman. The local government had failed to confront an emerging vigilante spirit that had clearly threatened rights presumably guaranteed by the Constitution and law. Government officials had taken no precautions, and an undeterred white mob had murdered a Black man.

Black residents became more restless and fearful Sunday afternoon when they learned that the coroner had decreed that "the deceased had come to his death by hanging at the hands of parties unknown." Blacks were furious at the injustice, and impatient with the excuses given for the inability to identify the leaders of the mob. The coroner had emphasized that the hanging had occurred very quickly and quietly, and that "the night was cloudy, threatening rain and intensely dark, it being almost impossible to have distinguished persons even without masks." They were upset by Mayor Lane's statement that "he had no intimation, in any sort of shape or fashion, that the lynching was expected." And they were deeply troubled to discover the white newspaper asserting that "it was evident that the majority of the whites regarded the fate of Louis Houston as fully deserved."

By Sunday evening white officials had become alarmed by unrest in the Black community and by rumors that "the jailer was to be punished" or that "the house of the woman who identified Houston as her assailant was to be burned." The chief of police and the mayor deemed the reports troublesome and called out two local white militia groups. Each assembled a full force of armed men, and "The artillery company brought out their Gatling gun mounted upon a carriage drawn by two horses and amply supplied with ammunition," and aimed it down Twentieth Street past George Evans's barber shop and the restaurants of Carrie Skinner and George Walters. All night people who peeked out of their windows could see armed militiamen patrolling the streets on foot and horseback. The Black churches, canceling their usual Sunday evening services, stood dark and empty, and the white newspaper reported that "It was a subject of general remark that not a dozen negroes altogether were seen on the streets after 10 o'clock, and none were to be found at the places where they usually congregate on Sunday night."[6]

No Black retaliation occurred, but the Black community was incensed. It compared the feeble force mobilized Saturday evening to protect Houston with the massive force assembled Sunday evening to discourage retaliation. The Black *Gazette* asserted that, "Had the Birmingham authorities put themselves to half the trouble or care to save the life of the man mobbed there Saturday night as they did afterwards on the groundless apprehension of lawlessness from colored citizens, the Magic City would have saved itself a lasting stain and disgrace." On Saturday night the air had been filled with "earnest" threats of hanging. That night had been the time that "the gattling [*sic*] gun and militia were needed." But despite the many public threats, the "masked men found the jail unguarded and the jailer alone," and they easily captured the prisoner and hanged him "without trial by judge or jury."[7]

Blacks took no comfort from the conciliatory words of white leaders and white newspapers. The white *Iron Age* seemed to want to forget the entire affair and reminded readers that, "A few days ago, a large number of witnesses who were examined before the United States Senate Sub Committee on Labor and Education testified without exception that good feeling existed between the whites and blacks of this community." The *Iron Age* announced that it "still holds to that belief in spite of the events of Saturday and Sunday," and the newspaper sought to end the matter by saying "There is no need to say let us have peace. Birmingham is a peaceful community, and means to remain so."[8]

WESLEY POSEY

Within a week, however, community peace was shattered by a new white mob, provoked by an allegation that a Black man named Wesley Posey had assaulted a nine-year-old white girl, the daughter of a section boss on the L&N Railroad, at Grace's Gap, three miles from the city of Birmingham. The girl "reported to her mother" that "a negro had outraged her person," and, said the *Iron Age*, "The child's statement proved to be true." She said that "the negro requested her not to tell, saying he would give her candy." At the time of the incident "she was away from home in the house of some negroes." A neighbor

spoke of the daughter as "a beautiful child, with a sweet and lovable disposition, and the picture of health." But now, said the *Iron Age*, "the act of one
demon has, perhaps ruined her young life and blighted a happy home."[9]

Posey, who was described as "half-blind," fled into the woods, where he
hid for twenty-four hours without food while a sheriff's posse of one hundred
men searched for him. Eventually Posey stopped at a Black cabin for food.
The posse learned where he was, captured him, took him to Birmingham,
and imprisoned him in the county jail. At once "rumors began to circulate in
the city intimating that the prisoner would be forcibly taken from the jail and
hung by mob violence." This time the city authorities did promptly mobilize
the local militia, with its Gatling gun, to guard the courthouse.

Despite the show of force, by 6 p.m. Monday evening a crowd of more
than a hundred white men was assembling two blocks from the courthouse,
at the corner of Twentieth Street and Second Avenue, right in front of Carrie
Skinner's Black boardinghouse and restaurant. Numerous speakers harangued
the crowd, and, according to an eyewitness, a local attorney "asked that all
who wished to protect their wives and daughters by hanging Posey would
hold up their hands." Many hands went up, and most of the white men, yell-
ing and brandishing pistols, followed the speaker along Second Avenue and
up Twenty-First Street to the courthouse. Blacks stayed inside their houses
and looked on in anxious amazement as the white mob, growing to five hundred, attacked the jail with drawn guns. The militia fell back and allowed
some members of the mob to batter down the door and enter the jail. The
rest of the mob, now grown to almost three thousand, stood on the courthouse lawn shouting "Bring him down, we've got the rope." Lights in the
courthouse windows showed the progress of the searchers as they rampaged
through courtrooms and offices, and climbed to the top of the belfry. Soon
they emerged empty-handed and in great frustration stormed across Twentieth Street, past the Black business block and the Black First Baptist Church to
City Hall. They searched City Hall but found nothing. Finally word spread
that the sheriff had earlier hidden Posey in the country. The exasperated and
sweaty white crowd broke up, swearing to return in the morning to resume
their mission.[10]

The next day, which the *Iron Age* called "one of the ugliest days in the
matter of public feeling that Birmingham ever saw," an even larger mob assembled outside the courthouse and chanted "Hang him!" Anxious Blacks

gradually learned, by rumor and later by newspaper report, that in the county courtroom, where ten days earlier N. R. Fielding and Pastor Isaiah Welch and their friends had discussed race relations with Senator Blair, the circuit court judge had convened a meeting of the local bar and other white citizens to discuss the crisis. A committee of leading citizens, including Mayor Lane, two aldermen, and a former governor, was appointed. The committee drew up resolutions denouncing the alleged rape by Posey but also deprecating "the lawless conduct of the mob at the jail Monday night, as well as the lynching of Lewis Houston on the night of November 24." To the disappointment of Blacks, however, reports said the majority of the assembled citizens had opposed the denunciation of the mob. One prominent attorney had defended the mob, declaring proudly that "he was one of 'the mob.'" The judge backed off and formed a new committee which revised the resolutions to ask simply for a speedy trial by the court and patience on the part of citizens while the trial proceeded. The assembled citizens adopted the new resolutions, but the *Iron Age* observed that "Those, if any, who believed that the action of the meeting would have a sedative effect soon found the fallacy of this trust, as the agitation in favor of lynching the negro was not suspended for a moment."[11]

The court convened and read a grand jury indictment against Posey while outside the white crowd continued to grow, still chanting "Hang him!" That evening two full companies of Montgomery militia arrived by train under orders of the governor. Commanded by a former Confederate colonel, the militia marched up Nineteenth Street past Fielding's grocery store and past the Black Congregational and Baptist churches to City Hall. From there, they established patrols and sentinels on all the side streets and camped on the courthouse lawn. Members of the mob hurled stones at the militia, but for three hectic days the state militia held the shouting mob away from the court-house. Inside, the judge read the indictment to Posey, who had returned from the country. The judge then assembled a panel of one hundred jurors, selected a jury, conducted a trial, found Posey guilty of rape after only a few minutes of deliberation by the jury, and sentenced him to hang. Finally, the Montgomery militia took Posey in charge, marched him past the shouting mob to the depot, and took him on the train to Montgomery for safe keeping during the legal thirty-day wait until the hanging.

The Birmingham Black community, while no doubt partially relieved that the ordeal was over, was deeply disturbed by the series of events: the appear-

ance of a new white mob so rapidly after the Houston lynching, the ineffec-
tiveness of local white moderates, the support of the mob by important local
whites, and the precipitous nature of the trial in an atmosphere in which, as
John Henry Thomason, editor of the Birmingham *Weekly Pilot*, put it, "there
was certainly *great* prejudice against the unfortunate man." White officials had
gone through a charade of respecting Posey's rights, but again the fury of a
white mob had incinerated the rights of a Black man.[12]

Posey was not, in fact, brought back to Birmingham in thirty days for
hanging. Some high-level white state officials, Governor Edward A. O'Neal
probably among them, raised questions about "a verdict rendered while bay-
onets held an angry mob at bay" and arranged appeals. Even the Democratic
Mobile *Register*, an advocate of social exclusion of Blacks, condemned the
Posey trial, declaring: "Every occurrence of this sort is a disgrace to the State in
which it occurs." Such a trial "is the very essence of lynch law—hang first and
investigate afterwards. We, the mob, declare him guilty; therefore hang him."[13]

Higher state courts ultimately set aside the Birmingham verdict and or-
dered a new trial in another city. Blacks were glad to see evidence that some
whites did deplore mob threats. The *Pilot* declared that "Too much credit
cannot be given to Governor O-Neal [*sic*] for his promptness in suppressing
the Birmingham riot and protecting Wesley Posey from the mob." But Blacks
also anticipated another sham trial and found no comfort in pious white sentiments and actions.[14]

Before the new trial could be arranged, Posey died in jail, saying at the
end, "I die an innocent man." Those who had visited him in jail said that he
"has not been himself since the terrible ordeal he passed through." On the day
Posey died, the white *Iron Age* revealed information that must have caused
many Blacks to reflect bitterly upon the angry certitude of the mob, and upon
the confidence with which white authorities had rushed to convict. A physician
who had attended Posey had told the *Iron Age* that a conclusive medical point,
which the newspaper considered unprintable, had convinced him that "Posey
was innocent of the crime charged against him," and that at his trial "he did
not have justice."[15]

Meanwhile, in August of 1884, half a year after the Posey trial, county
officials had placed five alleged mob members on trial for riotous assembly
and unlawfully meeting to plan murder. Numerous witnesses, including the
sheriff, the county jailer, and the city marshal, identified the defendants as

vocal members of the mob, but the jury, after only a few minutes' consultation, announced "a verdict of not guilty as to all the defendants."[16]

To J. H. Thomason, editor of the *Pilot,* it seemed that "The lynching of Houston" had "turned the white people wild for colored blood." Enormous energy festered around the image of Black male sexual threats to white women. Whites used that energy to reinforce and to justify their social protocols that forbade any close social interaction with Blacks. And on those rare occasions when a white woman accused a Black man of violating the sexual taboo, masses of whites stood ready to assemble in lawless mobs to inflict the most awful possible retribution. Any Black man had to contemplate the grim possibility that he himself could face such an accusation and its consequences.

The Houston and Posey episodes, coming in such rapid succession, generated fears that lingered long after the events. Six months later, in July, Blacks heard a new rumor of possible mob action against a Black man, John Parker, who was being held in the city jail for shooting (but not killing) a white man. J. H. Thomason feared that white mob activity and frustrations in the Houston and Posey incidents "did not increase their love for the colored people," and "they have only been waiting an opportunity to make good on some other man the threats they failed to execute at the time against Posey."

As it turned out, the July shooting produced less intense white anger than had the earlier allegation of rape, and the mayor and police did promptly protect the jail. Birmingham Black men again demonstrated their resilience in the face of mob rumors. Several armed themselves with shotguns and rifles and hid in the tall grass of a vacant lot across from the city hall to guard Parker. The police became alarmed about Black men "lying ambushed in the dead hours of night with guns in their hands." They arrested one man, locked him in jail, and charged him with "riotous conduct." The next morning, however, Mayor Lane, viewing the matter in the light of day, concluded that the evidence was "insufficient" to sustain the charge and dismissed the case. The correspondent to the *Gazette* wrote that "There is still a strong feeling among Negroes over Parker's supposed danger," and J. H. Thomason warned, "We are opposed to the serious trouble in Birmingham and if this mob business is not stopped the colored men don't intend to stand it any longer." The armed Black men stood guard several more nights, and the lynching rumors subsided.[17]

An accusation that a Black man had shot a white man could provoke white anger and could stir up lynching talk. But Parker was not lynched, and research has never discovered an example in nineteenth-century Birmingham of a white mob lynching, or attempting to lynch, a Black man unless he had been accused of assault upon a white woman.

GEORGE MEADOWS

The third lynch-mob episode, in 1889, involved an invasion of the community of Blacks who had taken up coal mining in the village of Pratt Mines, six miles northwest of Birmingham. The general tension between white and Black miners at this time no doubt helped set the stage for this episode.[18] But, regardless of its sources, the mob violence demonstrated the ability of an organized white lynch mob to threaten a Black community broadly. A mob squad could scour through streets and homes, sweeping up any Black man who seemed to fit only the vaguest of descriptions.

On a Saturday morning in January 1889, a white woman, Mrs. J. S. Kellam, and her six-year-old son went looking for a stray cow in the woods near the village. According to Mrs. Kellam, a Black man attacked them, killed the boy, assaulted her, and left them both for dead. Somehow she revived and told her story, and in short order more than four hundred armed white miners, accompanied by barking bloodhounds, were searching the village and scouring the countryside for men who fit Mrs. Kellam's description of her attacker—"a short, yellow negro about 20 years of age, heavily built, with a clean-shaven face, with a yellowish-brown shirt on."[19]

The *Age-Herald* reported that "Little knots of rough, determined men could be seen anywhere and in every street of the little village. There was no boisterous excitement, but the grim countenances and measured words of the spokesmen for the groups said more plainly than clamor could have said: 'When the murderer is caught, and his guilt is established beyond a peradventure, he must die, and die at once. The nearest tree or faggot pile will be his place of doom.'"[20]

Blacks, staying off the streets as much as possible, watched in horror as "dozens" of young men were summarily arrested because they loosely fit some part of Mrs. Kellam's description. Each suspect "would be closely questioned by the authorities and then taken to Mrs. Kellam's residence for identification," said the *Age-Herald*, "but each time the answer came from the weak, suffering woman, a word from whose mouth was more powerful than a death-warrant from a judge on the bench, 'He is not the man.' The prisoner would then be quietly led away and dismissed." There was "no disposition to act hastily," said the *Age-Herald*. "Every prisoner was treated with the utmost kindness and consideration, and no demonstration will be made until the right man is caught and convicted by identification, and when this is done no power can save him."[21]

Blacks shuddered at their community's exposure to capricious danger. They protested against the flagrant violations of the rights of all the arrested Black men, and they dismissed the claim that every prisoner was treated "with the utmost kindness and consideration." The search, said the Birmingham *News*, was "creating quite a feeling among the colored population, who led by a few, object to these wholesale arrests." But the bizarre search and arrests continued through Saturday afternoon and evening, through all of Sunday, and into Monday.[22]

The sheriff's deputies dismissed Black protests, and the *News* reported that "in the interest of justice they will arrest a thousand if necessary." The deputies asserted that "No innocent man can complain, and besides can readily show that he was not connected with the crimes." But the *Age-Herald* noted that "the negroes had aroused themselves and were congregating to protect their brother, should he be captured. They say that he shall have a fair trial if it costs them their lives."[23]

On Monday afternoon the report went out that Mrs. Kellam had reacted in horror when shown a suspect named George Meadows, a former furnace worker. Meadows had been arrested because it had been noticed, two days after the murder, that "he fit the description, even to his clothes." Ironically, Meadows had first drawn attention to himself by his "undue diligence" in "swearing his fealty to the white men and vengeance on the negro they were after."

When asked if she could positively identify Meadows as the attacker, Mrs. Kellam said, "If it is not him it is his twin brother." Then came the surprising word that George Meadows did in fact have a twin brother, Rufus. Vigilantes quickly tracked down Rufus Meadows and brought him before Mrs. Kellam, but she cleared him, and attention again focused on George Meadows. "Great excitement is now prevailing at the mines," said the *News*, and "crowds of negroes are congregating demanding a fair trial for the accused."[24]

Late that afternoon the mob leaders took Meadows back to Mrs. Kellam. Now she was less confident. She said she was "unable to identify him positively," but added that he very closely resembled her assailant and she thought he was the man. Both Mrs. Kellam and her husband, however, appealed to the citizens of Pratt Mines, verbally and through a newspaper letter, not to lynch the suspect but to turn him over to the authorities and "Let the law take its course."[25]

Local deputy sheriffs had participated in the search, and the county coroner had been present when suspects were shown to Mrs. Kellam. But the leaders of the white mob were the ones holding Meadows in custody, and they were determined not to let him fall into the control of the sheriff's deputies. Monday night the mob selected sixteen armed guards to hide Meadows in the woods so the deputies could not get him.[26]

At nine o'clock Tuesday morning the mob again took Meadows before Mrs. Kellum. She remained "unable to identify him positively." But "She thought . . . he was the negro." After the "partial identification," reported the *News,* "the mob grew furious," and "It was easy to see that they meant blood. They intended to hang the negro, and there was no resistance" from the sheriff's posse. According to the *News,* the posse "'seemed' to go ahead along the road, and when they were far in advance, the crowd 'suddenly' concluded that they had better hang Meadows. They selected a white-oak tree, with a straight outreaching limb. They threw the rope over; put it about Meadow's neck." They allowed him to kneel to pray. When he arose, "in an instant ten men grasped the rope and Meadows' body shot up into the air." A fusillade from the Winchester rifles and the Smith & Wesson 38s in the mob riddled Meadows's body with "about 100 shots," turning it "into pulp."[27]

This sickening climax did not bring an end to the episode. On the same day that Meadows had been captured, the search, which had spread to downtown Birmingham, had led to the arrest of another "yellow man" at the train depot, because he "very closely answers the description of the man wanted," indeed, "he comes nearer the description than any man yet arrested." When arrested, the frightened and bewildered suspect "could give no satisfactory account of himself or where he had been," so he was held to be shown to Mrs. Kellam. However, she was so distraught that she refused to look at him until two days after the lynching of Meadows. During those days the whites and the newspapers speculated openly as to whether the mob had hanged the wrong man, even as pictures of the hanging were being displayed in the windows of a large downtown clothing store and attracting large crowds. When Ms. Kellam finally viewed the new suspect she declared him "not the man." Those words served to convince most whites, finally, that the true criminal had paid the price and that the matter was concluded.[28]

Unrest continued, however, in the Black community. Black spokesmen stipulated that they had not wished a felon to escape, if he was in fact guilty. But they expressed their horror that Meadows had not been allowed a fair trial but had been "left to the mercy of hasty conclusions formed by the people at large." Declarations of Black anger were so widespread that "serious trouble was apprehended." The newspapers reported that "many pistols were bought by negroes," and that "a great deal of shot and ammunition had been bought by the negroes from the merchants who finally declined to sell to them." Whites responded by buying still more Winchester rifles and other firearms, and "considerable excitement" prevailed in Pratt City.[29]

Some law officials and numerous "cool and conservative citizens" sought to calm both Blacks and whites. Alabama Governor Thomas Seay issued a proclamation offering a $400 reward for the arrest of each or any one of the murderers of George Meadows.

A group of white "Citizens of Jefferson," however, defied the governor. They wrote: "The brightest page in the history of the state to which our children's children will point with pride will be written indelibly on their hearts, that the chaste mothers and pure daughters of the white people of Alabama are under the sovereign control of her noblest and best citizens, and shall be protected against the assaults of black demons, regardless of reward."[30] The Knights of Labor newspaper, the *Alabama Sentinel*, seconded the defiance, writing: "The good citizens of Pratt Mines have only done their imperative duty; they have arisen in their might and inflicted well-deserved punishment on a murderer of innocence and a violator of chastity.[31]

The Birmingham chief of police, at the request of the sheriff, sent several policemen to try to apprehend some of those suspected of carrying out the lynching. But, the police chief cryptically said, his suspects "proved their innocence." They then sued the chief for $5,000, and the chief had to spend $50 defending himself against their suit. Eventually the board of aldermen reimbursed him for that expense.[32]

Vivid memories of the Meadows lynching lived on. Two years later, a white newspaper reporter observed that in the village of Pratt Mines a new wide and smooth dirt path had come into being. Departing from the main road near the school and the business section, the path zigzagged along a gully for ninety yards into the woods, and ended at the large white oak from which Meadows had hanged. The ground around the tree had been "packed hard" by the tread of many feet, and the four-foot trunk had been "scarred in innumerable places" where visitors had used knives and axes to extract bullets for souvenirs. The reporter observed that nearly every day "somebody walks down to the wild and weird spot where the demon in human form ceased to breathe."

Blacks as well as whites visited "the Meadows oak." A reporter wrote, "Negroes visit it in crowds," and he speculated on the reasons. "Some of them go purely from curiosity. Others have invested the tree and the ground with a superstitious quality and go as a sort of worship, and still others who possess a little more of the reflective are said to go and review there the wrongs they imagine are done them by the white race and renew cowardly vows of revenge."[33]

The reporter's insight into the thinking of the visitors was no doubt imperfect, but certainly many Birmingham Blacks, even those who did not visit the Meadows oak, reflected upon the awful week that it symbolized. The ordinary day-to-day interactions of Blacks and whites had been disrupted by white frenzy. Every individual Black man who had become the focus of the mob had found himself completely defenseless unless and until one disturbed white woman declared him "not the man." The fragility of Black rights had become obvious, and a sense of helplessness permeated the Black community.

WHITE MEN AND BLACK WOMEN

Accusations of rapes of white women by Black men were rare in early Birmingham. The few accusations that did occur, like the three in Birmingham between 1871 and 1901, were highly dubious. Blacks had good reason to conclude that the ultimate purpose of the sexual taboo and of the white readiness to lynch was not to protect white women from real sexual danger or to maintain the purity of white blood. Rather, the purpose was to mobilize the most intense of human emotions behind the enforcement of the central social boundaries that designated people of African ancestry and slave heritage to be humans of debased worth who had to be relentlessly subordinated.

In the mid-twentieth century, Gunnar Myrdal's analysis of the "white man's rank order of discriminations" provided support for such an interpretation. The highest priority in the rank order, Myrdal declared, was "the bar against intermarriage and sexual intercourse involving white women." Thus, said Myrdal, the rank order was "very apparently determined by the factors of sex and social status, so that the closer the association of a type of interracial behavior is to sexual and social intercourse on an equalitarian basis, the higher it ranks among the forbidden things." Sex and the doctrine of "no social equality" became "in this popular theory the principle around which the whole structure of segregation of the Negroes—down to disfranchisement and denial of equal opportunities in the labor market—is organized."[34]

Myrdal noted the intensity of "the average white person's psychological identification with the 'white race,'" and "his aversion to amalgamation." But, said Myrdal, "the anti-amalgamation doctrine is merely a rationalization of purely social demands, particularly those concerning social status." The southern white desire for superior social standing was "psychologically dominant to the aversion for 'intermarriage.'" Southern whites utilized "the dread of 'intermarriage' and the theory of 'no social equality' to justify discriminations which have quite other and wider goals than the purity of the white race."[35]

Thus, asserted Myrdal, the popular southern white anti-amalgamation doctrine, with its preoccupation with sex, was a rationalization that did not actually reveal the fundamental motivation of whites: *"what white people really want,"* he argued, was simply *"to keep the Negroes in a lower status."* Sex was merely the vehicle by which whites would systematically deprive Blacks of power in all spheres of life. Whites would use the emotions surrounding sex and marriage to force an entire *"system of deprivations . . . upon the Negro group."*[36]

Support for that interpretation could be found in the lack of white concern about sexual approaches by white men toward Black women. Some whites frowned upon such approaches, but white society established no taboo against them and generated no mob outrage to punish them.[37] Blacks saw shameless hypocrisy in this. They knew that numerous white men, despite their sanctimonious talk about racial purity, casually indulged in sexual exploitation, including rape, of Black women and considered it to be one of the prerogatives permitted them by the white supremacy code. Blacks understood that, when whites insisted upon "no social equality," they were in fact concerned far less with protecting white biological purity than with preserving the prerogatives of privileged white social standing, and that they were particularly concerned with maintaining the opportunity to exploit the vulnerability of the African Americans who were kept in such degraded status.[38] To justify sexual exploitation and assault by white men, whites stereotyped many Black women as "Jezebels"—women inherently promiscuous and incapable of being raped. That image, paired with a "Mammy" stereotype, constituted what historian Grace Elizabeth Hale has described as "a racialized transcription of that old feminine dualism, the mother or the whore."[39] As historian Leslie Brown wrote, the "Mammy" stereotype of Black women servants as "desexualized and innocuous" assisted white employers in reconciling "their beliefs in black immorality and hypersexuality with their personal needs to have African American women as household laborers in intimate contact with their families."[40]

At the same time, the "Mammy" stereotype helped obscure the reality that major venues for white sexual assaults on Blacks were the white homes employing Black women and girls in domestic service. In these homes, Black women were highly vulnerable because of their race, gender, and class. Working in subservient, poorly paid positions, Black maids experienced sexual approaches from the white males of the households. These might be accompanied by offers of badly needed money, but the approaches could be repulsed only at some risk to continued employment. Black leaders were acutely aware of the reality. In 1887 the *Negro American* admonished: "Too much cleaning up-stairs rooms among our girls and married women. Let them engage in some other work that will lead to more virtue. Husbands and parents see to this matter at once."[41]

At the 1883 Senate hearings in the Birmingham courthouse, a Black carpenter, James K. Green of Montgomery, boldly articulated Black dismay. "Here is the only thing that we are troubled about now, about our civil rights," he said:

> A colored man and his wife may go to work to get a little home, may go hungry and naked to educate a daughter, the dearest treasure that they have got, and the very moment that she begins to come up there is an inroad made upon her by the whites of this country, and we have got no redress in the world. They can't deny that. Now, I want as much civil rights and rules to regulate and protect my family as any white man does, and if I catch a man under such circumstances I won't hurt him but once! . . . That is what we want to protect the virtue of our girls. That is the rights I want. I don't want no social equality with the white people, and I don't want them to have none with me. I see the influence of this thing every day. There has been a

time when they were opposed to such thing, but now that we are free the parents of the children can't even protect their children, and there ain't a white man here can deny it. That is the trouble in this country.[42]

To Black leaders, shameful evidence of the degrading vulnerability of Black women also appeared out in the settlements known as "Buzzard Roost" and "Scratch Ankle," which were beyond the city limits and the jurisdiction of the city police. The brothels employed Black women, but most of the establishments were owned by white men and wholesale liquor companies. In 1889, a white *Age-Herald* reporter tramped through the alleys in the company of a policeman, who took him into several of the "lowest dives," including the "Hole in the Wall" and the "Crow's Nest." The reporter described crude one-story frame buildings, divided into as many as ten small rooms by rough board partitions. Floors were dirty and stained with the remains of spilled drinks. The women smoked, drank whisky, lolled on beds "covered with filthy disordered quilts," and entertained young white workingmen. At the "Crow's Nest," the officer's knock on the front door created a panic. Three men ran out the back door and jumped the back fence, while "seven more marched gravely out the front way."

A higher quality "dive" was that of the "notorious courtesan" Jennie Beale, known as the "Speckled Queen." Her "palace," in a substantial brick building over a store, four blocks west of Main Street, was "lighted for a fete" when the reporter arrived and was "well furnished with some pretension of ostentation." The queen, he found, "has sixteen maids of honor, ranging from the purest ebon hue to that of a new saddle." The maids were visited by "only white men," and that evening the reporter discovered "at least twenty" white clients in the halls and reception rooms. Jennie Beale, he concluded, "has accumulated considerable money, and let it be said to the shame of the city, not a small amount of it has been contributed by men who are well known about the city."[43]

Such reports caused white tongues to wag, but they mobilized no mobs to hunt down and punish the seven white patrons who had exited from the Crow's Nest by the front door or the numerous "well-known" white clients of Jennie Beale. White violation of Black women never stirred up talk of a lynching. Several times church-oriented Blacks appealed to the white authorities to enforce the law against the Black brothels, but with little success.

In 1891 the board of aldermen recorded the receipt of "A petition . . . from colored citizens, numerously signed, asking that bawdy houses kept by colored women for white men be broken up." But the aldermen buried the petition in committee for six weeks, then disallowed it. In 1894 and 1900 they did the same with similar Black petitions.[44]

Black business and professional people found it a bitter irony that the most respectable Black businesses had almost no white clients, and had to scrape along on the patronage of poor Black people, but that the least respectable enterprises had plentiful white customers and flourished precisely because they engaged in the degrading business of selling the sexual services of Black women to white men. To Black leaders the irony seemed most bitter when the newspapers carried reports of yet another lynching somewhere in the South, reminding everyone once again of the alleged intensity of white determination to protect the purity of the white race.

In 1894, H. Sebastian Doyle, pastor of the St. James Colored Methodist Episcopal (CME) Church in Birmingham, secretary of the Black Pastors' Union, and editor of the Birmingham *Negro-American Press,* seized upon a contrast between two current newspaper reports to make the point. One report related how nine Black men had been lynched in Louisiana for the murder of one white man. The other report described how six young white men had taken a young paralytic Black girl, dragged her into a room, and raped her one by one until she died. Said Doyle: "If six negroes had even made the proposition to a white female, they would have been burned and tortured with the very refinement of cruelty." But "white men use no means to punish" the six white rapists. "White men," he asked, "do you not blush for shame?"[45]

Pastor Doyle was no stranger to the terror of a white lynch mob. As recently as 1892, he himself had been the lynching target of angry Georgia whites. His provocation had been political, not sexual. He had been making zealous campaign speeches on behalf of Populist Congressman Thomas E. Watson. When white Democrats had threatened to lynch Doyle, Watson had called out an opposition army of white Populist farmers to guard him. Thus protected, Doyle had continued speaking for Watson, even though during one speech a shot intended for him struck and killed a nearby white man. Doyle was impressed by Watson's protection, and he clung to a belief that exposure of the paradoxes and the fundamental social chaos portended by mob violence could mobilize whites like Watson to take a strong stand against it.[46]

For two weeks, Doyle reflected upon what the contrasting news accounts about whites lynching nine Black men and whites raping a helpless Black woman implied for the status of Blacks. He then he proclaimed his profound distress:

> Southern justice resolved to its essence is this; Negroes, look at white women and you die; white men, seduce, outrage, ravish negro women to death—yes whole bands of you lie in wait to seize helpless, infirm negro women and outrage till death ends the misery and you go free. By heavens, if you are convicted that won't matter; we'll turn you loose. White women mustn't be looked at; negro women must not be defended. In short, the spirit of Roger Taney is abroad. Negroes have no rights which white men are bound to respect.[47]

Doyle's invocation of Justice Roger Taney's 1857 Dred Scott decision may have seemed hyperbolic. Emancipation had given Blacks some important rights that many whites normally respected. But Doyle voiced the reality that any Black man could see all those rights crumble into dust the moment he encountered an accusing white woman, or the moment he violated a crucial boundary taboo, whether through blunder or audacious protest.

Doyle's rhetoric rang true as an expression of the deep frustration of African American men and women who continually found that their ancestry and their history as slaves caused whites to consign them to a dishonored social status. The social debasement brought in its train more than social exclusion, denial of respect, and institutional segregation. The dishonoring also brought vulnerability in all aspects of life—vulnerability to circumscription of economic opportunity, vulnerability to debilitating abridgment of electoral and legal rights, and vulnerability to systematic discrimination in allocation of government resources and services.

Doyle invoked Justice Taney's Dred Scott language to declare a grim reality. Because Doyle was Black, he lived with constant vulnerability to loss of his rights; he coped daily with the awareness that terror could destroy him; he suffered discrimination in every realm of life; and from most whites he received no respect.

CHAPTER 4

SCHOOL SEGREGATION

During Reconstruction, southern whites, invoking and asserting values and images of the powerful inner social color line, promptly segregated every public institution in the social realm. Then, building on the segregation of those specific social sites and institutions, southern whites expanded, connected, and sharpened the patterns of racial separation so as to establish in the late 1870s and early 1880s the segregation of schools, urban housing, and the labor force in Birmingham. These were the three broad and fundamental types of segregation. Powerful combinations of socio-emotional and instrumental motivations—the latter of which included economic and political self-interest—motivated their architects. All three emerged from thousands of confrontations and interactions between Black and white individuals and groups who were struggling over boundaries old and new.

THE SOCIAL SETTING

The school stood out as the *public* institution into which whites most resolutely extended the values and the boundaries of the *social* realm. Whites conceived of the school as an extension of the family, charged with responsibilities for the socialization of the coming generation. Moreover, school classrooms contained family-like groups of impressionable children who interacted socially on an equal basis and who formed deep and often enduring friendships. Thus, whites emphasized that the daily interactions among children in school classrooms

69

were inherently social. In schools, postbellum southern whites said, Blacks were unworthy to mix with whites and must be set aside in separate units.

When teachers imparted skills and prepared children for lifetime occupations, they were also performing a crucial economic function. And when city or state officials governed schools and financed them with tax revenue, they were providing the most significant and costly service rendered through the political realm. But the tax-supported public school incorporated functions and features so complex and so diverse that it could not be categorized neatly in any one realm. Different groups, placing different emphases upon the various functions of the public school, conceived of it as falling into different realms of life.

When southern whites thought of the public school in the context of race relations, they typically emphasized the social aspects. To allow boys and girls of African ancestry and slave heritage to enter the familial setting of the white school classroom, white parents said, would violate the right of American parents to determine for themselves who was worthy to be admitted into intimate association with their family. Government, they believed, had no legitimate authority to interfere with that sacrosanct right. To incorporate African American children into the familial interactions of the school classroom would bring social degradation and shame upon white children. Many whites asserted also that Blacks learned more slowly. If schools were integrated, they argued, the learning of all children would be impeded.[1]

FEDERAL POLICY AND SCHOOL SEGREGATION

In theory, the federal government could have blocked southern whites from segregating public schools. Because they were undeniably part of the political realm, the federal government could have done so by invoking the constitutional guarantee of equality under state law. In fact, during Reconstruction, Senator Charles Sumner of Massachusetts proposed requiring racial integration of public schools. He argued that it was essential to American democracy that public schools be open "to all without distinction of race or color." Beginning in 1867 he spearheaded an eight-year campaign to pass federal civil rights legislation that would prohibit states from segregating public schools by race. Racial separation of schools, said Sumner, "cannot fail to have a depressing effect on the mind of colored children, fostering in them and others that they are not as good as other children." Also it would have an evil effect upon white children, undermining the crucial principle of "equality" upon which democracy must rest. Sumner's Massachusetts colleague George S. Boutwell agreed and urged integration of schools so that "Negro and white alike" would in time "be assimilated and made one in the fundamental ideal of human equality."[2]

African American leaders at the national and state levels recognized the enormous positive impact integrated schools could have, and many of them endorsed Sumner's campaign. In 1874 a statewide convention of the "colored people of Alabama" met to debate whether to support the specific "mixed school" clause of Sumner's civil rights bill. It was at that convention that Pastor Isaiah Welch, then living in Selma, received notice as a star orator, speaking in favor of giving Black children the right to attend public schools with whites.

A reporter for the Montgomery *Advertiser,* a conservative, white, and Democratic newspaper, provided a derisive report on the convention. He highlighted another speaker at the convention—a Black legislator named Walker, who hailed from Dallas County. "Colored children should have access to all schools," declared Walker. "He was," wrote the reporter, "in favor of teaching the white and black children together in the same school, in order that that idea of inferiority of the latter might be broken up. Unless they were put together, there would be no equality of privileges and accommodations." The reporter pointed out that the *"unanimous drift"* of most Black speakers was to endorse Walker's sentiments in spirit, as their true goal. But some cautioned that they should "go slow" in proposing to integrate schools because of intense white hostility to the idea. Even white Republicans had stomachs too weak to take such strong whiskey "straight," said one speaker, and "required much water in it."[3]

Congressional Republicans shied away from supporting Sumner's mixed-school campaign. They were acutely aware of the intense southern white hostility to mixed schools, and knew that most northern voters saw the ideal of school integration to be at best a low priority. Sumner's "mixed school" clause won a majority of Republican votes on only a few procedural votes on which support for it proved tactically advantageous to the Republican Party. The clause never came close to passage.[4]

Southern white Democrats in Congress highlighted the social issue posed by mixed schools. Missouri Congressman John M. Glover argued that Sumner's mixed-school bill was an improper attempt to give the government power "to regulate the association, companionship, tastes and feelings of the people." John D. Atkins of Tennessee asserted that God had "stamped the fiat of his condemnation" upon mixed marriages, which brought "decay and death," and he urged that the states must have "the power to keep the races apart in the schools and elsewhere." Senator Thomas N. Norwood of Georgia argued that, if Black and white children attended mixed schools, the resulting "familiar association" would monstrously suggest that there should be "no impediment" to interracial matrimony.[5]

White southern educators, including many committed advocates of Black education, warned Republicans that southern white opposition to racial mixing in the social milieu of the school classroom was so wide and so deep that, if Sumner's mixed-school clause did become law, the South would simply shut down its public school systems.[6] In essence the white southern educators asserted that in the hearts and minds of southern whites the social aspect of school towered above all others. If closing schools should become the only way to prevent socially unworthy Black schoolchildren from mixing with white schoolchildren, educators in the South would not shrink from the destruction of the system, despite its enormously valuable political and economic functions. They used the threat to persuade the federal government to permit the whites to construct an exclusionary social boundary through the center of the public school system, even though the boundary would divide it into competing and unequal fragments.

After Sumner's death in 1874, Republican senators did enact the Civil Rights Act of 1875, partly as a memorial to him, but without his mixed-school clause. They left the matter of mixed or segregated schools to the states, and all southern states continued to require segregation in all public schools. Only in the North did states gradually prohibit school segregation, but even there states generally maintained racially discriminatory funding.[7]

The defeat of Sumner's proposal represented a far-reaching victory for the mobilization by southern whites of the intense emotions that fueled social separation. The emotional pressure did more than reinforce exclusionary boundaries in the social realm. The pressure helped southern whites embed them elsewhere within the public realm. Just as Senator Charles Sumner had foreseen, the policy decision to allow states to segregate public schools by race had a profound long-run negative impact on African Americans in all areas of life.

Throughout Sumner's campaign to prohibit school segregation, the state of Alabama had been actively creating a segregated public school system, confident that the South's arguments for separate schools would prevail. In the fall of 1875, soon after the Republican Congress had dropped Sumner's mixed-schools clause from the 1875 Civil Rights Law, Alabama Democrats, having regained control of ("redeemed") state government, created a new constitution explicitly requiring that "separate schools shall be provided for the children of citizens of African descent."[8] This separate-school clause was arguably the most significant postbellum "Jim Crow" law enacted by the state of Alabama. It involved the most important and costly of all state and local government services, and it was embedded right in the state constitution. More generally, by the end of Reconstruction every southern state had used laws and budgets to establish the institutional structure, including administrative policies and government bureaucracies, for a Jim Crow system of rigidly segregated Black and white schools.[9]

ALFRED B. JACKSON AND
SCHOOL REFORM IN BIRMINGHAM

During the 1870s, Alfred B. Jackson, a skilled bricklayer and plasterer, became Birmingham's leading advocate of improvement in Black schooling. He moved to Birmingham in 1873, two years after the boomtown had been founded. New residents were crowding in daily, and a housing shortage had become so acute that anxious tenants sought to occupy new buildings even before they were completed. Jackson's construction skills had been in great demand. He had prospered, gaining considerable economic independence. He aspired to have his children and all of the next Black generation acquire comparable skills and achieve comparable success within the new Black middle class in Birmingham.[10]

In 1873, during Birmingham's initial boom, a group of white laboring men held a mass meeting to call for the establishment of a "Free White School." White working-class children were growing up unschooled, said the workers, because laborers could not afford the tuition charged by the small private schools to which local businesspeople sent their children. The white workers had convinced the town's most prominent attorney, Colonel John T. Terry, to lead a civic campaign to gather school donations. Terry had persuaded Mayor

James R. Powell, who was also the president of the Elyton Land Company, which had founded Birmingham, to believe that the new "workshop" town would not grow and prosper unless it could attract and retain white working-men. They would not come or stay unless the town provided an affordable public school.[11]

Colonel Terry mounted an intense community campaign. From civic-minded residents he collected $3,000. He convinced the Elyton Land Company to donate a lot for a new school, and he talked Mayor Powell into donating his entire mayoral salary for school maintenance. Such feats became legends recited by white boosters to affirm Birmingham's remarkable enterprising spirit. With the $3,000 the aldermen began construction of a handsome brick two-story, four-room school building, and when the $3,000 ran out they issued $2,500 in city bonds to complete it.[12]

In the spring of 1874 the new Free White School opened, and in the eyes of many proud white citizens it was "the keystone of our new community." Each year after 1874 the Free White School ran ten months with four classes taught by four highly esteemed teachers. And each year the aldermen used city revenue to provide teachers' salaries, furniture, supplies, coal, water, repairs, and maintenance of the school.[13]

From all this the Black children of Birmingham faced categorical exclusion. During 1875 and 1876 their only instruction was a separate, informal class that met a scant four months in a small African American Church furnished with bare benches. There a few pupils of widely varying ages were taught by a modestly educated Black man whom the parents themselves, rather than the aldermen, had recruited.[14]

During the 1870s, Birmingham Blacks would have had no schooling at all except that during Reconstruction the Alabama Republican Party had established a state school fund and provided it with enough tax revenue to spend at the level of one dollar per year per child of school age. The Republicans had required by law that the annual state school fund be distributed among counties strictly according to population, and that counties and cities in turn must divide it between the races on a strict per capita basis. In 1875–76, Birmingham had had approximately three hundred white and one hundred Black school-age children. That meant the Free White School received $300 from the state fund and the Black school $100.

The white aldermen supplemented the state's $300 for the Free White

School with approximately $2,000 of city revenue, but for Blacks the aldermen provided no city supplement. During 1875–76 the Black class limped along with only the state's $100. With that amount, Black parents had hired the one teacher and had paid him $25 a month, the going wage for unskilled labor. In four months the money ran out and the class had to be shut down.[15]

Alfred Jackson was determined to make the city do better. During the hot August evenings of 1876 he walked from cabin to cabin in the Black settlements of Birmingham, persuading other fathers to sign a petition requesting "the establishment in this city of a Public School for negroes."[16]

Jackson knew there was no point in asking permission to send Black children to the Free White School. In postwar Alabama whites insisted more adamantly upon racial separation in school than in many other aspects of life. White men did not like to see Black men show up at the ballot box and play a role in politics, but often they put up with it. White men did not like to work beside Black men, but often in the new industrial city of Birmingham they put up with it. But white men and women refused to put up with having Black children mingle with white children in a school classroom.[17]

Any suggestion that even one Black child might seek to enter the Free White School would have provoked white outrage. Congress had decided against requiring school integration, and the Alabama state government had explicitly forbidden it. Alfred Jackson and the African American parents had no choice but to take on the task of convincing the aldermen to use city funds to build and operate a separate "Free Colored School." In late August of 1876 Jackson placed that request before the aldermen. He took his school petition down to city hall and handed it in. Jackson and the other Black parents hoped that their newly acquired leverage as voters casting one-fourth of the votes in city elections would enable them to claim access to the crucial government service of education, even though they realized that they would realistically have to accept separate schooling in inferior facilities.[18]

The aldermen, all white businessmen or lawyers or skilled workers, referred the petition to a committee and asked for a report at their next meeting, one month later.[19] On the Monday morning following the meeting, Blacks observed two hundred white children converging upon the northeastern corner of town to attend the opening day of the fourth term of the Free White School, which the white newspaper, the *Iron Age*, extolled as "the pride of our citizens" and "the ornament of our city."[20]

By the October aldermanic meeting, Ellis Phelan, who chaired the school committee, had a report ready. In a huge leather-bound minute book the city clerk recorded that "Alderman Phelan then read the following report of the committee in response to the petition of Alf Jackson and other colored citizens for the establishment of a Free School for colored people in this city."[21]

The city clerk's inscription of Alfred B. Jackson's name as "Alf," which probably reflected the way in which it was read out in the meeting, stood in contrast to the clerk's consistent style of identifying every white man by last name only or by last name preceded by two initials, but never by familiar nickname. Jackson knew very well that, when aldermen and officials called him "Alf," they were following an unwritten white social rule designed to implement the principle of social separation of the races. By calling Blacks by first name or nickname, while insisting that Blacks address whites with a title such as "Mr." or "Mrs.," whites indicated the social dishonor that they assigned to people of African ancestry and slave heritage. In the meeting the use of the undignified name "Alf" denoted Jackson's marginal and incon-sequential status and excluded him from the membership of worthy citizens deserving the full respect of the aldermen. Whenever Jackson had any control over how his name appeared in a record he insisted on a much more dignified style, either "Alfred B. Jackson" or "A. B. Jackson." But typically records created by whites consigned him to "Alf."[22]

Ellis Phelan, an attorney and local Democratic Party leader, had written a civil and careful report. He knew that war and Reconstruction had trans-formed the petitioners from slaves into full-fledged citizens, and he went through the motions of according them their full rights under the law. He emphasized that the aldermen were carefully following state law by dividing the Alabama state school allocation between Blacks and whites on a strict per capita basis. He also argued that, by using the lawful portion of the state fund to finance the four-month Black class, the aldermen had fulfilled their state-mandated obligation to Blacks. The clear implication of Phelan's report was that city officials intended to do nothing more for Black schooling. For the single Black class, no city revenue would be forthcoming. If Blacks wanted more school funding, Phelan advised, they should look not to the city but to the philanthropic Peabody Fund. Jackson knew very well that Phelan realized the Black school had no chance to qualify for Peabody money without the city funding Jackson sought.[23]

The white mayor and aldermen defended their denial of local funding by asserting that Blacks contributed nothing to city revenue. In fact, in 1876 not one of the city's five hundred Blacks owned any real estate in Birmingham, not one had their name on the list of city property owners, and not one paid a penny of property tax or of mercantile license tax into the city treasury. Most Black men, whether single or married, were unskilled workers who rented cabins on the eastern or western edges of town, cabins owned by white land-lords, who paid the property taxes. In 1876 all city revenue came from white property owners and white merchants, and that reality could be invoked as a seemingly natural economic distinction that would justify the continuance of the boundary that excluded Blacks from the educational benefits financed by city revenue.[24]

It was also true, however, that most of the white workers who sent their children to the tuition-free Free White School also owned no real estate or houses and paid no property tax or license tax into the city treasury. The Free White School had been created primarily for the benefit of the white workers who could not afford the tuition of the local private schools. The abolition of slavery had sharply reduced the legal and economic distinctions between white laborers and Black laborers, but the color barrier of social exclusion that surrounded the public school gave white workers ongoing economic, educational, and political advantages over free Black laborers.[25]

Disappointed Black parents and their children had no option but to hold once again a four-month school session on the benches of an African Ameri-can Church. By the time the state allocation finally arrived in late December, the economic depression had reduced property tax revenues and the state had cut the school allotment in half. Consequently, in 1876–77, Blacks were able to pay for only two months of teaching at twenty dollars per month.[26]

During 1877, 1878, and 1879 the one Black class barely managed to sur-vive with only the state money, which in 1878–79 paid one teacher thirty dol-lars a month for three months. The Black population's eagerness for education was growing steadily, and 106 Black pupils enrolled in 1878. On a typical day, 82 children were present, which meant that the teacher had to work extremely hard for the thirty-dollars-per-month salary.[27]

If Alfred Jackson or other Black parents dropped by to find out what the lone teacher was actually doing with the daily throng of 82 children, they saw that the main activity for all pupils was routine drill in "Orthography"—

learning to recognize the written letters and the sounds they made and memorizing the spellings of basic words. Approximately half of the Black pupils were at the very beginning level of orthography and spent their entire day on it, receiving no instruction in any other subject. When the school shut down after three brief months, those beginners were probably still at that rudimentary level, and they were there at the same level nine months later when the school finally reopened. The slightly more advanced Black pupils, who varied enormously in age, mostly worked their way through simple stories in a reader, each pupil going it alone at his or her own pace, with minimum attention from the harried teacher. Only one-fourth of the children received any instruction in "Arithmetic" or in "Writing," and only 14 percent had advanced to "Grammar."[28]

Neither Jackson nor any other Black person would have been allowed to visit the white school to make comparisons. But school reports showed that, in contrast with the Black teacher's class of 106, each white teacher taught 42 pupils. Like the Black pupils, all white pupils drilled on orthography, but they all also received instruction in reading. White classes had been graded according to reading level, and in each class most white pupils read and discussed the same assigned stories and received direct instruction from the teacher, something that could not happen in the Black class of 106 pupils reading at many different levels. Three-fourths of the white pupils (compared with only one-fourth of the Black) also received instruction in "Writing" and "Arithmetic," and nearly one-third, compared with 14 percent of the Black pupils, had advanced to "Grammar."[29]

Even without firsthand observation of the forbidden zone inside the white school, Jackson would have known that the typical 42-pupil, ten-month white classroom provided more intense instruction, more effective guidance, and more rapid advancement through the common school curriculum. The Black school's hectic, thin, and spasmodic instruction gave Black children much less instruction in basic skills, much less support for intellectual growth, and much weaker preparation for employment in Birmingham's new urban economy. Consigning Black students to socially separate schooling meant that they would be vulnerable to discrimination in the political realm and inadequately prepared for roles in the economic realm.

During 1880, Alfred Jackson's family celebrated the sixth birthday of their daughter Missiana. She had reached school age, but in the spring of 1880

Jackson had no choice but to take her to exactly the same crowded and hectic one-room, one-teacher, three-month church-bench operation—financed entirely by the meager state school appropriation—that he had been observing and working to upgrade since 1876. The Black school had made no real progress and had fallen further behind the white school.[30]

A NEW GENERATION OF SCHOOL REFORMERS

Despite the political obstacles, during the early 1880s the Black school began to make some modest progress. The confluent efforts of three extraordinary boosters of education were responsible. One was Black, and the other two white. The Black advocate was Burton Henry Hudson, who organized a Black board of school trustees with himself as treasurer, became a teacher and then the principal of the Black school, and in 1882 mounted a successful fundraising campaign and finally constructed a small Black schoolhouse. One of the two crucial white advocates was Mayor Alexander O. Lane, who served from 1882 to 1888 and again from 1890 to 1892. He presided over the most intensive period of education development in nineteenth-century Birmingham history. The other crucial white advocate was John Herbert Phillips. He had been born in Kentucky but was educated in Ohio, where he had become a teacher and high-school principal before Mayor Lane appointed him superintendent of schools in 1883. Phillips, with the financial support of the Lane administration, transformed the Birmingham education system into one of the most progressive in the South.

Hudson arrived in Birmingham in 1880 at age thirty and soon stood out as a quiet but effective leader. Along with Pastor Welch, he was one of a small handful of Black college graduates in town. Hudson had graduated from Talladega College, a school supported by the American Missionary Association and the Congregational Church. In Birmingham he demonstrated his church commitment and his organizational talent by founding a Congregational parish, the African American Church. The church remained small, attracting mainly people of professional and middle-class standing, but played a major role in Black community life.[31]

Hudson had the business skills and enough money to begin purchasing residential lots and houses and renting them out. He handled every transaction with an efficiency and a close attention to detail that became legendary within the Black community. Hudson's renters, like his many customers throughout his long and varied career in business and education, found him dignified, straightforward, soft-spoken, courteous, and observant. He was careful about the upkeep of his property and meticulous in keeping accounts. When rent came due he promptly called for payment, always approaching his tenants politely, with a smile, but firmly.[32]

By 1884 the city tax-assessment list revealed that in four short years Hudson had become the city's largest Black property owner, holding real estate assessed at $1,708. It was worth several times that in market value. Hudson's deliberate and efficient business style, and his financial success, challenged the stereotype of Blacks as unreliable, incapable of supporting themselves, lacking in initiative, and burdensomely dependent upon whites.[33]

A notable feature of Hudson's leadership was that, unlike such Black leaders as Alfred Jackson, he steered clear of politics. His avoidance was absolute and complete. Throughout the late nineteenth century, both Black and white newspapers frequently published lists of Blacks involved in political meetings, conventions, and rallies. But not once was Hudson included in such a list or mentioned in connection with politics, even though his business and school and church activities earned frequent notice. The available record contains no comment from Hudson about his aloofness from politics, but the pattern suggests that he was pursuing a consistent strategy, perhaps believing that an apolitical reputation would be better for his business ventures and would enable him to get a more sympathetic hearing for his Black school initiatives.

Hudson almost certainly recognized that many whites believed the privileged group position of whites would be threatened if a Black man, despite his social exclusion, played an active role in politics, particularly if he should attain an office in which he would exercise some authority over whites. Any Black man who did become visible in political activities typically found himself subjected to ridicule and satire in the white newspapers. They played upon the white sense of threat and intensified the dishonor of any conspicuous Black politician by smearing him with negative images drawn from and designed to reinforce an array of traditional hostile stereotypes.

Hudson understood that during the late 1870s the regimes of an anti-elite "Independent" faction within the Democratic Party had refused to allocate any city revenue to the Black school even though Black voters, under the leadership of politician James Harper, often gave decisive support to the faction. He learned as well that in the late 1870s Black school expenditures per child had been less than 20 percent of white expenditures. Of course, everyone could plainly see that Black children had no schoolhouse at all.[34]

Recognizing that organization would be needed to advance the cause of the Black school, in August of 1880 Hudson established a "board of trustees for the colored free school," with himself as treasurer. He soon persuaded the white board of aldermen to "recognize" the trustees, and the trustees appointed Hudson as teacher of the small Black class that still met in a church.[35]

Hudson recognized that building a Black schoolhouse would be very difficult, but made it his top priority. He had learned that each white schoolhouse in town had originally been financed and built in large part through the volunteer fundraising efforts of white citizens, who had thereby convinced city officials of their commitment to creating and sustaining a school. During the spring of 1882, Hudson launched a volunteer fundraising effort among Blacks. He sponsored potluck suppers; he buttonholed individual Black citizens; and in a few months he raised a few hundred dollars. He persuaded the white *Iron Age* to publish a statement from him appealing to whites. Hudson declared: "There is not a foot of ground, nor a school house in this city for the education of the colored children. We have begun a struggle to raise the money to buy a lot and build a schoolhouse thereon." He presented a rationale that he hoped would motivate Blacks and that would appeal to the self-interest of at least some whites. "Feeling as we do that there is no other way of bringing our people up to the desired standard of education, intelligence, and morality but to build school houses and educate them," he wrote, "we therefore present a most urgent appeal to the white citizens for aid to build a school house in our city. If you want us to make better citizens then help to educate us!" As his fund approached the $1,000 required, Hudson wrote in a second *Iron Age* statement that Blacks "do with all the ardor of our hearts call upon the white and colored citizens to help us now, for if we ever needed help we need it now. It is an absolute necessity and would be a gift of the highest kind."[36]

During the fall of 1882, Hudson approached the aldermen. He had demonstrated Black voluntary initiative, and he had raised several hundred dollars. Significantly, he had won some support among white industrialists, including Frank L. Wadsworth, who sat on the board and believed that improved Black education could enhance the reliability and productivity of Black labor, and could help the city attract and retain higher-quality Black labor. In

September of 1882 Wadsworth took the lead in getting the aldermen to agree to allocate $250 for construction of a new Black schoolhouse.[37]

With the Black donations and some small emergency loans from Black businesspeople, the $250 gave Hudson the $1,000 he needed. Soon he and the Black trustees commenced construction of a three-room wooden schoolhouse at Fifteenth Street and Second Avenue, one block from Hudson's own house, on the inner edge of the large Black settlement growing up near the Alice Furnace. In October the *Gazette* joined the Birmingham Black community in rejoicing that "Work has begun on the new colored schoolhouse in Birmingham. Prof. Hudson's worthy efforts are meeting with success." By Christmas the Spartan three-room wooden structure was completed, and in January 1883 Black children for the first time assembled in a real schoolhouse.[38]

In early December 1882, while Hudson was finishing the Black schoolhouse, the city, for the first time in ten years, elected a Conservative Democratic mayor, attorney Alexander Lane. Lane quickly established himself as a popular leader and championed increased government investment in civic improvement projects, particularly schools. Lane had grown up in the Black Belt plantation country, the son of a small-town physician in Barbour County. He had attained considerable education, graduating from high school, attending the universities of Georgia and Alabama, then reading law for two years while teaching in his hometown high school. When he became an attorney he moved to the new boomtown of Birmingham. There he courted and married the daughter of the leading attorney, Colonel John T. Terry, who had led the campaign to build the Free White School, and joined the colonel's law firm. Lane was a dynamic speaker, became a Democratic workhorse, and edited the Democratic *Iron Age* for a year before running successfully for mayor.[39]

In his campaign Lane had arranged behind the scenes to have a majority of Black voters support—for the first time in Birmingham history—a Conservative Democratic candidate. Thus, he had added Blacks to the usual Conservative Democratic constituencies of churchgoers, white businessmen, and industrialists. Lane had recognized that Black families regarded their school system as "very insufficient," and that what they wanted "more than anything else" was education, as Alfred Jackson testified a few months later, in 1883, to Senator Blair's Committee on Education and Labor. During his 1882 campaign Lane quietly promised increased support for the Black school, and Blacks provided a decisive component of Lane's winning coalition. In 1884 and 1886 he relied on the same coalition to win easy landslide reelection victories over white workingmen's factions. Astute political observers recognized that only the steady support of Blacks enabled the business-oriented Lane to defeat the workingmen's candidates and sustain a Conservative Democratic regime.[40]

Mayor Lane was determined to upgrade the Birmingham education system, which he regarded as a key to continuing industrial and commercial development, as well to his electoral success. His crucial move was to recruit John Herbert Phillips to reorganize and uplift the entire Birmingham school system. Lane made Phillips his new, full-time superintendent despite strong anti-northern protests from many citizens.[41]

Phillips arrived in Birmingham in the summer of 1883 and swiftly accomplished a thorough school reorganization and professionalization. He arranged for the highly political board of aldermen to delegate school matters to an appointed, and less political, board of education. He became the dominant influence on the board. He centralized power in the superintendent's office, which was the administrative authority over all the schools, white and Black. He prescribed a standard sequential graded curriculum for all schools, instituted a rigorous system of examination and selection of teachers, systematized teachers' salary scales, and launched an ambitious, centrally planned school-construction program. All this cost money, and Superintendent Phillips was fortunate to have the political backing of Mayor Lane, who took advantage of a cycle of booming Birmingham prosperity and growth to undertake increased city allocations to education.[42]

As part of the reorganization, Lane and Phillips pulled Hudson's small school into the city system. They maintained strict racial segregation while insisting on a minimum floor of professional standards far above the level at which the Black school had previously languished. But the professionalization still left the quality of the Black school significantly below that of the white. During Phillips's early years in Birmingham, the average Black teacher's salary hovered around 75 percent of the average white teacher's salary. Regarding pupils per teacher, he established the rough rule of thumb that each white teacher should have an average daily attendance below thirty, and each Black teacher an average daily attendance slightly above forty students. Under the Lane/Phillips regime of the 1880s the Black/white ratio of per capita expenditures for teachers' salaries jumped from below 20 percent under the mid-1870s Independent regimes to approximately 50 percent by 1884.[43]

The new ratios and rules of thumbs were still, of course, highly discriminatory. They suggest that Lane and Phillips and the school board had persistent ideas about the proper levels of the Black/white ratios, notions based
upon implicit prognoses about the future role of Blacks in the society and the
economy, and upon calculations about the lesser worth, honor, capacity, and
potential of Black children.

The Birmingham Black community could easily make positive and negative comparisons. On the one hand, a comparison of Black schools under
Lane and Phillips with Black schools under the earlier Independent regimes
indicated enormous improvement. On the other hand, a comparison of Lane/
Phillips Black schools with Lane/Phillips white schools revealed that Black
schools were still only half as good.

Climbing even to the 50 percent level had been made possible only by a
remarkable convergence of unusual local prosperity and leaders of the caliber
and persuasion of Burton Hudson, Alexander Lane, and John Herbert Phillips.
Lane had tacitly included Blacks in a governing political coalition. Hudson had
mobilized Blacks organizationally. Phillips had invoked minimal professional
concepts and standards. Only such a confluence of short-run Black political leverage, Black organizational initiative, and educational professionalism
could boost the educational provisions of a people deemed so dishonored that
they must be consigned to a separate school.

As Hudson had recognized, schoolhouses were significant both practi-
cally and symbolically. Before the advent of Superintendent Phillips, every
Birmingham school building, white and Black, had been the product of volunteer fundraising campaigns. After his arrival, Phillips, confronting exces-
sive crowding in white classrooms, declared that the city must take charge
of planning and funding school buildings. In 1883 he arranged for the city
to construct a two-story eight-room wooden building at a cost of $5,000, or
$625 per classroom. The school board named it the Henley School in honor
of Birmingham's first mayor.[44]

Two years later, Phillips and the school board and aldermen for the first
time extended to Black schools the new concept that the board should plan,
initiate, fund, and construct new school buildings. During the summer of
1885, the city built a new wooden six-room Southside Black school, modeled
after the hastily constructed white Henley School, at a cost of $3,500, or $583
per classroom. It was by far the largest and most attractive Black school yet

constructed in Birmingham, and the first funded entirely by the city. When the new school was completed in October 1885, Black citizens indicated their gratitude by having the board of education name it the Lane Grammar School in honor of Mayor Lane.[45]

By 1885, Superintendent Phillips had begun planning new white schools of much more substantial brick and stone. He persuaded the school board to send a delegation, led by him, to spend three weeks visiting seven northern cities to examine the most modern school designs in the most progressive school systems. Selecting a design that "combined most perfectly all the essentials—heat, light, comfort and convenience," they put architects and contractors to work constructing an elegant three-story red pressed-brick structure equipped with the most up-to-date heating, ventilation, and sanitation, at a cost of $50,000.[46]

The "noble" new brick structure became the model for two more modern brick white school structures, one of which replaced the wooden Henley structure. By 1891 the three new structures were completed and all white students were comfortably housed in stately and safe brick structures with central heating and efficient sanitary plumbing. Mayor Lane, doubling as school-board president, felt justified in saying that "we can well boast the handsomest school buildings in the South." Phillips was particularly relieved that he had removed all white pupils from the light-frame wooden structures heated by pot-bellied stoves that created acute fire danger, a danger that had for years caused him to order incessant fire drills.[47]

During the years that the city was constructing handsome brick buildings for whites, it responded to booming Black enrollment by replacing Hudson's original three-room Fifteenth Street Schoolhouse with a new two-story six-room wooden building, at a cost of $5,500, and by constructing a third new wooden Black school just like it. For a much-needed fourth Black school the board of education salvaged the white wooden "firetrap" Henley School, moving it to a new site and renovating it.[48]

The construction program of Superintendent Phillips ended in 1891. To Blacks it was clear that since 1883 his efforts had improved their school's physical plant, but it had improved the white physical plant far more. The three brick-and-stone white schools had cost approximately $60,000 apiece, or $3,300 per classroom, while the four wooden Black schools had cost approximately $5,000 apiece, or $513 per classroom.

The Black/white ratio of value of buildings per student had gone up and down in a volatile fashion. Back in 1882, before the arrival of Phillips, before Hudson had launched his volunteer campaign to construct the Fifteenth Street Black school, the city had owned no Black school building and only one white school building, worth $4,000, and the Black/white ratio of the value of the buildings per student in attendance had been zero.[49] By 1887, at the end of Superintendent Phillips's first hurried round of school construction, the city had owned three white schools, valued at $23,000, or $28.54 per white pupil in daily attendance, and two Black schools valued at $4,500, or $12.68 per Black pupil in daily attendance. Under the initial impetus of Hudson, Lane, and Phillips the Black/white ratio had risen to 44 percent.[50] But by 1891, at the end of the second and more ambitious Lane/Phillips round of school construction, the city owned four wooden Black buildings worth $19,500 and three much larger brick white buildings worth $175,000. For Blacks the value of school buildings per student in attendance was $18.70; for whites it was $114.38, a ratio of 16 percent.[51]

By 1891 J. H. Phillips had established himself as one of the most dynamic, visible, and progressive urban school superintendents in the entire nation. He had made the Birmingham school system the best in Alabama, and one of the best in the entire South. The Black schools of Birmingham were the best Black schools in Alabama. But the enormous disadvantage that a system of racial segregation inevitably imposed upon all separate Black schools was highlighted by the reality that even the best Black schools in Alabama, presided over by one of the most progressive school superintendents in the South, were housed in buildings valued at only 16 percent as much per student as those of the white schools.

Phillips deemed the smaller investment in Black buildings to be appropriate. Even though he asserted that "Birmingham is committed to the task of providing equal [school] opportunities for all the youth of the city regardless of color," he also declared the new Black buildings constructed between 1885 and 1891 to be "quite creditable" and "sufficient," and he announced that Blacks were "amply provided with school accommodations." In his mind Black schools should not be compared with current white schools, but rather with the Black schools of the past, which had been improved upon, and with the current standards implicit in other buildings in the Black community. In 1891 the simple, lightly constructed, but new and "commodious" Black schoolhouses were as dignified and impressive as the newest and largest Black churches. If the new brick schoolhouses for whites were comparable in construction and style to the newest downtown brick department stores, certainly the new wooden Black schoolhouses were superior to the small wooden back-street shops of the few Black businesses.[52]

Phillips believed that schools should be, and could be, powerful agencies of moral, social, and economic elevation for all races. But if the physical quality of the Black school was far enough above that of the average Black home and community to exercise uplifting leverage, that was sufficient, in his view.[53]

Phillips would never have sought to excuse any deficiency in the quality of schoolhouses by arguing that the physical quality of buildings was inconsequential to the learning that occurred within them. On the contrary, he laid great emphasis on the valuable symbolic and educational functions performed by good school buildings. In his 1891 annual report he defended the high cost of Birmingham's handsome white-school structures by writing: "As grand mountain scenery inspires ideas of grandeur and sublimity which take possession of the soul, so a good school building, massive and well appointed, contributes largely to the child's education. Unconsciously the child drinks in the ideas of beauty, of neatness, and of order which his surroundings inspire, and his character is daily growing by the absorption of indirect as well as direct instruction. A good school building commands respect, and inculcates self-respect in the child. It educates the community at large by emphasizing the value and importance of childhood."[54]

Superintendent Phillips distributed his attractively printed annual reports widely, and Black leaders who received them and who read between the lines could see that, in light of Phillips's eloquent words, the four wooden Black schoolhouses stood as more testimony to weak Black political power, and as yet another expression of the general white belief that African Americans had less human worth and potential. The sharp contrast between the Black and white buildings reflected a white view that the "elevation of the moral side" of the child's nature could not proceed as far with the Black as with the white, that the character-shaping school surroundings of Blacks need not inspire ideas so "grand and sublime" as should the school surroundings of whites, that while the white child should attend a "massive and well-appointed" school building that "inculcates self-respect," it was permissible to have Black children attend a less-respectable building which would foster diminished self-respect. Moreover, while a magnificent white school "educates the community at large by emphasizing the value and importance of childhood," it was acceptable that the "quite creditable" Black buildings educated the community to the lesser value and importance of Black childhood. The contrast between the best that well-intentioned educators considered appropriate for white and for Black children demonstrated that southern whites, even those most sympathetic to Blacks, fundamentally regarded them as humans of low status, debased worth, and meager potential.

By 1891 two decades of the policy of segregating public schools by race had brought forth in Birmingham a profoundly discriminatory institutional structure, a potent Jim Crow "state-way." Day after day, white children, going to separate superior brick schools, absorbed pervasive reinforcement of the lesson that they were inherently superior to Black children. And day after day, Black children, entering their "sufficient" schools, were exposed to dispiriting evidence that they were of less value than white children. The daily Jim Crow impact upon the minds and hearts of children, and the larger Jim Crow lessons for the Black and white communities, had not only reinforced the tense boundaries of the social realm, they had penetrated deeply into all aspects of community life, including both the economic and the political.

IMPACT OF DEPRESSION, 1893–1897

The depression of the mid-1890s was the worst in the nation's history, and it devastated the finances of the city of Birmingham. The city's elementary schools, Black and white, had been completely tuition-free ever since Superintendent Phillips declared them so in 1886. A desperate mayor and the aldermen cut school appropriations and, to preserve the bare bones of the public school system, levied monthly tuition charges of $1.00 to $3.00 per student, depending on the grade. As a consequence of the imposition of tuition and decimated family incomes, Black attendance plummeted. Meanwhile, the Black/white ratio of per capita expenditure for teachers' salaries dropped from the 50 percent level of the Lane administration of the mid-1880s to a level of 25–30 percent in the mid-1890s.[55]

In the fall of 1897 the school board decided to try to restore some of the lost Black attendance and potentially increase the pay of the Black teachers. The board encouraged attendance by cutting the Black tuition for each elementary grade to half the white tuition.[56] An explosion of angry protest greeted the announcement, and a white supremacy organization, the Regents of the White Shield, sprang to the forefront. It sponsored mass meetings, attended by hundreds of whites, to protest both the charging of tuition per se and the "grievous error in discriminating against the whites."[57] Local labor organizations immediately endorsed the White Shield protest. One labor meeting, held in the hall of the Brotherhood of Locomotive Engineers, attracted 250 angry white workingmen. The Birmingham Trades Council—the central organization to which each local union sent delegates—welcomed a committee from the White Shield and officially endorsed its position.[58]

The local labor newspaper, the Birmingham *Labor Advocate*, asserted that differences in costs of Black school buildings or in Black teachers' salaries did not justify "the act of discrimination between the black and the poor white children of Birmingham, as in favor of the negroes, which our . . . board of education in its wisdom made manifest." The *Labor Advocate* protested against the differential tuition in a long editorial on "The Race Problem." This polemic illustrated that the deliberate exclusion of Blacks from schools both expressed a deep emotional sense of social distance and served instrumental goals.[59]

"Educated negroes have always been most active in fomenting race difficulties," wrote the editor. He observed that generally "it is only as a laborer or serving man that the presence of the negro among the whites creates no friction," but he qualified his observation by adding: "except in so far as he comes into competition with the white workman."

The editor went on to predict that, because Blacks had public schools, it was inevitable that they would rise, and that Black/white conflict would intensify. "The rise of the negro will mean that he will contend all the stronger for equality," declared the editor. "If the whites resist all the stronger there will be conflict, and if they relax in their contention for supremacy, there will be a state of things under which the present white generations would certainly not like to live." With that explosive topic in mind the labor editor looked north, observing, he said, that Wisconsin was experiencing conflict between Scandinavians and the native white population. He dismissed the importance of that conflict, predicting that within fifty years the two groups would have "amalgamated and there will be but one people, white and harmonious." But he warned "there can be no such solution to the problem in the South," not even within fifty years. Here, "it is only a question of time when there must come a clash between the races, and come it will, for the negro cannot be socially assimilated and two distinct races, held apart by a natural barrier, cannot inhabit the same country without more or less antagonism."

Thus, the labor editor embraced as a permanent "natural barrier" the socially constructed boundary by which whites excluded all African Americans from close social contact. Consistent with his approval of the barrier against Blacks, who "cannot be socially assimilated," the editor asserted, "The only ground on which" the two races could peaceably inhabit the same country "is for one race to be in a degree subservient to the other."[60]

In response to the raucous uproar over differential tuition the mayor and aldermen dug deep into scarce resources and allocated enough extra funds to enable the board of education to abolish tuition in all schools, Black and white, except in the high school. But long thereafter white organized labor in Birmingham continued to take a dim view of Black education, and continued to endorse the social exclusion of Blacks, even though that exclusion inevitably made difficult their effort to foster economic cooperation in biracial unions.[61]

The attitude of Birmingham's labor movement toward Black education illustrated that endorsement of the exclusionary racial boundaries of the social realm could sway even hard-headed labor leaders into espousing sharp discriminations. In turn, such discriminations estranged white and Black workers and made difficult any effort to foster biracial cooperation. This was one way in which segregationist policies in education fostered further racial subordination and the enhancement of negative racial images and attitudes. More generally, establishing the racist Jim Crow schools institutionalized and perpetuated the inferior social standing of Black children, just as its white advocates intended it should, and just as Senator Sumner had warned it would.

The implementation of the rules and protocols of racial exclusion in education had helped solidify the inner core of Jim Crow belief and practice that shaped images, feelings, and behaviors in all realms of life. The sight of Blacks attending impoverished schools reinforced white belief that African Americans were inherently unworthy. This conviction fortified and perpetuated the principle of social exclusion that had originally built the wall splitting the education system into competing and deeply unequal white and Black components.

CHAPTER 5

URBAN RESIDENTIAL
SEGREGATION

In the economic realm, the old slave-era boundaries persisted into the late nineteenth century somewhat less tenaciously than in the social realm. Emancipation transformed slaves from property that was legally controlled by slave owners into economic agents who were theoretically free and autonomous. But former slaves, now technically free, faced the handicaps posed by their lack of accumulated wealth, by the limited skills they had been able to acquire while enslaved, by the failure of the federal government to redistribute plantation lands to the former slaves and provide economic compensation for its previous sanction and support for slavery, and by the stigmas that continued to bleed outward from the social realm into the economic realm. Housing was a significant part of the economic realm of life in Birmingham and the other swiftly growing cities of the New South.

HOUSING: ECONOMIC AND SOCIAL FACTORS

Housing was a crucial concern in the personal economy of every family and individual in New South cities. Therefore, economic factors and pressures played major roles in shaping housing configurations, and instrumental intentions to gain economic benefit and advantage helped to motivate the thousands of individual decisions that shaped racial housing patterns and fostered housing discrimination.

But concerns from the *social* realm and motivations from the *socio-*

emotional component of prejudice also shaped racial housing configurations. Since postbellum whites persisted in dishonoring people of African descent and slave heritage as socially unworthy, they did not regard them as "neighbors" with whom social fellowship could be fostered. The concept of "neighborhood" was subjective and imprecise, but it incorporated the notion that only people of equal honor and social standing, with whom close social fellowship would be welcomed, could be legitimate members. Since social criteria disqualified Black people from close social fellowship with whites, the criteria also excluded Black people from membership in white neighborhoods.

The groups of houses that white people regarded as their neighborhoods were sites of social interaction among relatively stable sets of white families. White men of the neighborhood got together to talk about work and politics, to smoke and drink, and to help each other with house repairs. White women of the neighborhood borrowed sugar and flour, shared news, helped each other with childcare, and arranged joint celebrations of children's birthdays. White children of the neighborhood grew up together, played with the kids next door, walked to school together, helped each other with schoolwork, and sometimes became romantically involved with each other.

Whites did not want to see Black faces in such neighborhood social activities and strived to maintain separation and detachment from the homes of Black people. The powerful economic factors that shaped the myriad individual decisions that configured Black and white housing were intricately intertwined with a major social factor—the intention of white people to exclude socially stigmatized Black people from neighborhood fellowship.

EMANCIPATION, BLACK IN-MIGRATION, AND
RAPID RESIDENTIAL SEGREGATION

Immediately after emancipation, unprecedented numbers of African Americans migrated into southern cities, significantly increasing the Black portion of the urban population and completely overwhelming the antebellum "compound" pattern, which could not accommodate them.[1] Most urban whites were upset by the influx. Historian Howard Rabinowitz found that "White Southerners experienced a sense of siege as they spoke of 'swarms' of Negroes who were 'engulfing' them and disrupting the previous pattern of urban life." They believed "the Negroes 'infested' the cities, 'clogged' the streets, and threatened the attainment of peace and prosperity." Indeed, "White opinion was virtually unanimous that the city was no place for blacks," and Blacks would certainly not be welcomed into white neighborhoods.[2]

Entrepreneurial white developers, however, saw long-run opportunity in the housing needs of the unwelcome Black in-migrants, and began building clusters of rental cabins on the outer edges of cities. They bought up inexpensive land, much of which had become environmentally degraded by close proximity to railroads, lowlands, factories, and dumps. Once established, the developers expanded these rental clusters, packing more and more cabins into them. The result was a segregated and congested substandard residential world which Black migrants, lacking capital to create any alternative, promptly filled. Very rapidly the developers established a racially segregated housing pattern that was destined to persist.

In *The Strange Career of Jim Crow*, however, C. Vann Woodward sketched a very different view of postbellum southern urban residential patterns. In 1966 Woodward fashioned an interpretation that emphasized the extent to which in antebellum southern cities the races had learned tolerance by living in close physical proximity and intimacy. The tolerance, he asserted, had persisted far into the New South, particularly in older cities, where it fostered a continuing "pattern of residential mixture."[3] But evidence clearly shows that postbellum southern whites had created southern urban residential segregation long before the political battles and the disfranchisement of the 1890s, and they had done it without the assistance of any segregation law.[4]

LINES OF DEMARCATION

In the rapid development of early Birmingham, developers who purchased blocks of land and built houses to rent or sell understood that white renters and white buyers would want some territorial demarcation to separate their houses from any nearby houses of African Americans. The demarcation could derive from the grid of streets and avenues or from topographical features. A difference in house design might make a satisfactory demarcation, or a rise or fall in the elevation of the land, or a screen of trees might work. Sometimes arrangements created by historical "accidents"—earlier purchases of specific pieces of land or earlier erection of specific buildings—had placed white and Black areas near one another but had also established graphic mental maps that provided demarcation between the races. For example, early in Birmingham's history several white skilled workingmen had purchased lots and built houses on the relatively inexpensive land in the square block circumscribed by Third and Fourth Avenues and Twenty-Fifth and Twenty-Sixth streets, on the eastern periphery of town. Over the years more white workmen purchased lots in the block, and together they sustained the white identity of their block, even though the comparably cheap land in the blocks just to the south had led developers to include them in what the city directory referred to as "Negro Quarters."[5] Whatever had been the historical signs or signals of demarcation, there now had to be a clear demarcation or whites would avoid an area. The powerful social desire of white renters and buyers to exclude Blacks from white neighborhoods operated as a strong factor shaping the pattern of residential location, and it did much to produce Birmingham's untidy but racially clustered housing pattern.

Within the overarching pattern of vividly demarcated *social* separation, the *economic* motives of white developers and landlords often intensified racial segregation. White developers knew that no Black businesses commanded enough investment capital to undertake development of substantial tracts of Black rental housing. They knew that Black residents, having limited budgets, would have no choice but to rent within whatever tracts and houses the white developers set aside for them. Thus, white developers, including white furnace owners Henry F. DeBardeleben and James Sloss, found it easy and profitable to build cheap cabins for Black workers on inexpensive land that lay close to heavy industries, which steadily provided jobs and steadily dumped pollution on the cabins.[6]

BLACK RESIDENTIAL CLUSTERS IN BIRMINGHAM, 1883

African Americans were pulled and pushed into the new segregated peripheral clusters. The pull came from the many "Negro" jobs available at nearby industrial sites. The push came from whites who excluded Blacks from white neighborhoods. Black residents, who collectively had no savings to invest in their own housing developments, rapidly filled the Black residential clusters constructed by white developers. These rapidly growing clusters congealed and persisted, creating an enduring pattern of racial separation. Such clusters show up on map 2 (A and B).[7]

MAP 2 (A AND B). Black and White Households, Birmingham, 1883

Such a detailed plotting creates an untidy picture with ragged edges. Birmingham, like most southern cities, did not generate a compact Black ghetto. The several Black residential clusters were not contiguous with each other, but rather spread out here and there in environmentally substandard areas, creating an impression of dispersal of the Black population. Moreover, many Blacks found some whites living in relatively close proximity. Several white grocers and saloonkeepers, for example, increased their accessibility to Black customers by locating in the interface of the white and Black residential areas.

At first glance, map 2 might seem to confirm C. Vann Woodward's description of persisting postbellum "residential mixture," casual "proximity and confusion," with considerable "intimacy of contact and association." But Woodward's description seems to have been based on observations by puzzled travelers of superficial scatter rather than analysis of central tendency.[8] The central tendency shown in the map is a strong clustering of Black households in three main types of highly congested, inferior, and uncomfortable residential environments. The three types were, first, the company-owned "Sloss Quarters" next to Sloss Furnace; second, the Black residential clusters or "Quarters" built by many individual white developers on inexpensive land on the outer edges of the city, near heavy industry; and, third, the rows of "Negro shanties," as the Sanborn Map Company referred to them, built by well-to-do white families along alleys next to their backyards.

ENVIRONMENTAL INFERIORITY OF THE
BLACK RESIDENTIAL CLUSTERS

In comparison with white residential areas, each type of Black residential area was distinctively inferior in location, physical attractiveness, quality and style of structures, and level of services and amenities. Dense crowding of cabins, often twenty or thirty per square block in what the city directory called "Negro Quarters," was often the first negative feature that stung Blacks. At no place in town were white houses packed together as tightly. Less intense congestion occurred in the alley type of Black cluster, but sometimes even there two or more families lived in the cabins.[9]

Rough ungraded, unpaved, and untended streets and alleys provided glaring indication of the quality of the infrastructure in Black residential areas. According to the season, the streets were deep with mud or thick with dust. As of 1889 in the eastern and western Black clusters the only street improvement undertaken by the city had been a bit of grading and the spreading of some slag on a couple of the worst street blocks. Blacks felt the disrespect even more acutely when they saw that the streets of the downtown business district had been paved with granite blocks or bricks or else macadamized. The streets and avenues in the main white residential section north of the business district had been carefully graded, and many of those close to Twentieth Street had been macadamized.[10]

Darkness reigned every night in the Black residential areas. The city installed streetlights only on the main thoroughfares that bordered the clusters—on Twentieth Street or First Avenue, for example—but not on streets inside them, and not in any alleys. The all-white city government considered a truncated level of services to be appropriate for areas of Black housing.[11]

Shabby, unpainted, and smoke-stained houses provided further negative demarcation of the three types of Black housing. White developers typically spent only a hundred dollars to build each flimsy, light-frame Black cabin, and the cabins soon became rickety and dilapidated. The Sanborn Map Company indicated the poor style and quality and the potentially high flammability of the cabins by applying to them the label "Negro shanty." "Shanty" indicated substandard appearance that set the cabins far below even the least pretentious white houses and cabins. The implication, sensed daily by Black people, was that whites believed that "shanties" were not only all that Blacks could afford, but also all that they deserved.[12]

Capping the shabby, congested, dark, and untended aura of the Black residential clusters was the stinking presence of unsanitary outdoor toilets, long after the modern technological innovation of indoor plumbing and indoor flush toilets had become standard in most white houses. To connect a hundred-dollar Black cabin to a sanitary sewer and to provide it with indoor plumbing and a flush toilet would add seventy dollars to the cost. The Black renters could not afford such an outlay, which in any case should not have been the responsibility of a renter. The white owners, however, balked at adding an improvement that would increase the cost of the cabin by two-thirds, and they perceived traditional outdoor privies to be perfectly adequate for Black folks. The reeking outhouses stood as a constant demarcation of the derogated Black housing clusters and of the downgraded lifestyle that whites considered standard for Blacks.[13]

The most foul of the clusters was the company-owned "Sloss Quarters." (They appear on map 1 and are magnified in the insert on map 2B.) In 1883 this cluster consisted of forty-eight rental cabins huddled close to the furnace, which constantly engulfed them in noise and smoke. The company packed 114 Black men, some with families, into those rooms. Often 3 or 4 unmarried Black men lived together in a single cabin, sharing cooking duties. Sloss included no indoor plumbing or toilets in its quarters. Instead, the company dug pits next to the cabins for outdoor toilets and provided a few outdoor water faucets atop bare pipes that poked up out of the ground. The company found the close proximity of its 114 workers convenient for two reasons. At hectic work times and emergencies the laborers could be rousted out quickly, and the company could collect rental income from land that was so polluted that it was otherwise useless because only employees who had no choice would live on it.[14]

The Sloss Company steadily built more and more cabins, spreading its "Quarters" north to Third Avenue and east to Thirty-Fifth Street. The management eschewed "coddling workmen," and by 1912 the labor analyst John Fitch declared the Sloss housing to be an "abomination of desolation." Surrounding the cabins were "a slag dump for a rear view, blast furnaces and beehive coke ovens for a front view, railroad tracks in the street, and indecently built toilets in the back yards." Further, "The houses are unpainted, fences are tumbling down, a board is occasionally missing from the side of a house." Nonetheless said Fitch, the rent for the disgusting accommodations yielded "a very liberal return on the investment" of the company.[15]

Slightly less foul than the "Sloss Quarters" were the cabins that many separate individual white speculators and developers had packed into the several square blocks of the eastern Black residential cluster. This lay between Pastor Welch's church on Twenty-Fourth Street and the rowdy Buzzard Roost saloon shantytown next to the eastern city limits at Twenty-Seventh Street. Heavy smoke from the Birmingham Iron Works had diminished the value of the property and made it repellent to white renters, a main reason that white developers had filled it with cabins for Black workers. One deadly consequence of crowding so many people onto land saturated in industrial smoke was that tuberculosis ran rampant, and Blacks were five times more likely than whites to die from it. Congestion, rough untended streets and alleys, nighttime darkness, shoddy cabin construction, and the sprawl of privies characterized the eastern quarters, just as they did the Sloss quarters. Similar conditions prevailed in the western Black cluster along Second Avenue between Sixteenth and Thirteenth streets. That neighborhood lay in the smoke penumbra of the Williamson Iron Foundry, the Linn Iron Works, the Alice Furnace, and the Birmingham Rolling Mill and next to the Birmingham Gas Company. The neighborhood included Birmingham's only Black schoolhouse and the Scratch Ankle dives.[16]

The third major Black residential pattern consisted of rows of cabins in back alleys within white residential areas, as depicted on map 2. Middle- and upper-class white families generally did not cook their own food, clean their own houses, or do their own laundry. For those chores they mobilized, on a daily basis, an army of Black women who labored as servants. The Black women spent a large portion of each day working in the large white houses out on the street fronts, and each evening they retreated to the cabins that the white families had built along the alleys.

The close proximity of alley cabin and front house provided some convenience for the daily forays of Black servant women into white homes, but the proximity did not foster close neighborly association among pairs of families, Black and white. White families sometimes thought it helped them recruit reliable Black women servants if they built a cheap Black rental cabin back on the alley. But seldom did all members of a Black alley household work primarily for the white family in front. At least half and probably as many as three-fourths of the Black men who lived in the alley cabins of the white residential district worked down near the railroads in heavy industry. For many years the housing shortage in Birmingham made the alley cabins a useful alternative for Black industrial male laborers, especially when their wives could pick up domestic service employment near their alley cabins.[17]

In 1883 the population of the world of Birmingham alleys, Northside and Southside, was overwhelmingly Black—in fact 93 percent Black, and only 7 percent white. This was true even for the alleys that bisected the major white residential district. The alleys were densely Black and contained nearly two-fifths (actually 39 percent) of the entire Black population of the city. It should be noted that some Black alley dwellers lived not inside a major white residential district, but rather in alleys within the Black residential clusters, or in alleys built on patches of low-value land scattered throughout town.[18]

FACE BLOCKS AND ALLEYS IN
THE PRIME RESIDENTIAL DISTRICT

Map 2 (A and B) shows the location of Black and white households in Birmingham in 1883. In the Northside residential district, where most middle- and upper-class white families lived, the Black households (represented by black dots) were located almost exclusively in alleys (represented by gray bars). On the map, the rows of "×" symbols that wrap around the street fronts of most blocks indicate the overwhelming white presence in the handsome two-story houses that typically stood there.

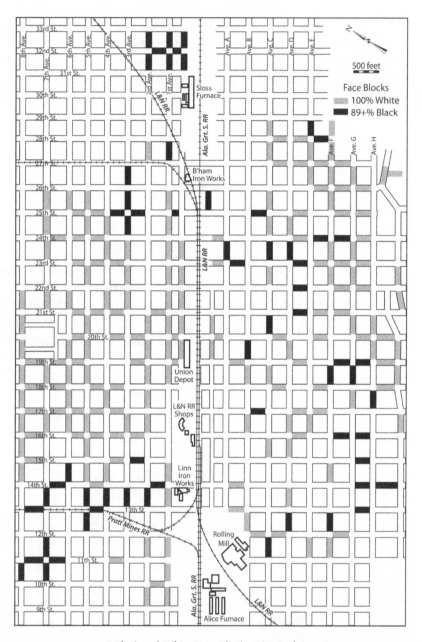

MAP 3. Black and White Face Blocks, Birmingham, 1891

On map 3 a different technique, using data from a "Street Directory" section that appeared in the 1891 *Birmingham City Directory*, intensifies the image of white domination of the space along the street fronts. Map 2 was built upon data from the *Birmingham City Directory* of 1883, which provided only alphabetical lists of Black and white residents, giving their names, occupations, and addresses. On map 2 the unit of analysis was the individual household, and the plotting of all household addresses revealed cumulative spatial geographic configurations of the residential clusters—such as the "Sloss Quarters," or the eastern and western clusters or the alleys in white residential areas—into which households had become arrayed.

By contrast, map 3 employs the "face block" as a unit of geographic analysis. Such face blocks were meaningful spatial units in the everyday life and perception of white urban inhabitants. Residents tended to know and interact with most families who lived up and down and across the street of such face blocks, and when residents were concerned about keeping Blacks separate, they particularly wanted to exclude Blacks from neighborhood face blocks.[19]

Beginning in 1891 the directories of many southern cities, including Birmingham, incorporated a separate and supplemental "street directory" which facilitated tabulation of the racial population of face blocks. The street directory listed each street; then for each street it listed in order each linear block that was defined by cross streets. Then within each linear block it listed house numbers in order, and next to each house number it listed the names of inhabitants and their race. With such post-1891 street directories a researcher can avoid the tedium of plotting each household on a map. For each linear face block it is possible to tabulate the percentages of Black and white, and indicate the percentages with systematic symbols on a map.[20]

This technique was used to construct map 3 for Birmingham in 1891. This map presents a highly segregated visual image. But the stark image of wall-to-wall segregation is actually incomplete because of a major omission in the new "Street Directory" section of the *Birmingham City Directory* for 1891, and of most southern city directories: The street directories did not list alleys. Cutting corners in a way that indicated disdain for alleys and for alley residents, the directory company published a street directory that omitted the hundreds of people that lived in the east-west alleys that bisected every Birmingham block.

The names of alley dwellers did, however, appear in the *City Directory*'s 465-page alphabetical listing of all Black and white residents, and this list allowed documenting two crucial matters—first, the extent to which the alleys of 1891, like the alleys of 1883, were overwhelmingly populated by Blacks, and, second, the extent to which the Black cabins in the alleys and the white houses of the surrounding face blocks were juxtaposed in a sharp pattern of racial separation.[21] Map 4 is the product of the comprehensive location of Black residents. The map designates two separate Northside districts—a business-and-government district (B) and a prime residential district (R). Primary attention goes to the residential district, within which the location of every alley address was plotted.[22]

Within the prime residential district, map 4 designates all face blocks that were 100 percent white. In 1891 fully two-thirds of the face blocks were 100 percent white. The map represents the Black households in the alleys with broken black bars that lie across the center of blocks. Between 1883 and 1891 crowding had increased as many more Blacks had moved into cabins in the alleys behind the large street-front houses. Within the residential district thirty alleys contained substantial numbers of Black shanties. By count, nine alleys contained from two to five Black households, eight alleys contained from seven to ten Black households, eight alleys contained from eleven to fifteen Black households, and five alleys contained more than fifteen Black households each.

Map 4 has been built upon two variables of classification. One variable classified people into races, "white" and "black." The other variable classified living space into "alleys" and "face blocks." The classification and the analysis to which it is applied pose a crucial question: Are the two principles of classification independent, or are they related? Are the criteria upon which the classification was built meaningful, and are the race and space criteria effective at sorting people and places into meaningful categories? Applying a statistical test to the data behind maps 3 and 4 yields the conclusion that a strong relationship held between the two variables of race and space.[23]

A confirming indication of the presence and the nature of Black alley cabins comes from the Sanborn Fire Insurance maps, which meticulously identified "Negro shanties" because such flimsy wooden structures always posed a worrisome fire risk. Map 5, traced from an 1891 Sanborn map, shows the prestigious Episcopal Church block, between Fifth and Sixth avenues and Twentieth and Twenty-First streets.

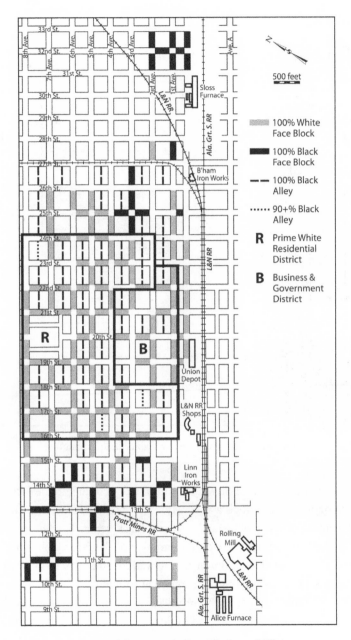

MAP 4. Racial Patterns in Face Blocks and Alleys,
Northside Birmingham, 1891

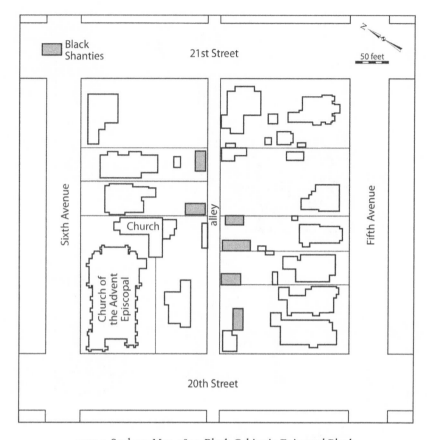

MAP 5. Sanborn Map, 1891: Black Cabins in Episcopal Block

According to the 1891 Street Directory and according to the face-block pattern on map 5, the block was nearly all white. The face blocks on three sides were 100 percent white, and only one Black person lived on the fourth side, tucked into a tiny house on the far edge of the face block, across the street from the main block. But map 5 showed that the alley inside the block contained six Black shanties which housed at least ten families.[24]

Map 6 shows another apparently very white block, between Fifth and Sixth avenues and Seventeenth and Eighteenth streets. On two sides the face blocks were 100 percent white, and the other two were 67 percent and 75 percent white. But map 6, traced from an 1891 Sanborn map, reveals that the inner alley of the block contained eleven Black shanties.[25]

MAP 6. Sanborn Map, 1891: Black Cabins inside White Block 45

The heavy presence of Black people in the alleys of a major white residential district is very much at odds with Woodward's description that suggests "casual" and congenial "confusion."[26] A pattern of close proximity did exist, but within that pattern the races were juxtaposed in a rigidly segregated pattern. Alley and face-block defined two separate types of space, two distinctive residential environments. Strict segregation prevailed with sharp clarity and no confusion between them. And the world of the alleys was intensely Black. In 1891 only three transient white households, headed by a widow, a carpenter, and a brickmason, had taken up residence in the alleys. Little can be discovered about the three white alley households, and within a year all three had disappeared from the city. The cabins in the alleys were packed with

305 Black households. The alley population was 99 percent Black and 1 percent white.[27]

Surrounding the 99 percent Black alley world was a contrasting white world of large houses spaciously arrayed on well-landscaped face blocks, two-thirds of which were 100 percent white. Around the edges of the white residential district and in a few scattered corners lived 89 Black households that had found street or avenue addresses available to them. But 701 white households dominated the world of the face blocks on the streets and avenues, and that world was 89 percent white.

Segregationist intentions, not confusion, had sorted 305 Black households and only 3 white households into alley cabins. Such intentions had fostered enough proximity so that white ladies could conveniently mobilize the Black alley women into white homes to do cooking, cleaning, and laundry. The quality of Black housing graphically demarcated a strict residential separation of the races and reflected an unwritten but firm conception in the minds of whites that Blacks were permanently disqualified from social fellowship with whites and from membership in white neighborhoods. The packing of Black people—only Black people—into the deprived world of the alley demonstrated that the principles of racial separation and subordination were powerful in the minds of the whites who designed and controlled Birmingham's housing.

Some historians might be tempted to portray the Black alley cabins of Birmingham as perpetuating the essence of the old slave-era compound model. But neither the slave masters of antebellum cities nor Richard Wade, who wrote the leading history of these cities, would agree. To antebellum urban slaveholders, alleys were actually anathema, and most slave cities purposely built no alleys. As Wade pointed out, creating alleys led to the opening of rear entrances to residences, and rear entrances enabled slaves to come and go inconspicuously. "Whenever alleys were opened, they created an alternative center for slave activity," and the isolation and control of enslaved people provided by the compound was lost. "Soon Negro life in the neighborhood gravitated to the middle of the block and away from the supervision of slaveowners or white authorities." Consequently, urban slaveholders minimized the construction of alleys in their cities.[28]

The designers of Birmingham, in contrast with the leaders of slave cities, cut east-west alleys through every block of the city, and the white families of Birmingham who built backyard-alley cabins for Black servants never attained the degree of control over those servants that slave masters had sought, and sometimes achieved, over the enslaved people inside the compounds. And the construction of Black cabins in alleys behind white houses did not foster close association between the white families in the front houses and the Black servant families in alley houses. The Black families living in the alleys interacted mainly with the other Black families in the alleys, and the alley neighborhood became distinctly separate from the white street-front face-block neighborhood. It was contrary to the culture and the sensibility of white ladies to make themselves guests in the Black homes, or to reciprocate in any way the constant presence of Black servant women in white houses.[29]

Observers noted this pattern. In 1916, when city sanitary officials were seeking, with little success, to eliminate alley outhouses, an upper-class reformer, Mrs. J. B. Reid, observed the conditions in the servant quarters in alleys. "One of the greatest evils of this city is the 'alley quarters'—the homes of our cooks and washerwomen," she wrote. "They are huddled together, and are seldom 'kept' at all." The Black servant cabins suffered "dense neglect," and from them "germs are disseminated over the entire city." Mrs. Reid recognized that white women neither visited in the Black servant cabins nor concerned themselves about the vile sanitary conditions in them. "We simply take for granted that the negro quarters are not our business," she complained, but in fact "they are the hotbeds of germ life, and sources of spreading them into thousands of homes in the city."[30]

BLACK HOUSEHOLDS ON WHITE STREETS

A number of Black households were located on the heavily white streets and avenues of the residential district. Map 7 plots the locations of these eighty-nine households and shows them in relation to the many 100 percent white face blocks. Many of these households were owned by middle-class individuals or families, all of whom lived outside of the alleys of the residential district.

The eighty-nine households tended to cluster on the edges of the prime residential district, rather than in the center. They huddled primarily in older commercial and industrial areas around the downtown business district. There they usually occupied older rundown structures that had outlived their original commercial and industrial purposes but still had enough structural integrity to survive into a second career as second-rate housing, which was

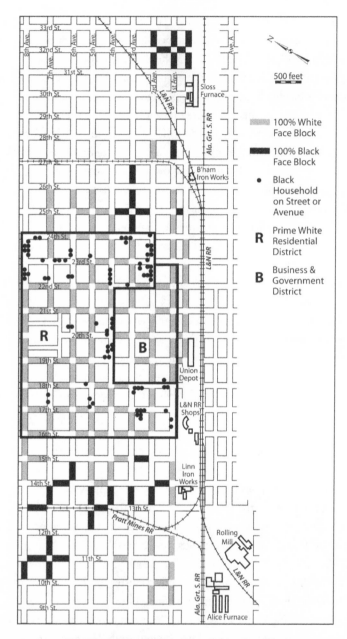

MAP 7. Black Households among White Face Blocks,
Northside Birmingham, 1891

considered appropriate for Blacks. The Black households that grouped in the upper right corner of the district were bunched around two brick factories. While the rather anomalous presence of 89 Black households on the street fronts of the prime residential district did indicate some scatter and untidiness in the housing pattern, it did not significantly alter the pattern of separate and distinctively inferior housing for Blacks.[31]

BLACKS AND WHITES IN
THE DOWNTOWN BUSINESS DISTRICT

Analysis of the 1891 Street Directory for the downtown business-and-government district, which is highlighted on map 4, reveals patterns in which white men predominated heavily. Most people listed at downtown addresses were not residents, but businesspeople occupying offices and stores. A total of 1,079 white people and only 46 Black people occupied addresses on the streets and avenues of the business-and-government district. There were several face blocks in the business district that were not exclusively white. Several Black barbers, for example, had shops there. Another 21 Black residents occupied addresses in downtown alleys, which were exclusively Black. In the downtown district as a whole, 94 percent of occupants were white, 6 percent Black.[32]

SEGREGATION, LAW, AND PUBLIC SERVICES

Following C. Vann Woodward's example of paying careful attention to the legal dimensions of segregation, it is important to ask whether during the 1870s and 1880s the white residents of Birmingham used law or the coercive power of government to create the tight 1891 pattern of residential segregation. Did they rely on law to pack Black families into alleys surrounded by white face-blocks?

The answer is no. American reverence for the sanctity of property rights was profound, and during the late nineteenth century, Birmingham, like all American states and cities, created no law or ordinance that attempted to mandate housing segregation or that sought to place any restriction upon the right of property owners to sell their property as they saw fit. Any property owner of any race could legally sell any piece of property to any buyer of any race, regardless of whether the property was located adjacent to white or

Black houses. Such legal permissiveness could theoretically have produced a rather mixed Black/white pattern that conformed to Woodward's descriptive terms—proximity and confusion.

That did not happen, as map 4 and the related analysis make clear. Why not? Because the real estate market was powerfully shaped by a nonlegal factor—the intention of most whites to implement the central belief behind the inner citadel of the three-color-line system. This belief was that African Americans were unworthy people who must be systematically excluded from social fellowship with white people, and must therefore be disqualified for membership in white neighborhoods. The exclusionary principle of the inner social circle was not embedded in any real estate law, and it did not need to be. Even without law it could powerfully influence housing patterns.

Although Birmingham's segregated residential pattern was not created by law, once it was in place, politicians could follow its lines in distributing city services and infrastructure. The pattern of distribution reinforced and perpetuated the environmental inferiority of every Black residential cluster. One significant example of this is the building of the city's sewage system.

During the 1880s most white houses in the prime Northside residential district converted to indoor plumbing and indoor toilets as a standard convenience. But most Black cabins continued to rely upon substandard, uncomfortable, inconvenient, and dangerously unsanitary outdoor toilets. City government did not directly prescribe this outcome. But well-established government traditions and procedures—particularly a deep tradition of seeing the government as primarily the agent of the local property holders—let it happen, and in fact encouraged it.

Whites were able to convert to indoor plumbing because during the 1880s and 1890s the mayor and aldermen constructed an underlying infrastructure of Northside sanitary sewers, shown on map 8.[33] Birmingham's Northside was topographically simple, sloping gradually downward from east to west. Just beyond the western city limit, at the end of Fifth Avenue, rose the large Valley Creek, which flowed southwest from Birmingham toward the town of Bessemer. The city engineers ran the sanitary sewer pipes from east to west, and then dumped all the sewerage downhill into Valley Creek.[34]

Laying sewer pipes required digging up streets. It was much more efficient to dig up and repair unpaved alleys than to dig up paved streets, and accordingly Birmingham's efficient city engineers ran most of the sewers be-

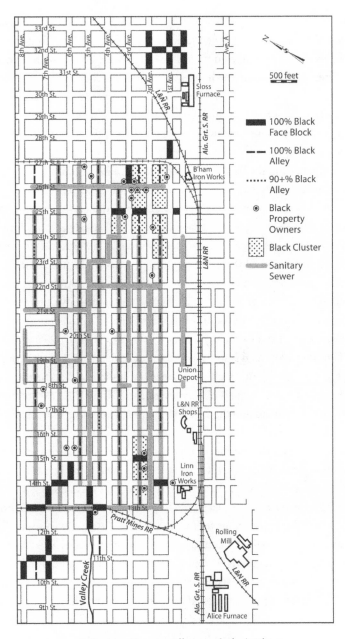

MAP 8. Sanitary Sewers, Alleys, and Black Clusters,
Northside Birmingham, 1891

neath the east-west alleys. Ironically, as a result, the dwelling units closest to the sanitary sewers were the Black cabins along the alleys. But few if any Black cabins were connected with the sewers or fitted out with indoor toilets. Instead the whites in the houses out on the street-fronts had ditches dug and pipes laid from their houses across their backyards to hook up with the sanitary sewers. They then installed indoor toilets, which became regarded as standard equipment in white houses, and which transformed the sanitary routines and habits of most white families.[35]

Compounding the lack of access of Black cabins to sanitary sewers was the failure of the city to extend the network toward the densely settled Sloss Quarters, as shown on map 8. City officials excused themselves, pointing out that as of 1889 the Sloss Furnace and quarters lay outside the city limits and not within the scope of city-government responsibility. But in fact the initiative for excluding the Sloss properties from the city limits had come from the company itself, which had worked to remain exempt from the city property tax and to remain out of the potential reach of any future city regulation about connecting Sloss cabins to sanitary sewers. The city government chose to acquiesce in the Sloss Company strategy.[36]

The city also denied sewer access to most of the several highly congested blocks in the eastern Black cluster. However, it did build a short line along Twenty-Sixth Street from Third Alley to First Alley. The exception is revealing, but to understand the exception requires knowing how Birmingham financed its sewers.

The Alabama Redemption Constitution restricted the city property tax rate to an unreasonably low level. Mayor Lane, who came into office in 1883 eager to construct city improvements, tried financing street paving and sewers by issuing long-term bonds that would be paid off with future general property taxes. But the bond payments bit too deeply into the tightly restrained property tax revenue, and finally Lane and the city aldermen convinced the legislature to pass laws that granted Birmingham the authority to assess an increasing portion of improvement costs directly onto the owners of adjacent property.[37]

The laws established a special assessment system similar to that which many American cities already used. Typically, the cities administered the special assessments separately from its regular assessment of property taxes. The crucial point is that under this system city governments acted, in effect, as agents of the local property owners. In Birmingham, when a majority of property owners on a particular linear city block agreed, by signing a petition, to pay special assessments to finance street paving or a sewer in their block, the city government would survey, design, and build the improvement, then would sell a short-term bond to finance it, and finally would bill the land-owners for the cost, which they could pay in ten annual installments. In many residential areas filled with white landowners, the system fostered prompt con-struction of sewers and of other amenities like sidewalks and street paving.[38]

The sewers under the Northside alleys were not financed by the African Americans who lived in those alleys. Not a single Black alley family owned the house in which it lived. To whom, then, did the city engineers look to pay the special assessments to build the major east-west sanitary sewer lines? To the white owners of the street-front face-block houses. All of these owners signed petitions to lay the sewers, dug ditches across their backyards, and hooked up to the new sanitary sewers running under the alleys.[39]

The one exception to this pattern was the one mentioned above—the short line along Twenty-Sixth Street from Third Alley to First Alley. This stretch had the city's largest cluster of Black property owners, and they may have helped to get the sewer along their street. But probably equally important was the influence of the white owners of the Buzzard Roost saloon shantytown between Twenty-Sixth and Twenty-Seventh streets and between First Avenue and Second Alley. The white owners of saloons, dance halls, and brothels needed sewer access to dispose of the waste produced by their crowds of cus-tomers. In all likelihood, the vibrant commercial activity in the "Roost" en-abled the white owners to convince the city to provide them a short sewer arm.

The shanties packed into the blocks on either side of Twenty-Sixth Street did not find a way to connect with the sewer. City officials held firmly to the tradition that city government should not require property owners to pay for services that would mainly benefit non-property-owners. With regard to sewer connections the city meticulously honored the wishes and initiatives of property owners, and the white owners of the Black residences had no desire to spend the extra money to create sewer connections. For the 1880s and 1890s there is no record of any agency, public or private, pressuring landlords to eliminate outdoor toilets by connecting Black cabins to nearby sewers. Prob-ably few, if any, did so.[40]

In 1901 the editor of the *Age-Herald* deplored the very existence of the al-leys of Birmingham. The much venerated "founders of this town" had "made the folly and mistake of including alleys in its city plan." An "alley ... means unfit habitations, foul smells, and much riotous conduct in close relations with decent living," he wrote. "From these alleys come in one foul stream riotous noises and unbearable smells." Indeed, "No decent human being desires the world to know that he lives in an alley."[41]

As mapping shows, few whites would live in the alley world of Birmingham. The absence of indoor plumbing, the filth, and the odors demarcated a separate and derogated Black neighborhood and a downgraded Black lifestyle. The new technology of sanitary sewers, indoor plumbing, and indoor toilets became standard for most white homes, but most Black homes continued to rely on stinking backyard privies.

A PILLAR OF JIM CROW

In Birmingham and much of the urban South, severe segregation and discrimination characterized residential life from the post-emancipation era and long into the twentieth century. Discrimination in services and amenities delimited Black residential areas as second-rate, inferior, and unworthy, and warned whites that they should live elsewhere. Black residential clusters were segregated partly to facilitate an instrumental white goal of minimizing expenditures for city services and amenities for Blacks. A key result was that Black residential districts exhibited a negative and deprived ambiance. Elite whites led the way in shaping the discriminatory patterns through their real estate development practices and manipulation of the property tax system. But whites across the economic spectrum provided political support to the elites. The deprivation of Black neighborhoods saved money, and it stamped upon those neighborhoods a mark of unworthiness as places where unworthy citizens like Blacks would live. Southern urban residential segregation was so powerful and produced such appalling consequences that it could be described as a central pillar of Jim Crow.

CHAPTER 6

THE ECONOMIC REALM

Work and Property

"It is not worth a great deal to be black," said N. R. Fielding, Birmingham's most prominent Black artisan, at the 1883 Senate committee hearings. Blacks were "oppressed in our labor, in our work, and deprived of being advanced in skilled labor as we might be. We have no opportunities to learn trades as the whites have."

"They discount your color?" asked Blair. "Yes, sir," said Fielding.[1] Pastor Isaiah H. Welch seconded Fielding. Speaking as the leader of the nine Black witnesses, he told the committee: "The entrances to the different trades seem . . . to be closed against" Black men. He saw a "disposition" on the part of white laborers, particularly labor organizations, "to shut our people out." Black parents were "anxious to have their sons learn trades, believing that to be the best means by which they can provide for their future usefulness." But, in fact, "there are very few trades outside of the barber's occupation of which our young men have a chance to acquire knowledge." Therefore, "they are mostly engaged about here in mining and doing other subordinate work; very few of them are learning trades." And this, said Welch, "is very discouraging, not only to the young people, but to parents."[2]

RACIAL PATTERNS

Fielding and Welch denounced the everyday reality that Black workers continually encountered impervious boundaries—criteria, rules, stereotypes—by which whites sought to sustain and intensify an overall economic paradigm of white above Black. Judging by two major economic patterns, the whites largely succeeded.

First, in Birmingham, 75 percent of white males held skilled jobs while 90 percent of Black males held unskilled jobs. A similar pattern pervaded all the industrial areas of the New South. As economic historian Gavin Wright has written, "The southern industrial workplace was highly segregated," and the segregation was explicitly "racial." Moreover, the pattern of labor segregation indicated strong economic continuity between slave South and free South. A major factor was the thin on-the-job experience and training provided by the antebellum slave regime. Slaveholders used the vast majority of male slaves as unskilled agricultural laborers, providing neither skilled training nor rudimentary education, and the postbellum South had done nothing to undo that legacy of slavery. Most Black migrants to southern cities arrived without any industrial on-the-job training, and white employers considered it natural to consign them to unskilled work.[3]

Second, in Birmingham, whites owned 99.6 percent of all property, while Blacks owned the tiny remainder. The property ownership pattern likewise grew directly from slavery. The slave regime had denied Blacks the right to own property, and the federal government and the Republican Party had emancipated Blacks without attempting any significant or sustained redistribution of property or income. In 1865 African Americans found themselves upon the very lowest rung of the economic ladder. The postbellum South needed no period of experimentation with forgotten alternatives to subordinate freedmen to the bottom of the economic realm.[4]

N. R. Fielding's personal success in the economic world, however, demonstrated that the pattern of white above Black was not uniform. Fielding had attained high skill as a bricklayer, and he was part of an exceptional top 10 percent of skilled Black males who occupationally stood above the one-fourth of white males who languished in unskilled jobs. Fielding had become a prosperous building contractor who employed twenty-five men. He had built a house large enough to accommodate eight boarders, and altogether he owned property worth $1,054. He was thus one of an exceptional ninety-three Blacks, including ten women, who had become property owners and who stood economically above approximately one thousand adult white males who owned no property whatever.[5] By 1883, Fielding and a few other Blacks in Birmingham had established modest, but perhaps conspicuous, beachheads of Black economic accomplishment and property ownership along the Black/white economic borderline. This had become possible in the economic realm because emancipation had dismantled the rigid antebellum economic rules that had defined African Americans as property and that had rendered them legally incompetent to play an autonomous economic role. After emancipation, whites had to deal with Blacks as freedmen who could make some choices, albeit narrow, about jobs, contracts, and property, and occasionally achieve middle-class standing.

Still, in the economic realm the negative legacies of slavery—nonexistent education, deficient job experience, and no accumulation of property—handicapped freedmen and produced Black/white economic contrasts that showed considerable continuity with the slave system. Also persisting into the postbellum world were negative economic stereotypes that portrayed slaves and freedmen as lacking independence, initiative, thrift, and autonomy. The stereotypes continued to operate in the minds of postbellum white employers and laborers, influencing their judgments about the suitability of Black laborers for specific types of jobs, and causing whites to view Blacks as naturally destined for economic dependence and servile labor. The stern regularity of the social color line held.

BLACK PROPERTY OWNERS

In early Birmingham the economic dominance of whites revealed itself in the white domination of property ownership. In 1884 African Americans owned only $30,578 worth of property while whites owned $6,908,180. The 93 Black people who owned property accounted for only 7 percent of property owners even though Blacks comprised 41 percent of the population. Table 1 demonstrates the overwhelming supremacy of whites in property holding and the low value of the few Black holdings.

The small Black property holders, however, were highly visible in local life. This was so because they bent an important Black/white economic boundary, and their property ownership pointed to the threat of future economic advancement of more Blacks above the level of many whites. The top Black property owner—the school principal Burton Hudson—owned land and houses valued at $1,708. His valuation was less than one-third of the aver-

TABLE I. Distribution of Assessed Valuations of Black and White Property
Holdings, Birmingham, 1884

ASSESSED VALUATION	WHITE (NO.)	BLACK (NO.)
$500,001–$1,000,000	3	—
$100,001–$500,000	5	—
$50,001–$100,000	4	—
$20,001–$50,000	20	—
$5,001–$20,000	146	—
$2,001–$5,000	262	—
$1,501–$2,000	103	1
$1,001–$1,500	140	5
$501–$1,000	276	9
$251–$500	184	31
$1–$250	125	47
TOTAL OWNERS	1,268 (93%)	93 (7%)

SOURCE: Jefferson County, Concise Form of Amount of Taxes Due by Each Taxpayer of Jefferson County, Alabama, for the Year 1884.

age white valuation of $5,472, but it was more than the median white valuation
of $1,250. In other words, Hudson personally owned more property than did
half of the city's individual white property owners. When the one thousand
white nonowners are brought into the picture, Hudson as property owner
stood above three-fourths of adult white men. For a people only twenty years
removed from square one at emancipation, the acquisition of property by
Hudson and the other Black property owners in Birmingham was a significant
achievement.[6]

JOB SEGREGATION IN TRADES AND INDUSTRY

In the Birmingham job market, Blacks confronted subordination, but the pattern was complex. The subordination did not usually involve wage discrimination between Blacks and whites who held the same or similar jobs. The
brickmason N. R. Fielding told the 1883 Senate committee about specific instances of alleged wage discrimination between Black and white construction

workers. But studies of the postbellum southern labor market have concluded that Fielding's experience with wage discrimination was neither widespread nor typical. The more common pattern was that Black and white workers were segregated into separate industries or separate job categories or separate segments of the job market, with whites heavily dominating but not completely controlling all skilled categories. Within such a racially segmented labor market, Blacks and whites did occasionally hold the same or similar skilled jobs, and in those relatively rare situations Blacks typically did not experience wage discrimination. In the market for unskilled workers Blacks typically received the going wage.[7]

The dominant pattern of racial segmentation was not completely consistent, however. Conspicuous exceptions did exist, as demonstrated by historian Paul R. Worthman. He tabulated unskilled and skilled Black and white male industrial workers, subdividing the skilled workers into four major categories. As table 2 shows, in 1883, Blacks in Birmingham held 13 percent of all skilled jobs in the city, and they had made more substantial inroads into a few specific skilled categories.

TABLE 2. Black and White Male Industrial Workers in Five Occupational Categories, Birmingham, 1883

	WHITE	BLACK	PERCENT BLACK	PERCENTAGE OF WHITES	PERCENTAGE OF BLACKS
Skilled					
Building Trades	285	52	15.4	27.6	4.5
Railroad	156	20	11.4	15.1	1.7
Mechanics	330	20	5.7	31.9	1.7
Service	17	27	61.3	1.6	2.4
TOTAL SKILLED	788	119	13.1	76.2	10.4
Unskilled	246	1,024	80.6	23.8	89.6
Total	1,034	1,143	—	100	100

SOURCE: Reanalysis of Paul R. Worthman's tabulation from Birmingham *City Directory*, 1883, in "Working Class Mobility in Birmingham," in Tamara K. Hareven, ed., *Anonymous Americans* (Englewood Cliffs, N.J.: Prentice Hall, 1971), 176–79.

Nonetheless, the general pattern of white predominance was striking. Among all white male industrial workers, fully 76.2 percent held skilled jobs, while among all Black male industrial workers only 10.4 percent held skilled jobs. An overwhelming 89.6 percent of Black male industrial workers were employed in unskilled work.[8]

An exceptional 119 Black male industrial workers in Birmingham, however, had climbed into a skilled category. They typically earned $2.50 to $3.00 per day—more than twice the wage earned by the 246 unskilled white male common laborers. Thus within industrial occupations the color pattern was more jagged than in social institutions like churches and schools. Most whites disliked the jagged line, and the unskilled whites at the bottom probably grumbled. But no whites launched effective efforts to eliminate the exceptions and to make the economic color line as rigidly consistent as was the social color line.[9]

Behind many of the exceptions in the Black/white occupational pattern lay the straightforward economic factor of previous on-the-job experience and training, and behind that factor lay certain practices of the antebellum slave regime.[10] Some exceptional Black migrants presented skills in the building trades, skills fostered during slavery by a few urban masters who had found it advantageous to upgrade their slave labor force so as to use it in urban construction. Birmingham's early construction boom attracted several Blacks with such prior training, among them N. R. Fielding—brickmason, contractor, and boardinghouse owner—and Alfred B. Jackson, a plasterer. In those two special trades, Blacks in 1883 comprised more than 40 percent of workers. In other skilled construction occupations the percentage of Blacks was much lower, varying from 17 percent for painters to 7 percent for carpenters, and to o percent for plumbers.[11] Some of these tradespeople became highly visible leaders within the Black community. Fielding became a prominent political organizer. Jackson led school reform and served as the lieutenant (second-in-command) of Birmingham's Black volunteer militia company, called the Magic City Guards and organized during 1883–87 as part of the Alabama State Troops.[12]

Among the carpenters who brought slave-era experience was Jesse Claxton, another of the witnesses at the 1883 Senate hearing. In antebellum Richmond, Virginia, Claxton had been bound out by his master to learn carpentry, and he had become a finishing carpenter with such refined skills that when he arrived in Birmingham in 1873 he had been hired for $3.00 a day to make the ornate window frames that decorated the very courtroom where he gave his 1883 testimony. In the ensuing decade Claxton had become a successful contractor, employing several $2.50-a-day carpenters.[13]

In the service trades—barber, shoemaker, and tailor—the antebellum acquisition of skills had also fostered a relatively heavy Black presence. In 1883, 100 percent of Birmingham barbers and 38 percent of shoemakers were Black. Acquisition of such skills by slaves had been fostered by the belief of many antebellum urban whites that such trades provided a personal service that was appropriately received from a servant race. As of 1883 Birmingham had few tailors, and none were Black. Perhaps the raw boomtown was better known for its rapid construction than for its fine dress. But tailors would come. By 1895, 21 percent of them were Black.[14]

Most of Birmingham's twenty-seven barbers regarded themselves not as servants, but skilled artisans or small businessmen. Thus, a dozen of them listed their shops in the "Business Directory" of the *Birmingham City Directory*. Some of those dozen had shops at visible downtown locations where they catered only to white men, while others had shops in the Black business district where they catered only to Black men. Some of the "colored" barber shops were large, operating as many as ten chairs, and doing "a giant business." Several of them, like the shop owned by a political leader, James A. Harper, became customary places for Black men to gather for camaraderie, gossip, and political planning. Even if whites continued to view barbers as servants, the barbers saw themselves providing a high grade of service requiring considerable skill and finesse, and they were proud that they did not work in white homes like domestic servants, but rather maintained attractive shops where they received clients. Barbers typically charged 35 cents for a shave and haircut and earned as much as men in the skilled building trades. Some barbers catering to whites may have found advantage in the friendly relationship they could cultivate with prominent customers. The position of barber carried prestige in the Black community, and many barbers were leaders in churches and fraternal associations.[15]

Barbering proved to be an occupation too attractive for Blacks to keep to themselves. In 1884 one white barber moved to town and opened a downtown shop for white customers. There were three by 1886, twelve by 1887, and twenty-six by 1890. By 1890, 20 percent of barbers were white and 80 percent Black. Barbering became one of the few trades that underwent a change from 100 percent Black to part white.[16]

If tradition and prior on-the-job experience had enabled Blacks to establish a beachhead in a particular skilled trade, they often succeeded in sustaining it over time, but did not have much success expanding it. From 1883 to 1900 in the building trades, for example, Blacks were able to maintain only a 12 to 16 percent representation. In the specific trade of brickmason the percentage of Blacks would decline from 42 percent in 1883 to roughly 25 percent by 1890, but then it climbed to 30 percent by 1895 and persisted at that level until 1910, when it again rose above 40 percent.[17]

At industrial sites—the iron furnaces, rolling mill, foundries, and railroads—white domination of the higher-paying skilled positions was almost complete. At such sites large groups of Black unskilled common laborers earning $1.00 to $1.50 a day worked alongside a few white skilled workers who earned $2.50 to $4.00 a day. Seldom did a Black worker climb into a skilled position.[18] At the furnaces about 10 percent of the workers, "all white" according to furnace owner James Sloss, earned $2.00 to $4.00 a day as engineers, blacksmiths, machinists, furnace carpenters, or furnace tenders. The ladder of furnace positions open to Blacks was short, going up only to coke-oven tender, which paid $1.50 a day.[19]

At the Birmingham Rolling Mill, which employed 450 men, the crucial work of rolling and shaping the molten iron was performed by 91 highly skilled men known as puddlers, heaters, or rollers, as well as molders, who earned $3.50 to $5.00 a day. Only one of them was Black. The other 90 were white, many of them immigrants from Ireland, England, or Germany. Most Blacks did only unskilled lifting and loading. Typically the highest position a Black could attain, after several years of learning the ropes, was helper to the skilled whites, at a wage of $1.25 to $1.30.[20]

The railroads also tightly constrained Black opportunity. Blacks did nearly all the common labor of building and repairing tracks, at the $1.00-a-day wage, but Blacks had only limited access to jobs running and repairing the trains. Blacks got about one-fourth of the positions as firemen or brakemen, which paid from $1.20 to $1.50 a day, but whites got all the higher positions, such as engineer or conductor, which paid from $2.80 to $5.00 a day.[21]

IN THE MINES

Coal mining provided opportunities for Black advancement, but they came at a high personal cost. The mines provided some marginally skilled jobs, but they involved difficult, dangerous, and extremely dirty work underground.

To take up coal mining around Birmingham a worker had to move out to the coal-mine village of Pratt Mines, six miles northwest of the city. The Pratt Mines Railroad, the vital coal lifeline for Birmingham industry, connected the mines to the city. Every day half a dozen long trains with cars heaped with coal came down the six-mile railroad and fed the industrial fires. The 1883 *City Directory* showed that about 200 Black miners and about 370 white miners had moved out to Pratt Mines, where they lived in cabins near the mine entrance. Often a handful of single Black men, sometimes brothers or cousins, lived in one cabin, sharing rent and food.[22]

Black newcomers to the Pratt Mines found that most of the mine work available initially was at the level of unskilled mine "helper," which paid $1.00 a day. The helpers loaded and hauled coal, drove mules, and did odd jobs. Some Blacks eventually advanced to a higher skill level where, as full-fledged coal miners, they were paid on a piecework basis. In 1883 at the Pratt Mines they received 50 cents per ton of the coal that they got out. Income depended in part on strength, endurance, and motivation, and the average daily output per miner was four tons, which earned a miner $2.00—double the wage for common day labor, but less than the wage commanded by building skills such as carpentering and bricklaying.[23]

Many experienced white miners hired Black common laborers and paid them $1.00 a day to work as helpers, picking up and loading the cut coal and pushing trams in and out. With such assistance the experienced miners could concentrate entirely on the semiskilled task of cutting the coal, and could increase their daily output by several tons, enough to pay the helpers and still pocket extra take-home pay. Many strong but inexperienced Black men straight from the country got a start as unskilled helpers, and some of them learned enough of the tricks of cutting coal to go to work on their own as miners, digging coal, and receiving 50 cents per ton, thereby forging a route into the semiskilled component of mining.[24]

Looking only at the wage earners, however, would miss almost half of the laborers in the Pratt Mines. In 1883 only about 57 percent of the workers received any wages at all. The other 43 percent—about 500 men—worked under conditions of forced servitude. Those workers were convicts sentenced to hard labor by state and county courts. The legal charges that most frequently sent Black men to the life-threatening convict mines were assault and carrying a concealed weapon, which typically brought a fine of fifty dollars, or one hundred days working in the mines. But other offenses that sent Black men from the Birmingham courthouse to the mines in October 1883 were "disturbing public worship," and "unlawful use of abusive language."[25]

Under the sentencing arrangements the authorities leased the prisoners to coal-mine corporations, which housed them in several stockades. About 90 percent of the Pratt convicts were Black, about 10 percent white.[26] For the corporate employers, the convict labor system provided a low-cost supply of unskilled labor which they could organize in a fashion that closely resembled slavery. For the owners of the southern mines, employment of Blacks in that way was natural and, like slavery, the convict labor system was a means of profit maximizing.[27]

Historian Mary Ellen Curtin has found that by 1883 twenty-nine Alabama counties leased county prisoners to coal mines in the state. Pratt Mines leased 200 prisoners from fourteen counties while New Castle stockade, one of several convict prisons near Pratt Mines, leased 225 prisoners from fifteen other Alabama counties. Some of the prisoners leased to mining camps in the Birmingham area were women.[28]

In 1882 a report by Dr. Jerome Cochrane, state health officer, exposed conditions at New Castle stockade. Convicts at New Castle who failed to dig a quota of fifteen bushels of coal a day were flogged with "a thick leather strap, some three inches wide, and two feet long, attached to a wooden handle twelve to fourteen inches long." Each morning the convicts were bound together in chains to march from stockade to the mine, where they were separated to work. Back at the stockade in the evenings the convicts sat down without washing hands or faces and ate cornbread, peas, and coarse meat from tin plates set on unwashed tables that were "sprinkled with white lime."

The 25 white convicts at New Castle slept in one cell, the 105 Black prisoners in another cell that measured 7 paces by 17 paces. The Black cell had "no windows," the ventilation being "exclusively through the long open spaces or cracks between the logs." The Black prisoners slept on bunks stacked three high, on straw mattresses and "extremely filthy" coarse blankets "swarming with bed bugs" and "saturated with coal dust, human sweat, and grease." Iron buckets which received feces and urine stood unemptied until morning.[29]

Some Black women cooked and cleaned for numerous male prisoners in mining camps. For example, Annie Gilmore, a twenty-year-old listed as a "house girl," was the only woman living among 46 men at New Castle. Some of the female prisoners had to live with mining bosses. Mary Ellen Curtin writes that this made "them vulnerable to rape and sexual abuse," and concludes: "To be a black woman in an Alabama prison camp was a nightmare of hard work, bad treatment, and isolation from other women." In 1883, when prisoner Annie Tucker attempted to run away from the house of the Pratt contractor, the superintendent, according to the Board of Prison Inspectors, "stripped her, had her held down, and inflicted 56 lashes upon her with a heavy strap." As Curtin observes, "Such abuse inevitably recalls the days of slavery."[30]

Half a year after his first report, Cochrane found alarming mortality rates among Black convicts—at one prison 161.5 per 1,000 per year, and at another prison 360 per 1,000 per year. If this rate persisted, all would be dead in three years. Cochrane blamed the lethal pattern on white prison supervisors and guards who considered it appropriate to compel Black convicts, but not white convicts, to work even when the penitentiary physician had pronounced them ill. None of the white convicts had died, and among all the free wage-earning Pratt miners, Black and white, the death rate had been 20.6 per 1,000 per year—far below the mortality among Black convicts.[31]

After receiving the convicts they had leased, the corporations graded them and assigned tasks to them not according to race, but according to strength and ability. Men classified as first-class miners were given a quota to dig five tons of coal a day, those classified as second-class a quota of four tons, and so forth down through third-class men and "dead-heads." The company proceeded to teach strong able Black men all the skills of coal mining and to classify them as first-class miners, demanding five tons a day. If such convict miners survived to serve out their long sentences, they would emerge as highly skilled miners, and most of them chose to stay in the mine district working as experienced but now free coal miners.[32]

By 1883 approximately 200 such Black ex-convicts lived at Pratt Mines or in other mine villages and earned two to three dollars a day using the skills they had learned as convicts. The dreaded Alabama convict labor system brought death to an shockingly high portion of its inmates, but for some Black men who fell into its clutches and survived, it served also as a trade school, albeit a brutally harsh one. Of the various methods of acquiring the skills to rise above common day labor, only the coercive and dangerous school of the convict mines extended its training more generously to Blacks than to whites.[33]

During the 1880s the Black portion of full-fledged free miners grew steadily, the number of Black convicts increased, and Blacks continued to do virtually all of the common labor in the mines. This common labor became a special marginal occupation identified as "Negro work" because of the disagreeable and dangerous conditions, the marginal wages, the large presence of convicts, and the fact that a majority of miners were Black.[34]

UNION ORGANIZING

In general, the sharp line of social separation in Birmingham produced tension and fragmentation in the labor union movement. However, the patterns were complex, with variations depending on the industry and the categories of workers employed. The historians of labor in the Birmingham district have documented both competition and cooperation among Blacks and working-class whites.

Historian Henry M. McKiven Jr. studied union organizing among white workers in the iron and steel industry. Most of these workers lived inside the city of Birmingham. He pointed to powerful economic conflict between Blacks and whites, and argued that skilled white workers, rather than employers, provided the crucial initiative for excluding Blacks from skilled positions and preserving them for whites. His interpretation portrayed social and political color lines as largely instrumental echoes of the economic line.[35]

Daniel Letwin, however, found different patterns in his study of coal miners, Black and white. Most of them lived in small mining communities outside of Birmingham. Letwin concluded that most of the initiative for conflict between Black and white miners came from employers who strategically divided workers by race so as to weaken and dominate them. In 1890 many miners in Birmingham joined the United Mine Workers (UMW), organizing what was called UMW District 20. When unions gained power, as did UMW District 20, employers often imported Blacks as strikebreakers. They did so during a strike in 1894 that lasted for a hundred days. Labor leaders consistently sought to resist the employers' strategy by incorporating Black and white miners into a single biracial union and seeking to foster "a sense of shared identity rooted in common class experience." Black miners responded positively to the appeals for labor unity, and white coal miners became more interested in incorporating Blacks into a common biracial union than did any other category of skilled or semiskilled white workers.[36]

In 1895 the Birmingham Trades Council, composed primarily of white unions in the building trades, admitted unions that were composed of African Americans. A weekly labor newspaper, the Birmingham *Labor Advocate,* endorsed that move. Between 1897 and 1904 the coal miners' union, the UMW District 50, became a powerful force in the entire Alabama State Federation of Labor and in the Birmingham Trades Council. Letwin joined historian Paul Worthman in arguing that the miners' union had a vision of racial cooperation, and this promoted a policy of racial cooperation in the federation and the council and helped to mitigate conflict between Black and white workers.[37] In 1900, according to Letwin, the labor leader Henry C. West "advised black miners to ignore company efforts to turn them against 'poor whites.'" West reminded Blacks that "You have often heard the expression 'I'd rather be a negro than a poor white man.' Now, I'll tell you, the poor white man and the negro stands [*sic*] in the same column when it comes to earning bread." Black and white miners, he declared, should "shake hands over the pick and shovel or these companies will have us just where they want us."[38]

Letwin acknowledged, however, that white miners consistently rejected "social equality" with Black miners even while both groups were cooperating in union activity. He attributed the rejection primarily to external societal pressures to which the white miners accommodated, but he did recognize also an element of internal "true conviction" on the part of the white miners in opposing social equality. They did so, wrote Letwin, partly in self-defense against what they regarded as "cynical" attacks from their enemies, partly in simple straightforward dismissal of any desire for or toleration of interracial sex, partly as an attempt "to retain credibility in the eyes of a racist public," and partly also because of "the depth of the dominant racial assumptions held by the white miners themselves."[39]

Employers in the mining industry generally harbored the same fundamental racial attitudes as their white workers, but they also had a powerful instrumental motivation to fuel racial hostility within their workforce. In 1903, a large coal company, the Tennessee Coal, Iron & Railroad Company, launched an effort to destroy the United Mine Workers, and the union responded with a strike, supported by Black miners, which lasted two years. The employers prevailed in part because of their continuing ability to rely on convict labor, and their success in eroding the spirit and practice of labor cooperation across the racial divide. Another strike followed in 1908. Black miners also supported this one, but the strike failed and left the Alabama UMW in shambles.[40]

Whatever the nature of racial cooperation within the labor market, the cooperation did not extend beyond the workplace, as evidenced in 1897 by the support of the Birmingham Trades Council and the *Labor Advocate* for protecting the segregation of schools. In fact, the council and the *Labor Advocate* never endorsed any challenge to the inequitable funding of Black schools—or to their segregation. And Henry C. West changed his message after 1900. In 1906 he articulated a deep sense of social and economic distance between Blacks and whites, particularly with regard to education. He ran for the state legislature on a platform that included the statement: "This is a white man's country. I am opposed to negro education, because it is an established fact that an 'educated negro' is as a rule a worthless imp." With those sentiments he won the strong endorsement of labor unions.[41]

BLACK IMMOBILITY IN A SEGMENTED LABOR SYSTEM

Altogether in the Birmingham Black community of 1883 less than 10 percent of the adult males had obtained skilled positions that gave them the margin of comfort and respect afforded by a wage of $2.50 per day, a wage that would support a family without a spouse having to work for white folks.[42]

Many Blacks who arrived during the early 1880s tried to take the seemingly logical step up into the skilled trades, but found the step blocked. The Black skilled carpenter Jesse Claxton blamed the blockage upon white workers rather than white employers. In his view, "The people here that owns the works, I don't suppose they would have any objection to taking in colored apprentices, but the class that works there won't work with them as a general thing." Claxton pointed to instrumental competition between white and Black laborers, with whites seeking to exclude Blacks from skilled trades, thus trying to keep the skill boundary as tightly congruent as possible with the color boundary.[43]

Testimony supporting Claxton's assessment came from a white industrialist from Tennessee, H. S. Chamberlain of the Chattanooga and Knoxville Iron Company, which did work similar to that of the Birmingham Rolling Mill. Chamberlain reported: "It has been difficult to get the colored men into the skilled work, because there was such a prejudice against teaching them the trades." He explained that "there are only a few departments of the iron business, puddling, heating, and rolling, and into those you could not put colored men, because if you did the white men would strike."

Chamberlain, however, had broken from common practice. In 1880, when the Chattanooga and Knoxville Iron Company's skilled white ironworkers had gone out on strike, his company, after studying the situation thoroughly, "made up our minds to put in the negro." We "shut our teeth," discharged all the whites except a small skilled nucleus who were willing to work with and train Blacks, and then "put the colored men into the puddling, and into the heating, and into the rolling departments—into every place about the mill." And the experiment worked: "We find the colored men . . . are fully as good as white men; their yield is as good; they are as steady workmen; they are as reliable in every way, and their product is fully as good." He added: "We have never had more successful working of the mill than during the last two years, when we have had colored labor almost exclusively."[44]

In Birmingham, according to Henry M. McKiven, skilled white iron and steel workers sustained a tight color boundary that systematically denied Blacks the opportunity to climb into skilled positions. In 1890 there was only 1 Black iron puddler out of 155 puddlers listed in the *City Directory*, 2 Black heaters and rollers out of 21, and no Blacks among the 37 iron molders. Likewise, in the iron and steel fabricating industries, in 1890 there were no Blacks at all in the key skilled positions of boilermaker or patternmaker, and there was only 1 Black among the 258 machinists. Only in the position of blacksmith had Blacks make any inroads, by 1890 holding 28 of the 132 positions, or 21 percent. In the skilled railroad positions, Blacks climbed from 12 percent of the positions in 1883 to 15 percent in 1890, but those of that 15 percent were all in the lower-level fireman and brakeman positions. Thus whites monopolized the most attractive skilled positions in the iron and railroad industries.[45]

Guidance for understanding the dynamics and motivations that could produce such a labor market can be found in the segmented-labor-market model of sociologist Edna Bonacich. The model focuses upon economic competition in a labor market that contains "at least two groups of workers whose price of labor differs for the same work, or would differ if they did the same work." If the two labor groups are ethnically identifiable, then the economic competition between them will tend to intensify ethnic antagonism. Typically the lower-paid group may be newcomers to the labor market, seeking to make inroads into it. The newcomers may have weaknesses—lack of resources, deficiencies in job skills, or lack of political clout—that make them vulnerable to unfavorable wage bargains and that make them willing to sell their labor cheaply, a weakness which makes them attractive to employers. In times of labor tension employers are likely to try to recruit the low-wage group as strikebreakers. The higher-wage labor group will respond by seeking to weaken the threatening low-wage newcomers even more drastically. They will attempt to exclude the lower-wage group from desirable jobs and to restrict it to undesirable low-wage jobs. As a means to that end, the high-wage group will foster a broad system of ethnic subordination that will handicap the newcomers not only economically, but also socially and politically.[46]

Conditions in Birmingham's labor market corresponded closely with the conditions of the segmented-labor-market model, and it helps in understanding the group dynamics that by the early 1880s had already split the Birmingham labor market by jobs. White laborers had gained almost exclusive access to more desirable and higher-wage skilled jobs, while the weaker Black newcomers were relegated mainly to undesirable low-skilled jobs. At the same time, urban working-class whites embraced restrictions that handicapped Blacks socially, and had tended to throw their political weight against crucial government services to Blacks, particularly schools. In 1888, when white workingmen helped to institute the city white primary, they threw their weight against the Black franchise.

Paul Worthman provided one measure of the effectiveness of white working-class strategies to block Black advancement in his study of upward occupational mobility among unskilled Black and white workers who lived in Birmingham in 1880 and 1890. Among those who stayed in town at least ten years, only 17 to 19 percent of Black workers, as compared with 50 to 63 percent of white workers, climbed upward at least one occupational step, either to a more skilled manual labor position or to a nonmanual position.[47]

Many factors blocked opportunity for upward mobility by unskilled Black workers and reinforced the strategies of working-class whites to keep

Blacks weak and subordinate. A major economic factor was the lack of Black on-the-job experience in skilled tasks. However, even more powerful were the negative stereotypes and a deep stigma of social unworthiness generated within the social core of Jim Crow. The pattern of exclusion of Blacks from skilled jobs was not as sharp as the school pattern, which excluded 100 percent of Black pupils from white schools. But Gavin Wright has correctly labeled the exclusion of African Americans from skilled employment to be what it was—"segregation." It stood, along with schools, as an example of a type of segregation that was imposed promptly and thoroughly after the Civil War.[48]

COMMERCIAL AND DOMESTIC SERVICE

As of 1883 approximately one hundred Black men of Birmingham had taken up service as porters, servants, stewards, or waiters in white downtown businesses, restaurants, and hotels, or as servants and gardeners in white homes in the prime residential areas north of the business district. Such work was cleaner and lighter than common industrial labor, but often it involved still longer hours and even lower pay. It was usually on the low side of the dollar-a-day standard, a daily wage that translated into twenty to thirty dollars a month, an income that meant a very constrained budget. And domestic service placed the Black person more constantly in the presence of whites in the white family milieu, and thus it allowed less independence. The Black worker had to face an expectation of behavior that required an elaborately subservient manner. The Black service worker had to endure constant supervision. Every posture and tone had to communicate deference, and the service had to be sensitive and responsive to the whites' every whim, mood, and desire.

Single men who earned such wages in either industry or domestic service had some budget leeway, spending roughly half of the wage on room and food—often living with several other men and sharing expenses—and the other half for clothing, incidentals, and amusement. But an unskilled Black family man faced much tighter constraints. Even families that lived in the plainest two- or three-room cabins in the Black "quarters" would spend most of the man's monthly wage for rent and food. Therefore it usually became vital for Black mothers to find ways to supplement family income.[49]

Many Black families took in a boarder, whose presence added to the mother's cooking and washing chores, but who paid the family several dollars a month. Beyond this, most Black mothers added a crucial ten to fifteen dollars to monthly family income by taking jobs as domestic servants in white households, or else by taking in the washing of white families.

Through long tradition, southern white women of business and professional families, and of some working families, had defined cooking, cleaning house, and doing laundry to be slave or "Negro work"—work too exhausting and tedious to be proper for the hands of white women. Emancipation, and the subsequent growth of New South cities, drove a dramatic expansion of the employment of Black women as domestic servants. In Birmingham, white households recruited most of the adult Black women in town, mustered them daily into white homes, and directed them to perform the drudgery of keeping up those homes. Probably a heavy majority of the approximately twelve hundred adult Black women of Birmingham worked outside their homes at least part-time in menial domestic labor.[50]

In their places of work, Black women, like Black men, sought to maintain as much autonomy from whites as possible. For example, most Black women, married or unmarried, refused to follow the slave pattern of "living in" where they worked, perhaps in a small room near the kitchen. "They seem to think that it is something against their freedom if they sleep where they are employed," observed one white man, "they think it is more like being free to have their own homes and to go to them after their work is done."[51] And, they may well have wanted to reduce the risk of sexual aggression on the part of white heads of households or their sons.[52] Black women prized the independence that came from their ability to quit work at one house and to change jobs, and in Birmingham they found the demand for domestic service great enough to allow them to change jobs frequently, to the great consternation of their white employers.

Preeminent among those employers was Mrs. George R. (Margaret Ketcham) Ward, whose husband ran the best hotel in town, the Relay House, across from the depot. Mrs. Ward, forty-two years old in 1883, had grown up in a notable antebellum Georgia family, and in Birmingham she had established herself as the leading social arbiter. When the US Senate subcommittee held its 1883 hearings in Birmingham, the senators, like all distinguished visitors, stayed at the Relay Hotel, and one evening at the hotel Senator Blair arranged to have Mrs. Ward give testimony, particularly on the "servant problem."[53]

"In old times in the South," recalled Mrs. Ward, the slave servants "were generally very nice about their work, . . . they were trained to understand that they must obey and give attention to their work; and, on the whole, they were really splendid house servants; I do not think there was ever a better set of house servants anywhere than the old house negroes."[54] But since emancipation, exclaimed Mrs. Ward, "it is just growing worse all the while. . . . The servants are growing more and more incorrigible all the time." They were not properly conscientious or responsive to reprimands. "If you dare to correct them or to suggest that their mode of working is not the best, or not the one you approve, they will leave you, or else be insolent about it."

Mrs. Ward was the only female witness to testify in Birmingham, and the committee heard only her side of such encounters. But her description afforded the perceptive listener some insight into the feelings on both sides. "Tell them to wipe up the floor," said Mrs. Ward, "and they will splash away from one end of the room to the other; and if you tell them that that is not the way to do it, they will either be insolent or perhaps give you a vacant stare as if they were very much astonished that you thought that was not the way to do it, and they will keep right on."

Mrs. Ward was particularly annoyed that the Black women servants "have no idea of the binding force of a contract or of any moral obligation. They leave us at any time they choose; they go from house to house, and we can place no dependence upon them at all." Consequently, "It is a very hard life that we housekeepers here lead; a life of dependence upon people that cannot be impressed with the importance of anything." She complained, "It is such a makeshift kind of life that it is actually dangerous to invite company three days ahead, because you cannot depend upon your servants staying with you so long."[55]

In her elegant hotel Mrs. Ward was trying to uphold the standard established by the best houses of the antebellum South, and her hotel ballroom was famous for the glittering social occasions that she orchestrated. At such occasions she had no problem excluding Black guests as completely as had antebellum hostesses, and she had no problem excluding all Blacks from the guest registry of her hotel. But she was finding that emancipation, which required her to deal with her Black servants as employees rather than as property, had seriously undermined her capacity to exercise the control that formerly had shaped enslaved women into such "really splendid house servants." At one point Senator Blair asked naively, "Couldn't you employ white natives?"

"Oh mercy!" exclaimed Mrs. Ward. "I wouldn't give them room. We would all go distracted if we had them for servants." White servants were "slovenly," they were incompetent, and, worst of all, "they think it is perfectly absurd that we should require them to do any other way than as they have been accustomed to do for themselves."

"Then the truth is that bad as these Negro servants are they are the best you can get?" observed Blair. "Oh, certainly," affirmed Mrs. Ward "I would not be without them. We are used to abusing them, too. It is like home to have the colored ones around us even though they are trifling."[56]

For Mrs. Ward the advantages provided by the persisting color boundaries remained crucial, even though they had crumbled somewhat. Black women on tight family budgets remained vulnerable both socially and economically, and Mrs. Ward could "abuse" the "trifling" Black servants in a way she would never dare to attempt with white employees. That made it "like home to have the colored ones around us," but not completely like the antebellum homes, because in them Black women had been slaves, not servants.

The ordeal with servants put Mrs. Ward in "a very fractious frame of mind." "I just feel as though I am wearing away years of my life that I am fitted to spend in a better way," she complained. It was "a constant fret and bother and annoyance to deal with these people." Her annoyance provoked an imperious manner that often had characterized spokespeople, male and female, of the antebellum planter class. "I do think that if a Southern woman ever arrives at the Celestial City," proclaimed Mrs. Ward, "she ought to go very high up. I think she ought to get up where she could look down on all the Yankees, for she will be one of those that are spoken of as coming up through great tribulation."[57]

Senator Blair asked her if she blamed northern folks for her troubles. "Yes," she replied, "I blame you for a great deal of it. I think if you had staid [sic] at home and let us go out of the Union we would have avoided all this trouble."[58]

The Yankee invasion had given Black servants enough independence to render Mrs. Ward "fractious," but Black women found that no amount of changing from service in one white household to another could relieve them of the menial nature of domestic service. Nor could it diminish the tension of maintaining constant deference, nor remove the sting of having to submit silently to the scolding by white employers whose standard had been established under slavery.[59]

A majority of the Black women of Birmingham labored in such menial domestic service. The labor boundary that subordinated Black women had persisted from Old South into New South, and it was severe, unrelenting, and completely one-sided. On the Black side of the boundary a majority of adult women spent a large portion of each day working as servants who cooked and cleaned in white homes or who washed the clothes of white families. On the white side of the boundary, women were systematically relieved of the drudgery and tedium of household chores. Not surprisingly, white women did not cross the boundary. Not one white woman in Birmingham did domestic service for a Black family. Only sixteen white women did domestic service at all, and all sixteen served white families.[60]

THE BLACK BUSINESS CLASS

At the top of the Black middle class in Birmingham in 1883 were about a dozen professionals. They included preachers and teachers in the segregated churches and schools; Burton H. Hudson, the school principal and real estate investor; John Henry Thomason, the editor of the *Pilot;* James A. Scott, the only Black attorney in Birmingham and the commander of the Magic City Guards; and an employment agent, who found Black servants for white households. They became major leaders in the Black community, and most of them have already appeared in this study as central figures in key social, economic, and political episodes. A larger group of about sixty Black people comprised the *business* component of the Black middle class. Most of them provided goods or services that the segregated white businesses were not offering. Most had gotten their start by developing some strong talent for producing or handling certain basic goods—groceries, meat, clothes, liquor, lumber, cooked meals—and then through energy, intelligence, hard work, and often a bit of luck, they had accumulated enough capital to set up as a self-employed small businessperson. Together, the professionals and the businesspeople accounted for all of the Black property owners in Birmingham.[61]

The creation and operation of Black boardinghouses illustrates the process by which several enterprising Black people entered the business world.

Boardinghouses offered opportunity for Black entrepreneurs because only houses run by Blacks would accommodate Black boarders. By 1883 about two dozen enterprising Black couples had followed a path forged by N. R. Fielding and his young wife, Carrie, who had moved from Athens when the Birmingham building boom took off. Fielding had used the skill of his own hands to build a large house, financing it in part with his income as a brickmason. Carrie Fielding had used her command of ordinary household skills and her talent for management to provide room and meals for seven boarders, thereby bringing in money to pay off the house. Soon Fielding's construction skills enabled him to become a contractor, and out of his rising income he bought several town lots. Birmingham's population boom not only augmented the demand for Fielding's construction skills, it also caused the value of his property to rise markedly. By 1884 he was the fifth-largest Black property holder in Birmingham, owning real estate with an assessed valuation of $1,054 and with a market value considerably more than twice that figure.[62]

The next largest group of Black businesspeople contained a half-dozen grocers and other dealers in foodstuffs. N. R. Fielding considered the food business attractive enough that in 1883 he sold some real estate to set up a grocery store "where I will keep on hand a full line of family groceries and confectioneries" and "will sell as cheap as any merchant in the city." Thus, Fielding added yet another line of business to his portfolio. Also J. H. Binford, who had brought some money when he moved to Birmingham from Huntsville, opened a grocery near Pastor Welch's church, on First Avenue and Twenty-Sixth Street, next to the Sloss Furnace and the Sloss settlement.[63]

Several types of small Black business, including Fielding's grocery store, clustered in the small downtown Black business center that spread around the corner of Nineteenth Street and Third Avenue. In 1883 that business neighborhood included Jake Lipman's "Cheap Clothing" stand; the ice cream parlor and day boardinghouse of Mrs. Alice Buckner and Mrs. Evelyn McQueen; N. R. Fielding's grocery store and confectionery, which had recently added a soda fountain and watermelon stand; James E. Bush's employment office, which helped Blacks find domestic service positions; the Gem Fruit Store that featured ice cream, soda, tobacco, butter, eggs, and chickens; the new grocery of J. J. Gayles and S. Woodruff; George Evans's "colored" barber shop, and the billiard saloon of Messrs. Robinson and Peterson. A few African American businesses were slightly separated from the Black business corner, among them Carrie Skinner's restaurant and boardinghouse; Taylor Boon's shop, "now prepared for dying clothes any color that is desired"; George Walters's restaurant, which promised "a good square meal for twenty-five cents," and the office of the Black newspaper, the *Pilot*. They included restaurants, more grocery stores, a newspaper office, an attorney's office, boardinghouses, clothes-dyeing shops, barbershops, fruit stores, ice cream parlors, and soda fountains, along with a large billiard saloon.

This small Black business cluster tucked into one downtown corner provided visible evidence of the emergence of a substantial, though still fragile, Black business community. But the modest one-story frame structures of the Black businesses stood in sharp contrast to the brick structures to the south. Only the white business district boasted banks, large dry goods stores, corporation office buildings, hotels, hardware stores, wholesale companies, commission merchants, brokers, dentists, doctors, engineers, utility company offices, printing companies, and warehouses. The contrast between the Black and the white business structures made clear the intangible but impenetrable boundary that separated the rich, highly diversified, and overwhelmingly dominant white business community from the Black business community's modest retail enterprises trading in food, clothes, and personal services.[64]

In 1886 the correspondent for the *Gazette* reported with pride that a group of Black Birmingham businessmen had organized "a colored Joint Stock Company with a capital stock of $2,500" to invest in new business opportunities, primarily real estate. "Its stockholders," said the correspondent, "embrace our wealthiest men," and he listed the officers and directors. This group had done well in Birmingham but had not risen quite to the level attained by N. R. Fielding and B. H. Hudson. The stockholders included W. S. Robinson and J. T. Peterson, the two owners of Birmingham's best Black saloon and billiard parlor; F. S. Hazel, the Black public elementary school principal whose monthly salary was $60; John H. Binford, a grocer who owned a house worth $1,000; Henry Hall, a small businessman who had been elected Black poll-tax collector and recently built "a neat cottage"; Jesse B. Claxton, a skilled carpenter who frequently undertook contracts for jobs large enough to enable him to employ several other carpenters; and Methodist Pastor T. W. Coffee, whose congregation was struggling to pay off the debt on its sanctuary and to build him a parsonage. The other incorporators included several more small businessmen, pastors, and skilled artisans.[65]

Obviously the local Black economic elite, which included a good portion of men who worked with their hands, was not rigorously exclusive. The extent to which the elite's moderate wealth and modest lifestyle exceeded that of the average Black person was slight compared with the extent to which the colossal wealth and extravagant lifestyle of the most affluent whites set them above and apart from most whites.

The contrast in the economic resources of the elites who perched atop the Black and the white economic hierarchies suggested the enormous contrast in the pools of resources contained within the two hierarchies. It pointed also to the white predominance at every level of wealth and income and at every job level. The labor market was segmented by skill level and by job, with whites dominating the skilled positions and Blacks mostly relegated to the unskilled. Economic rules and realities had created anomalous opportunities that had enabled a few Blacks to push above the submerged economic position to which whites attempted to restrict the Black population, and had thus made the economic color line more ragged than the social color line. But the general pattern of the local economic hierarchies revealed the overwhelming success of the white program of fostering ascendance of whites and subordination of Black men and women.

CHAPTER 7

THE ECONOMIC REALM

Social Space

Within the economic realm, whites and Blacks could come into close physical contact in various spaces. Among these were city streets, places of work, and commercial businesses. Whites designed some of these places as inherently "social" in nature. Important among these were, for example, residential neighborhoods, work-site lunch rooms or lunch benches, boardinghouses, and restaurants. In time, sites at which people sat in close proximity while traveling, such as streetcars and railroad passenger cars, also fell under the white definition of social. In such places whites sooner or later, but typically sooner, demanded and achieved physical separation of the races. The purpose, whites said, was to exclude African Americans from social fellowship, for which whites considered them unworthy. Only in that way did whites believe they could maintain the purity of the inner citadel of the color-line system.[1]

INDUSTRY AND COMMERCIAL BUSINESSES

In some spaces in which whites and Blacks closely interacted, economic principles of efficiency forced whites to compromise in pursuing the goal of physically separating the races. This was the case at many industrial work sites in Birmingham where Black workers were distinctly segregated according to skill levels. Whites relegated Blacks to low-skilled, low-wage jobs, but many production tasks required coordinated contributions from skilled and unskilled workers and required close Black-white physical proximity. At the iron furnaces the majority of the labor force consisted of unskilled Black day laborers who worked and sweated right beside the small contingent of white skilled workers. One of Birmingham's highly skilled white iron workers, Daniel Daniel, a heater at the Birmingham Rolling Mill, testified at the US Senate hearings in 1883 that he did not object at all to the hiring of $1.25-a-day Black common laborers "to help us in certain stages of our work where the iron gets so that we cannot handle it without help." Proximity was necessary, and the superior status of skilled white workers was self-evident. It needed no spatial separation from unskilled Black helpers to affirm it.[2]

At the same time, however, white workers might insist on drawing a color line through their work space when they took a break for eating or drinking, inherently social activities. At the 1883 Senate hearings the white industrialist John W. Lapsley, former president of the Shelby Iron Works, emphasized white workers' refusal to eat with Blacks, saying:

> Now a Southern man will not refuse to work with the negro. I had a young man with me, a very nice, intelligent young man, that I esteemed very highly on account of his moral worth. He worked day in and day out by the side of a negro and never made the slightest objection. . . . I have had to employ mixed labor several times, mostly negroes, but sometimes white men with them, and they have worked together right along, without complaint. . . . [But], if this man that I have spoken of had been asked to sit down at table with a negro he would have considered it a gross insult, but he did not feel at all insulted at being asked to work with him in the field. That man would come in and sit at the table with my family every day, and would go right out to the field and work with the negroes. He did that for two years, and he did not consider it any degradation at all; but he would not have gone to eat with them.[3]

Economics also complicated the goal of physical separation in Birmingham's shops. Many white storekeepers were eager for the trade of the 41 percent of the city population that was Black. Several druggists, pawnbrokers, and numerous merchants selling dry goods, clothing, shoes, watches, books, and tobacco advertised regularly in the Black *Pilot*, indicating that Black customers would be welcome in their stores. It was quite impractical, however, for such shopkeepers to set aside a separate Black section, or to segregate merchandise by race, so white customers in those stores often found themselves in close proximity with Black customers, both male and female. In such situations white shopkeepers and white customers relied not upon separate space, but rather upon elaborate rules of etiquette to maintain a racial subordination that they considered proper. Typically whites demanded that Black customers show great deference and stand back until all whites had been waited on, and clothing dealers usually would not allow Blacks to try on clothes before buying them.[4]

No white grocer advertised in the Black newspaper, but many enterprising Blacks had gone into the grocery business, and several of them advertised regularly in the Black newspaper. It was clear that only Blacks patronized the Black grocers. However, the available record does not indicate definitively whether Birmingham custom would have permitted a Black customer to shop in a white-owned grocery store. Food carried powerful social connotations, and mixing the races in a food store might have raised tricky social issues in the minds of some whites. Food also raised potent issues of health and sanitation, and white stereotyping may have caused white customers and white grocers to discourage Blacks from shopping in white-owned grocery stores.[5]

Likewise, no white restaurant advertised in the Black newspaper, but several Black restaurants did. Again the social nature of restaurants and the social implications of people eating in the same room caused whites to demand that such institutions be absolutely segregated, not by lines drawn through the space inside the buildings, but rather by lines drawn around the buildings, preventing the entrance of unwanted Black diners.[6]

Significantly, but not surprisingly, none of the numerous white boardinghouses of Birmingham ever advertised in the Black newspaper while many Black boardinghouses did. The social nature of a boardinghouse was self-evident. The overnight lodgings of all guests stood in close proximity, and typically guests shared meals around a common table. Accordingly whites would assume that only whites would be welcomed in a white boardinghouse, and Blacks would know better than to dare to seek lodging there. For white keepers of boardinghouses, the principle of no social equality took absolute precedence. They banished any thought of accepting Black guests, even if many rooms stood vacant and the potential income from them was desperately needed.

STREETCARS

In Birmingham, Blacks and whites contended over informal rules of separation regarding a local transportation space—horse-drawn streetcars. By the 1880s the informal but well-enforced rule on streetcars was that Blacks had to sit apart from whites and must surrender their seats to whites if a car became crowded. Failure to comply could lead to a nasty scene, as a Black woman named Mrs. Clayborne discovered in 1887. She had boarded the crosstown streetcar in the Black residential section on the west side for a ride into the downtown area. There some white women entered the car and the conductor asked Mrs. Clayborne to move to the other side, away from the white women. But she kept her seat. Someone summoned a policeman who moved her, using such robust force that she and several prominent Black citizens considered it appropriate to file charges of assault against him.

When the case came before the court of Mayor Alexander O. Lane, the policeman swore that he had calmly and courteously asked Mrs. Clayborne to move to another seat, and he swore also, according to the *Negro American*, that "she at once became boistrous [*sic*], and acted and spoke in a manner unbecoming a lady." Other white passengers, including a clergyman, "swore the same." In the light of this evidence, said the *Negro American*, "the honorable head of the municipality said that he saw nothing reprehensible in the conduct of the officer, and that he would dismiss the case." Worse yet, the mayor "added also a rebuke to the lady for refusing to comply with the reasonable request of the conductor, viz., that she give up her seat to a white lady."

"Our feeling is one mixed of pity and indignation," commented the Black editor. "Indignation that a woman, weak and defenseless, should be treated thus, and when so treated be unable to find redress at the bar of justice and pity that any people should be so treated." In the streetcar incident Blacks again saw in the abuse of a Black woman a powerful sign of white dishonoring of all Black people. The Black editor expressed deep distress that white people should be so blinded by "contemptible, unreasonable, unreasoning race prejudice as to permit such a thing to occur among them." The editor's pain must have been sharpened by the knowledge that the judge who had dealt so harshly with Mrs. Clayborne was Mayor Lane, the most favorably inclined white Birmingham politician Blacks were likely to encounter. His rebuke to Mrs. Clayborne for not promptly giving up her seat to a white lady was not the extreme language of an antiblack fanatic, but rather an articulation of the mainstream white determination that in any space that could be defined, however arbitrarily, as having a social aspect, Blacks had to acknowledge their inferior status by complying fully with white exclusionary rules.[7]

DISRESPECT FOR BLACK WOMEN

The failure of whites to extend normal courtesies to Black women on streetcars reflected a larger pattern of deliberate social exclusion. This pattern appeared in the nineteenth-century city directories, designed primarily to help businesses by listing all householders and their addresses and occupations. The lists of names reflected racial boundaries and lowered the status of women by virtue of both their race and their gender.

In 1883 the first Birmingham *City Directory* listed the residential and occupational information about whites and Blacks in two separate alphabetical lists, a "White Department" of ninety-two pages and a "Colored Department" of sixty pages.[8] Within the category of Blacks, the directory chose not to use the respectful titles of "Mrs." or "Miss" when listing Black women. Entries for white women typically read "Roden Miss Lillie, seamstress, bds Mrs. Mary Roden," or "Bailey Mrs. E. M., boarding house, res n s 4th av . . . ," or "Armstrong Mrs. Louisa, wid, bds Mrs. J. Parker." But the "Colored Department" used no titles for women and no identification of widows, following the forms: "Anderson Mary, cook, wks. J. Rockett," or "Brittan Mary, wash'n, res n alley C, bet 19th and 20th sts." If a woman in the "Colored Department" worked for a married white woman, the directory employed the form: "Henderson Alice, cook, wks Mrs. Mary Letson," which in one terse line made crystal clear the social disparity implied by the use of titles.[9] The racially discriminatory use of titles applied only to women. All men, both Black and white, were listed without any title. When Black married women had opportunity to indicate their own personal preference about titles, they made clear their wish to be called "Mrs." In 1883 the Black newspaper, *Pilot,* carried a weekly advertisement reading: "MRS. M. COKER, BOARDING AND LODGING, 4th Avenue bet. 19th and 20th Streets." Another advertisement read: "ICE CREAM PARLOR and DAY BOARDERS. Give us a call. Mrs. MCQUEEN AND BUCKNER." But the "Business Directory" of the 1883 *City Directory,* which listed a white female boardinghouse owner as "Mrs. J. A. Webb, cor 2d av and 20th st," listed the proud Black proprietresses as simply "Martha Coker, 4th av, bet 19th and 20th sts," and "Alice Buckner & Eveline McQueen." The middle-class economic standing achieved by successful Black female entrepreneurs failed to command for them the title "Mrs." which they had used in their newspaper advertisements.[10]

Occupation and economic standing did influence societal perceptions and directory conventions. For the specific menial occupations "servant," "cook," "domestic," and "washerwoman," the directory listed 350 Black women and only 28 white women. For the 28 white women, the directory had not established a consistent usage regarding titles. For 16 the directory used either Miss or Mrs., but for 12 it printed no title, following the form: "Schwartz Fannie, servant, wks A. Marre."[11]

The indignity implied by listing a woman without title was made clear by the fact that the only other white women to be denied titles were the most disrespected group in the entire "White Department"—a dozen white prostitutes. Those "fallen" women boarded in four houses run by notorious "Madames," and they were listed without title or occupation, following the cryptic form: "Jones Sallie, bds Madame Nanny Toney."[12]

The "Colored Department" had no convention for identifying married women, single women, or widows. Instead the directory imposed a social indignity on all Black women by listing all of them without title, no matter their marital status. During slavery white society had denied legal recognition to Black marriages. Even under freedom it continued to employ gender title practices that withheld from married Black women the full recognition of status which social convention routinely accorded to married white women. Blacks resented how the protocols showed disrespect for Black women and withheld full social recognition from Black marriage.

RAILROAD PASSENGER CARS

In a transportation space growing even more rapidly than streetcars—the passenger cars of railroads—the drawing of the color line was even more contested. Vital economic, social, and political principles conflicted. Railroads played a key role in Birmingham's development, and the railroad managers, who had interests that ranged far beyond Birmingham, rigorously pursued the principle of economic efficiency. At the same time, most whites insisted upon the principle of separation from Blacks in any situation that had social implications. Blacks invoked the political principle of the right of all citizens to equal access to public facilities. The complex interaction among this set of protagonists and principles produced inconsistent patterns of racial arrangement and delayed the decisive drawing of a color line until whites could defeat the legal principle of equal rights and overwhelm the economic principle of efficiency. Thus the slow steps toward the legal imposition of racial separation on railroad cars closely fit Woodward's proposed chronology of relatively late adoption of Jim Crow. But the reason for the delay in imposition was not a lack of white interest in separation, as Woodward indicated. Rather, it was the inherent difficulty of resolving the conflicting principles involved.[13]

Railroads designated railroad cars as either first class or second class, and formally distinguished them not by rules based upon color but rather by rules based upon the purely material matters of price of ticket and quality of accommodations. First-class cars had cushioned seats, carpeted floors, and water coolers, and they were kept clean; second-class cars had hard wood seats, bare wooden floors, no water coolers, and were usually dirty. Commensurate with the differences in price and accommodations, railroads also enforced different informal rules of behavior in the two classes of cars. Passengers in first class were expected to behave in a genteel manner, not smoking or drinking alcohol or using vulgar language. Women who could afford the higher price almost always rode first class, as did men who were accompanying ladies and genteel nonsmoking men. Men who wished to smoke or chew tobacco, drink spirits, or swear were allowed to do so in the second-class car among those who could not afford a first-class ticket. Second-class cars were jammed with crowds of diverse lower-income people, and the cars were often dominated by crude, loud white men.[14]

Passengers in railroad cars were not engaged in work but were idly sitting in close proximity for substantial parts of a day, using the same facilities, constantly observing each other, and hearing or overhearing the same conversations. Napping or reading could be difficult. For many whites, particularly the more genteel whites who sat in first class, it seemed a given that social rules should govern such space, and that the social rules should separate Blacks from whites.

The southern newspaper which most aggressively undertook to define railroad cars as social space was the New Orleans *Times-Democrat*. In July of 1890 the *Times-Democrat* explicitly incorporated the argument into its campaign for the passage of a Louisiana separate-car bill—the very bill that would in 1896 become the center of the *Plessy v. Ferguson* case. The *Times-Democrat* asserted that in a railroad car whites and Blacks were "crowded together, squeezed close to each other in the same seats, using the same conveniences, and to all intents and purposes in social intercourse." Further, "A man that would be horrified at the idea of his wife or daughter seated by the side of a burly negro in the parlor of a hotel or at a restaurant cannot see her occupying a crowded seat in a car next to a negro without the same feeling of disgust."[15]

There was a problem, however, with justifying the assertion that public space in railroad cars should be defined as social and thus governed by social boundaries. The problem was with the definition of "social." Encounters in railroad cars, unlike interactions in prime social institutions like churches and schools, occurred entirely by chance, were not long-term, were not designed to foster fellowship, could not be designated as extensions of the family, and did not involve a set of people who would necessarily develop relationships through close long-term proximity. Riding in the cars involved no institutional relationship among passengers, and no commitment regarding future interactions.

In the complaint of the *Times-Democrat*, the words "to all intents and purposes in social intercourse" and "feeling of disgust" betrayed the weakness of the definition of passenger-car encounters as social interactions. The negative Black stereotypes that whites used to justify and to reinforce social exclusion had prompted the writer to find the presence of Blacks in a closed and crowded space to be repulsive. But it was precisely his "feeling of disgust" that made it highly unlikely that any interactions between white men and women passengers with the nearby Black men and women passengers were truly "to all intents and purposes" social encounters that threatened to foster or signal social fellowship. The writer's attempt to define the railcar interactions as "social" illustrated the aggressive strategy by which whites often appealed to gender-sensitive situations to justify defining certain public spaces as social. The real goal in employing this aggressive definition of "social" was to enhance white privilege and power by excluding Blacks from allegedly "social" public space and relegating them to separate and visibly inferior space. That was the political intention of the *Times-Democrat* editorial.

Blacks and railroad managers agreed that railroad cars were public economic space. Blacks argued that such space should be governed by the political principle of equal access to public facilities while railroads argued that the space should be governed by economic boundaries. The railroads gave priority to economic efficiency and profits and were reluctant to go to the trouble and expense of providing separate cars for different races as well as for different economic classes of passengers. In Alabama the railroads, led by the L&N line, decided to deal with the problem by piling an informal racial rule on top of the economic distinction between first- and second-class cars. They simply refused to sell first-class tickets to Blacks. Thus all Blacks, including even affluent well-dressed, well-mannered Black women, found themselves relegated to the noisy, dirty, smoke-filled, and uncomfortable second-class cars.[16]

The rule provoked consternation in the Birmingham Black community, and its leaders undertook to apply the political realm's legal principle of equal rights of citizens within this contested corner of the economic realm. They knew that the state of Alabama had established a railroad commission to regulate railroad rates, an action which suggested that institutions and rules of the political realm had legitimate jurisdiction over such an economic institution as a railroad.

In 1883, just before the US Senate hearings in Birmingham, a protest meeting was organized and the new pastor, Isaiah Welch, was asked to deliver a keynote address before a broad array of community leadership, including four other Black pastors, the one Black lawyer, the Black newspaper editor, the Black bricklayer/contractor/merchant N. R. Fielding, and several Black workingmen, including a cook, a shoemaker, a fireman at the furnace, and a painter. Welch highlighted an important part of the context for the protest— the Supreme Court's decision in the civil rights cases overturning the 1875 Civil Rights Act. He voiced the Black dismay. "Loyal citizens are alarmed, bewildered, and partially discouraged," he said, "by a startling decision of the Supreme Court," which "comes upon us like a peal of thunder from a cloudless sky," which has "swept away by a few strokes of a Chief Justice's pen" one of the "recognized safe-guards to our liberty," and "from which an appeal is impossible." With prescient insight he asked "Is our political horizon to be covered with dark clouds, pregnant with danger and destruction? Is this decision the advanced winds of a terrible storm that will make the timbers of our national ship yield to its political pressure?" Welch went on to foster hope by highlighting Justice John Marshall Harlan's "learned" dissenting opinion. Harlan had demonstrated an "unusual degree of courage and manhood," said Welch, and his dissent, when published, might "disclose the necessity of a sixteenth amendment to the constitution." Then Welch identified one practical consequence of the decision and pointed to a practical response that the concerned Black citizens of Birmingham could take. The consequence was that "the general government is unable to protect its citizens without the concurrent assent of the several states." Therefore, in the future Blacks would have to press the states to defend their liberty and to uphold justice.

Welch recommended specific action in that regard. He proposed that the meeting adopt resolutions to send a special delegation to the Alabama state railroad commission in Montgomery. The delegates would be instructed to ask the commission to correct the discrimination that Blacks suffered when they were not allowed to purchase first-class train tickets. The delegates would point out that the discrimination conflicts "with a right of ours common to all men."[17]

The meeting adopted the resolutions and a petition, drafted by Black attorney James A. Scott. It explicitly invoked the major racial boundary changes wrought by emancipation and by the Reconstruction amendments to the US Constitution. "Certain Federal enactments," the petition said, had secured "equal civil and political rights" for "colored citizens." It asserted that, "Since the colored man has been fully recognized as a citizen by the State constitutions of the country, we feel that he should be protected in the enjoyment of public privileges as other citizens." In light of that constitutional principle, the petitioners asked the commission "for the correction of the following discriminating abuses, now uniformly practiced by the railroads of this State."

The petitioners specified that "colored people" could not purchase a first-class ticket, even if they could pay the higher price, and that they were therefore "forced to submit to the indignity of riding in what is commonly known as the smoking car." Moreover, they added: "While riding in the said 'smoking car' our colored ladies are not accorded the courtesy and protection which is shown other lady passengers."[18]

In the second-class cars, where all Blacks and all impecunious whites had to ride, the railroad had marked off separate white and Black sections. But white men inclined to engage in vulgar behavior also had to ride in the smoking car, where they smoked, drank, swore, or told off-color stories. Moreover, many white men ignored the Black/white division and intruded themselves into the Black section, where they harassed Black women. The petition asserted that "The division of the smoking car into two apartments has always been regarded by every sensible man as a complete failure in accomplishing the object had in view—the separation of the races. White men have always been allowed full and free access to the apartment designated for the use of colored passengers." The result, explained attorney Scott, was that "in the cars allotted to the colored people a white man comes in and smokes cigars, and chews tobacco, and curses and swears, and all that kind of thing," and the Black ladies had no choice but to endure the white men's smoke, their leers, and their "insulting and offensive language."[19]

The Black protestors were most troubled by the social insult to Black women. The insult delivered a powerful white message that the Black race was socially so degraded that even its most refined women should not be treated with courtesy or protection, but must be exposed to the unpleasant conditions of the smoking car and must be left vulnerable to the foul behavior and improper attentions of vulgar white men, no matter what their feeling of disgust might be. The petitioners perceived clearly that the debasing of their women was a white strategy to perpetuate the general subordination of African American people, built on the stereotype of Black women as, in the words of historian Blair Kelley, "immoral, unladylike, and undeserving of protection." Women suffered "stigmas of both race and gender on southern railroad," Kelley noted, and their demands "that they be treated as ladies worthy of first-class treatment provided a very striking challenge to the strictures of segregation."[20]

With the petition in hand, Welch led a five-man delegation to the state capital in Montgomery. They received a polite reception from the president of the railroad commission, who summoned the state superintendent of railroads to discuss means of settling this "vexed question." In addition, Welch managed to arrange appointments with both the governor and the state superintendent of education, seizing an opportunity to emphasize the intensity of Black educational aspirations. The appointments finished, the delegates were pleased at the hearing they had received but were physically exhausted. Then they learned from Pastor Welch that he had scheduled several of them to appear the next morning as witnesses at Senator Blair's hearing on labor and capital. They boarded a night train and arrived, in a sleep-deprived condition, barely in time to take their places at Blair's courthouse hearing. The mission to Montgomery had brought the Black leadership of Birmingham together in a collective and articulate effort, but it had little effect on public policy.[21]

By 1883, whites in Alabama had prevailed upon the railroads to impose a rule excluding Blacks from the social space of genteel whites. But the rule did not accomplish a final resolution of the problem. The rule clearly contradicted the constitutional principle of equal protection, and Birmingham's Black petitioners served notice that on those grounds they would continue to challenge the rule. The conflict between white demands for social separation, Black appeals to legal guarantees of equal rights, and the railroads' pursuit of economic efficiency created a tangle that would persist during the 1880s, delaying the imposition of tidy and stable rules regarding racial arrangements on passenger trains.

White insistence on separation that would benefit all whites in all classes of railroad cars intensified, and in 1891, the year after the Louisiana legislature enacted its separate-car law, the Alabama state legislature followed suit by making the racial boundaries on railroads more formal and clear. It passed legislation requiring railroads to provide separate Jim Crow cars for Black and white passengers, thus putting the principle of social separation ahead of the principle of economic efficiency. The votes in both houses of the legislature were unanimous, including both Democrats and Populists. In the House, a Populist legislator proposed an amendment to strike "equal" from the clause requiring "separate but equal" accommodations for Blacks. The amendment failed to pass after another legislator warned that failing to assure equal treatment of Blacks might result in a court ruling that the legislation was unconstitutional. In 1896 the US Supreme Court would, in *Plessy v. Ferguson*, endorse the concept that states could legally require separate but equal facilities for Blacks and whites.[22]

Thus the economic space inside railroad cars became subject primarily to social rules embedded in laws designed to separate and subordinate Blacks. But that resolution had been slow in coming because railroads and Blacks had been able to invoke contrary principles. The chronology of the process fits well with Woodward's argument that most states did not enact actual Jim Crow laws until at least a decade after the end of Reconstruction. But Woodward implied, in contrast to the interpretation presented here, that the delay occurred because many whites had rather tolerant attitudes and did not desire or demand segregation of passenger cars. In fact, he invoked the delay and the inconsistent patterns as evidence of a general lack of white insistence on segregation until the 1890s. But in so doing he failed to acknowledge the abundant evidence of white demands for racial separation in railroad cars, of tacit railroad compliance with racial norms well before laws were enacted, and of the role of contrary economic values and political principles, rather than lenient white attitudes, in causing the delay and the inconsistency in practice.[23]

Historian Michael Perman has pointed out that the timing of the adoption of railroad-car legislation in Alabama was similar to the process in three other Deep South states—Mississippi, Louisiana, and Georgia. Between 1888 and 1891, all passed laws requiring separate railroad cars. In these three states, Perman concluded, "the provision of separate coaches did not portend a change in the mode and tone of race relations in these states," and "no sense of crisis or urgency surrounded the decision." This was because "racial hierarchy and the separation of the races were so well established . . . that their application to public conveyances did not signify any new behavior or require any new policy." The timing for the legislation was explained largely by technocratic considerations. State laws were necessary because "African Americans could not be banned from trains" and "railroads were not confined to one town or locality."[24]

CHAPTER 8

THE POLITICAL REALM, 1871–1888
Organizing and Voting

In Birmingham during the 1870s and 1880s whites constructed three central pillars of the Jim Crow system—racial segregation of schools, urban housing, and the labor force. They also poured the foundation for a fourth pillar—political disfranchisement—and finished constructing this pillar in 1901. But throughout this period, Black migrants to the booming city, some of whom were able to establish a degree of economic autonomy and form the nucleus of a Black middle class, resisted political marginalization and became a significant political force in Birmingham.

ORGANIZING IN THE
FACE OF DISCRIMINATION, 1871–1880

Emancipation and Reconstruction, particularly through the adoption of the Fourteenth and Fifteenth Amendments to the Constitution, weakened old racial boundaries in the political realm more than they did in the economic and social realms. In 1867 Radical Republicans began to enable Blacks to vote and hold office, and to organize politically. By the time of the founding of Birmingham, many of the old boundaries in the political realm of life of Alabama had temporarily crumbled. But the racial stigmas and stereotypes of the social core of discrimination continued to be powerful, and the leaders of the Democratic Party continued to campaign within that socio-emotional context. In addition, they knew that Black voters in Birmingham usually supported opponents of the Democrats. So the Democrats had an instrumental as well as a socio-emotional motivation to minimize the Black vote and discourage or suppress Black political activity.

During the 1870s and 1880s, southern whites employed a sequential and cumulative array of tactics to circumvent the Fourteenth and Fifteenth Amendments. They crudely and sometimes cunningly made it more and more difficult for Blacks to vote and to elect candidates of their own race. They employed a series of suffrage-restriction tactics—violence, fraud, gerrymandered voting districts and wards, at-large elections, and statutory suffrage restriction. Such mechanisms diluted the Black vote, minimized its impact, and prevented Blacks from winning government positions. Ultimately all southern states (Alabama in 1901) would devise sweeping legal schemes to disqualify and disfranchise all Blacks.[1] But until the late 1890s the Fourteenth and Fifteenth Amendments somewhat deterred southern whites. Moreover, at various times, contending white factions within the Democratic Party saw a practical advantage in receiving Black votes. Consequently, the leaders of the Democratic Party did not seek immediately to deny Blacks the right to vote or to disqualify them as a class of voters.

Black activists in Birmingham alertly recognized opportunities in divisions that cropped up among Democrats. The activists proved to be resourceful and resilient in taking advantage of the divisions as they participated in the city politics. Even after 1874, when Alabama was "redeemed," Black voters played an important role in determining the outcomes of local elections, and in often defeating the elite establishment Democrats. As historian Michael W. Fitzgerald has written, "African Americans had lost most of what they had sought from Reconstruction, but they gained knowledge of the uses of state power and the ability to articulate it."[2]

James A. Harper, "Little Bill" Morris, and Anti-Democratic Politics in the 1870s

From the founding of Birmingham, the Democratic Party was the dominant party in the city and was consistently able to defeat the Republican Party at the polls because of its association with federal power and Black political aspirations. The Democratic Party, however, was divided into the regular Democrats, an elitist faction led by the most powerful business interests in the young city, and a faction known as the "Independents." The factionalism created opportunities for African American politicians.

In 1873, two years after the founding of Birmingham, James Harper emerged as the most important Black politician in the city. He mobilized Black voters in a way that often shaped the outcome of city elections. During the 1870s Harper demonstrated tenacity and energy that indicated not only personal enjoyment of an activity for which he had formidable talent, but also a strong belief that Blacks must assert the rights of full citizenship in American society. In 1876, Harper was thirty years old, his wife Julia was twenty-three, and they had a three-year-old son, Walter. Harper had grown up in Georgia, his wife in Alabama, and during the early 1870s they had lived in Tennessee, where their son had been born. At some point they heard the reports of Birmingham's promise and moved there. Harper opened a barber shop on Second Avenue and plunged into Republican politics, making his barbershop a center of African American political activity. He loved political camaraderie and had a knack for getting people's attention and generating excitement around the tedious chores of retail politics—going down to city hall to sign the registration list, attending rallies, and turning out the vote.[3]

Like many Black Republican leaders in the New South, Harper hated the Democratic Party, and pursued the strategy of mobilizing Black voters for the local Independent faction that opposed the local Democrats. In Birmingham, he persistently aligned Birmingham's bloc of one hundred Black voters with the local anti-elite Independent faction that opposed the local elitist Democrats. In 1873, in the countryside outside Birmingham, he helped the Republicans and Independents work to unite Blacks and whites against Democratic candidates. In Birmingham, white voters were rather evenly divided between the two Democratic and Independent factions, and after 1874, when "Redemption" had ended Reconstruction and the viability of Republican candidates, the Black bloc often provided the margin of victory for the Independent faction.[4]

The local Democratic Party faction was closely allied with the most powerful economic institutions in the young city. They included the Elyton Land Company that had founded Birmingham, the two railroads, the one bank, the nascent coal and iron companies, and the largest merchants. These regular Democrats also had the support of the leading newspaper, the *Iron Age,* and of the more respectable churchgoing, temperance-oriented element among local citizens. In 1873, during Birmingham's first spectacular boom, the city chose as mayor the flamboyant president of the Elyton Land Company, and former Confederate colonel, James R. Powell. His supporters celebrated his double role by dubbing him the "Duke of Birmingham."[5]

During the summer of 1873 a cholera epidemic struck Birmingham, ending its boom. This was just before the Panic of 1873 on Wall Street, and the two crises joined to drive Birmingham further into economic doldrums. The once popular "Duke" Powell became accused of having made conditions worse. In disgust, he had his party nominate a lesser-known man as the Democratic candidate for mayor. Soon a young upstart politician—warehouse owner W. A. Morris—seized the opportunity and mobilized an anti-elite Independent challenge to the Democratic nominee.[6]

The more respectable citizens regarded Morris, the son of a small-town hotelkeeper, as an ambitious but unrefined social climber. In politics he allied himself with the saloon interests and various small businesspeople and workers. He appealed to "dissatisfaction" with the cozy connections between the land company and the city, and he promised to "divorce" city from company. He had successfully organized a kind of economic class interest within industrializing Birmingham, taking advantage of the misfortune of epidemic and economic depression.[7]

The Democratic *Iron Age* denounced Morris as a demagogue. "A candidate who bases his pretensions . . . upon his opposition to the Elyton Land Company," declared editor Willis Roberts, "seems to us to have very little claim upon reasonable and unprejudiced voters." Indeed, "How can the growth or wealth of the city be promoted by opposition to the interests of the Elyton Land Company." Editor Roberts endorsed statements by Mayor Powell. "The interests of the two corporations [city and business] are identical," declared Powell. "What benefits one helps the other. What injures the one damages the other." Moreover, said Powell, the Morris faction was composed of selfish men "who seek their own gain without reference to your good," men who "look alone to their own individual advantages" and not to the broader welfare of the entire city.[8]

In early 1875, in the midst of continuing gloom in the stalled city, Morris's anti-elite campaign prevailed, capturing 64 percent of the voters. To knowledgeable observers it was clear that the Black vote had been a crucial component of Morris's majority, and that Morris had benefited from making an appeal, albeit vague, across racial lines.[9]

The Democrats wanted to discredit Mayor Morris and prevent his reelection in 1876, so they launched an extended campaign attacking him. He was lax in law enforcement against saloons, many of which were run by his cronies, said the *Iron Age*, which went so far as to accuse him of attempting "to run the city entirely in the interest of saloonkeepers." Democrats also aggressively linked Morris with another stigmatized group, Black voters. The *Iron Age* warned that Mayor Morris would "promise" Blacks "favor" and would "receive their entire vote." The other white Democratic newspaper, the Jefferson *Independent*, said white voters must "show colored aspirants for civic honors" that "this is now, always has been, and ever will be a WHITE MAN'S CITY."[10]

In his 1876 reelection campaign Morris denounced intrusive "Puritanism." The pro-corporation, intolerant, zealously self-righteous Democratic "Puritan Ring," he warned, was actually intent upon "abridging the rights of the saloonkeepers" and inaugurating officious surveillance over their clientele.[11] In the campaign James Harper worked to mobilize Black voters. He spoke robustly, with a style that whites called "ranting." In the 1876 city election, he spoke "so disrespectfully" about the Irish ancestry of the Democratic candidate James O'Connor that the town's leading Irish-Democratic politician "threatened to cut his [Harper's] throat." The newspapers referred to Harper as the "obnoxious Jim Harper" or the "notorious Jim Harper."[12] Caustic adjectives such as "obnoxious" and "notorious" were not in the vocabulary that newspapers used when discussing white politicians, even those they opposed and hated. But the newspapers applied these terms, and labels such as "the notorious Jim Harper," to consign Harper to an even more dishonorable social status. He seemed capable, however, of wearing the labels with equanimity and even pride.

With Harper's support, Morris won reelection with a majority of sixty. When Harper opened the postelection issue of the white *Iron Age*, he found the Democratic editor Roberts proclaiming: "Brigadier General Harper, colored, marshaled his colored forces last Monday," and the Democrats were "utterly routed—Waterlooed." Roberts was following a typical Democratic strategy of besmirching Independents by associating them with stereotypically slave-like "colored forces."[13] In the process he was also contributing to the reconstruction of the stereotype of African Americans. After that election, no one could refer to Harper as childlike or docile. Instead, the editor promoted him to "Brigadier General Harper, colored," in order to isolate him in a new way—the cunning, aggressive, and corrupt Black politician. Thereby, the editor dismissed Harper's aggressive behavior as exceptional, while keeping relatively intact the basic image of African Americans as incompetent, ignorant, irresponsible, childishly dependent, pliable, and therefore politically incompetent and irresponsible.

Morris's margin of victory had been close. This led observers to note that the Democratic attacks upon the respectability of the Morris regime had diminished his support among whites, and had made his Black support more crucial to him. The *Iron Age* blamed the Democratic defeat on Black votes and continued to link the Morris regime with Blacks and with other disreputable types like saloonkeepers, enterprising "lewd" women, and "croakers" (petty grumblers). This strategy resonated in part because Morris was vulnerable. He had, in fact, collaborated with the most socially dishonored group—Blacks.[14]

During 1876 and early 1877 the *Iron Age* continued attacks on the respectability of the Morris regime. The Morris leaders, claimed the editor, shamelessly appointed no-account cronies to important city offices and to the police force. For example, the son of the city marshal ran a well-known downtown "drinking saloon." Consequently, law enforcement was said to be lax. Notoriously, one of the mayor's close allies, Alderman James W. Butler, was a saloonkeeper. Twice, Alderman Butler was caught selling whisky on Sunday, and Mayor Morris, in his capacity as municipal judge, twice let Butler off very lightly. Morris allegedly also condoned derelict behavior by Blacks, and thereby endangered upright citizens. The *Iron Age* demanded "that the laws be executed by the Mayor, without regard to class, color, or previous condition." It dubbed the Morris administration "the little whisky ring."[15]

The *Iron Age* attacks succeeded in diminishing respect for Morris and his administration and weakening his appeals across lines of economic class. Consequently, the aldermanic ticket that had been elected along with Mayor Morris became unstable, and a series of resignations resulted in the elitist Democrats controlling an aldermanic majority.[16] In August of 1877 the Democrats and *Iron Age* launched a new attack against Morris. The Democrats accused the mayor of playing a devious behind-the-scenes role in mobilizing the Black vote in a county election in which an Independent faction challenged the regular Democratic faction. Despite the charge, in the election the Independents surprised the overconfident Democrats by capturing 45 percent of the county vote.[17]

Editor Roberts of the Democratic *Iron Age* saw a new opportunity to link Morris with the "ignorant rabble" of Black voters, and thus to insert the emotions of the social realm into the political realm. Roberts published an editorial headlined "DUPLICITY" in which he charged that in the county election Mayor Morris, while openly voting Democratic, had surreptitiously helped "Jim Harper" mobilize the Black vote for the Independents. Thus "His smallness, Mayor Morris, who now holds his office by virtue of 100 negro votes, is the negro leader in Birmingham, and through his Lieut. General, Jim Harper, polled the negro vote for the Independent ticket." Roberts warned: "Vote with the negroes if you want to Mr. Morris, but don't attempt to hold with the white folks." Editor Roberts published affidavits from several white citizens who alleged that on the day of the county election they had seen Mayor Morris give Independent tickets, or ballots, to Harper, which Roberts claimed provided conclusive evidence that the mayor had worked with "Jim Harper" to poll Black votes.[18]

Mayor Morris counterattacked. But his problem was that he had in fact worked with Harper to mobilize the Black vote for the Independents. His response was two-pronged. First, he refused to acknowledge cooperation with Harper, and managed to obtain affidavits to contradict his accusers. E. C. Mackey, who was a clerk in Morris's store and who had been appointed city treasurer by Morris, filed one of the affidavits. Mackey quoted the original accusation by three white gentlemen who said that they had "heard Morris call the negro, Jim Harper, over to his store," and had seen Harper come out of the store with Independent tickets in his hand. That statement, wrote Mackey, "does Mr. Morris an injustice." At the time "Jim Harper" came in the store, with tickets in his hand," Mackey said "the Mayor was holding his mayor's court in another building and knew nothing of it." Second, Morris declared Roberts's accusation to be an affront to his personal honor. Thus, while denying an association with Harper, Morris admitted that such political cooperation with him would have been shameful. Morris did not defend the legitimacy of Harper's political activity. Instead, Mayor Morris escalated the defense of his honor by invoking the southern ritual of dueling, He sent a letter, meticulously written along the lines dictated by the southern dueling code, to Roberts. Morris had turned the tables, challenging the editor's honor and calling upon him to defend it.[19]

Roberts refused to respond to Morris's challenge. According to dueling etiquette, a refusal to respond was a deliberate insult. It indicated that the editor considered the mayor to lack social standing as a gentleman, and to be unworthy to challenge the honor of a real gentleman. Roberts then went further. He obtained his own affidavits to justify his accusation in the *Iron Age* that Morris was "the leader of the negroes at the election last Monday, through his shadow Jim Harper." Roberts declared: "we let others speak and leave the public to judge whether the simple assertions of little Bill Morris are worth more than the statements hereunto appended and signed by gentlemen of undoubted veracity." Roberts's reference to "little Bill" was overtly insulting. Newspapers never referred to a respectable white man by his first name or nickname, let alone with an adjective like "little." But Roberts had printed a white man's name according to the customary style for Black names and appended the adjective "little." Roberts had indicated that he personally regarded "little Bill Morris" as on a social level with the "obnoxious Jim Harper."[20]

A Lapse in Maintaining Racial Boundaries

The Independents were losing white support, and possibly Black support as well because of the growing white solidarity on the issue of Blacks in politics. But the Independents retaliated by coming up with their own story of disgusting political behavior. They published evidence that W. C. Steward, a recently appointed Democratic replacement alderman and prosperous grain-mill owner, had violated racial etiquette. The violation was allowing Blacks to eat at his family table. The Independents deliberately thrust into the center of the political realm an accusation that a white man had failed to comply with one of the most routine and ubiquitous practices of social exclusion of Blacks. As a result, the historical record over several months is littered with evocative words about applying the protocols of racial exclusion within the political realm, about the fervor with which whites embraced them, and about the intensity with which whites would censure any white man who seemed to violate them.

Alderman Steward, who was new in town, had been born in Ohio of parents from New England and New York. He had lived in Ohio until his mid-thirties, marrying an Ohio woman and raising three children there. He had lived in the South for only eight years. In Birmingham he presided over a large and rather cosmopolitan household. It included several boarders who worked in the mill, including one from New York and one from Germany, along with Steward's three children.[21]

Independent politicians heard rumors that the household behavior of the Steward family was decidedly un-southern in manner, and they investigated. Steward had previously lived in the small country town of Woodstock, Alabama, thirty miles southwest of Birmingham. The Independent leaders found several former neighbors who gave affidavits alleging that they had seen members of a Black servant family, perhaps the children, eating at the same table with members of the Steward family. Brandishing the affidavits, the Independents called an "Indignation Meeting" that denounced Alderman Steward as "an open and avowed advocate of negro social equality."[22]

For politicians like Morris and his aldermanic allies, politicians who had endured months of denigration as accomplices of disreputable saloonkeepers and Blacks, being able to turn the tables was a political windfall. The pious and prosperous new replacement alderman elected by their righteous antagonists was vulnerable to an accusation that he had debased himself, his family, and his Democratic Party by engaging in intimate social association with African American servants, thereby violating the most sacrosanct boundaries of the social domain. Morris and the Independents anticipated that the accusation of "social equality" with Blacks in the private social realm would trump any accusation of connections with Black voters in the public political realm. They chose to exploit the "social equality" accusation to the fullest, confident that it would galvanize white workingmen, small entrepreneurs, and independent-minded anti-elite voters whose support for Morris had been declining. They hoped it would help mobilize such voters in opposition to the "Puritan" Democrats.[23]

White antagonism against the "social equality" alderman mounted abruptly, and it sent a shock wave through the Democratic camp. Alderman Steward denied the accusation, and the Democratic *Iron Age*, recognizing the power of the accusation, mounted a defense. Editor Roberts contacted former neighbors of Steward in Woodstock and found four who were willing to write letters for publication, affirming Steward's good character and testifying that they had never seen any hint that he allowed his Black servants to indulge in familiarity that implied equality.[24]

In the face of the moral implications of the "social equality" accusation, the key defense strategy of the *Iron Age* was to assert that the moral and economic elite of the city supported Alderman Steward, vouched for his good character, and believed his denial. The newspaper found ninety-two citizens, who owned two-thirds of the taxable property in Birmingham, as the editor accurately boasted, to sign a declaration that the accusation about "social equality" had been based upon "a mistake of facts." Men of such high standing were trustworthy, said the *Iron Age*. They had the good of the community at heart, and all citizens should believe them when they declared the accusation against Steward untrue and endorsed his good character.[25]

The Independents, in effect, had sought to redefine the components of respectability. They tried to shift attention to the need for vigilance in upholding social boundaries that subordinated Blacks and excluded them socially. Such vigilance, they argued, was vastly more important than were the alleged deficiencies in the civic rectitude of the Morris regime. In comparison with the disgraceful relaxation of moral standards involved in Alderman Steward's alleged mealtime intimacy with Blacks, they argued, allegations about connections with proprietors of drinking places and efforts to control the votes of Blacks paled into insignificance.

The conflict between the Independents, led by Mayor Morris, and the Democrats, led by editor Roberts, then proceeded to turn into an even greater tangle. Charges, countercharges, legal challenges, political maneuvers, and a near duel between Morris and the Democratic county chairman were followed in December 1877 by the resignation of Morris. He resigned in order to settle the extended fracas and made a statement of civic virtue in a widely circulated public letter.

In the letter Morris sought to emphasize the grave import of the Independent theme of vigilant racial boundary defense. He did so by employing explicit metaphors of insidious disease, exclaiming: "I have done all in my power to relieve this people from the incubus of radicalism and from the carbuncular infliction of *negro equality*, of which W. C. Steward is, according to the proof, a practical advocate," he declared. "I cannot serve with him, nor with men who by their actions seem to endorse his proclivities."[26]

The mayor's metaphors conveyed the message that his self-righteous Democratic-Puritan opponents had, by their endorsement of Steward's "proclivities," fallen so low that they were undermining the community's moral strength. The phrase "carbuncular infliction of *negro equality*" invoked the image of a malignant inflammation threatening to contaminate the community. The word "incubus," in late-nineteenth-century usage, referred to an evil male spirit or nightmarish demon who was "supposed to descend upon persons in their sleep, and especially to seek carnal intercourse with women."[27]

By invoking this powerfully sexual image into the public record, the re-signing anti-elite mayor sought to inflame his supporters by charging that Alderman Steward and his Democratic allies, like the radicals of Reconstruction, were undermining the most intimate of the crucial social boundaries that held Blacks in their proper subordinate places. Thus were the Democrats "fixing . . . *a curse* upon this people."[28]

In the mayoralty election of 1878 the Democrats continued to emphasize their superiority in economic power and entrepreneurial leadership. They nominated for mayor the celebrated "Duke of Birmingham," the former mayor James R. Powell. He knew that Black Republican leader James Harper was organizing Black voters for the Independent ticket and that Blacks might provide the margin of victory. But Powell had hopes of siphoning off the votes of some Black domestic servants who worked in the better hotels, the large businesses, and the homes of upper-class whites. Perhaps, he thought, employers might be able to pressure their employees into voting for him. Meanwhile, Powell's party quietly dropped Alderman Steward from the Democratic ticket.[29]

To counter the Democrats, Morris sponsored his partner in the lumber and sawmill business, Thomas Jeffers, to run on the Independent ticket against Powell. Like Morris, Jeffers was a master mechanic employed by the South and North Railroad, and enjoyed wide popularity among local workingmen. The Independents eagerly placed Alderman Steward's chief accusers—Captain Charles T. Hardman, a rival grain miller, and carpenter J. T. Hutchison—at the head of their aldermanic ticket.[30]

In the campaign, Jeffers and the Independents continued to emphasize their devotion to vigilant defense of racial boundaries and to denounce the Democrats for having elected "a social equality Republican to the office of Alderman." In responding, Powell published newspaper letters that further reinforced the postwar reconstruction of stereotypes in Birmingham. Powell addressed "my colored friends upon whom I know reliance is predicated for my defeat." He adopted the stance of a paternalistic former slaveholder, asserting: "Two hundred who were my slaves, of whom many are now in Montgomery, attest to my sincerity of friendship." He had "been generous to and careful of all in sickness and trouble," he said, and "the most faithful and dependent families have been the objects of my continued care and *support*." Blacks should trust him as a "real" paternalistic friend and protector.

Powell stigmatized Black political leaders like James Harper as sly false friends. During Reconstruction, asserted Powell, many "colored men" had blindly followed white carpetbaggers from the North, who had taken political advantage of them, and then "deserted" them and "departed" in "shame." But now the carpetbaggers had been replaced by "shrewd, unprincipled" Black politicians who stepped in "to manipulate and vote" Blacks "for money paid for services." "Jim Harper" in particular, he said, was a shady trickster using money and whiskey to sway "pliant negroes." Many Blacks were still "incapable of the exercise of independent suffrage," and they continued to line up behind such leaders. But, declared Powell, "I don't want the votes of such." On the other hand, some enlightened "colored men" had "had the good sense" to "consult, advise and act with their better informed white friends in municipal, state and federal affairs." Powell said he welcomed the support of such Blacks, and would protect their interests if he became mayor again. His words dripped with paternalism and accorded Blacks no respect or recognition as equals. With such words he inoculated himself against any complaint from whites about his quest for Black votes. The only Black voters welcomed by him, Powell implied, would be deferential "colored men." He was not courting pushy or venal Blacks who "will not be advised" by "real" white friends. Powell simultaneously sought some Black votes, appealed to white hostility against Black voting, and directed the hostility at allegedly "shrewd, unprincipled" Black leaders like Harper.[31]

The intensification of racial appeals by the Independents might have tempted Harper to withdraw his support from them, but he did not. Perhaps he felt Powell's direct personal attack on him left him no choice except to continue to cast his lot with the Independents. On election day Harper mobilized a large Black vote for the Independent ticket, helping it win a narrow victory, including the defeat of the "Duke." Powell had lost, but in the process he had made his own contribution to the evolving stereotypes of "pliant" Black voters and shrewd, aggressive, and corrupt Black politicians. Together, he and

Morris had contributed to the weight of racist metaphors in Birmingham politics. Any hints of economic class issues had disappeared, completely obscured by differences over strategies for maintaining color lines.[32]

Influence from the Social Core

The righteous accusations, the vehement denials, and the community-wide agitation over the "social equality" alderman had displayed the intensity of white determination to maintain meticulous enforcement of social exclusion. The white outrage against Steward had indicated that any white who stooped to behavior that implied his equal standing with a Black person brought social shame upon himself and his family, and gave the community reason to doubt the quality of his character.

The Independent accusers struck a responsive chord in the hearts of many whites when they warned that Steward's failure to enforce the rules of the social color line inside his household signaled encouragement to any Blacks who might aspire to challenge and subvert boundaries. In citing Steward's failure, the Independents described it as a threat to the community. The threat consisted not of menacing actions by allegedly criminal or dangerous Blacks, not of economic competition from Blacks, and not of Black political leverage. Rather, the Independents pointed to a threat to moral order posed by the laxness of a white Democratic Party official in enforcing the racial boundaries in the crucial inner realm of social life.

Whenever a white family in Birmingham gathered around the table for a meal, while the Black servants who had prepared the food deferentially disappeared, both groups quietly paid homage to a central ritual of social exclusion. When the Morris Independents destroyed Alderman W. S. Steward with the accusation that he had failed to comply with the ritual, they demonstrated that the commitment of most whites to unwavering conformity was so intense that it could, when unleashed in the political realm, disrupt factions and terminate careers. The daily domestic dramas of racial segmentation at mealtime expressed the superior status and social power of whites. The deferential daily Black affirmations of white superiority nourished the socio-emotional component of prejudice and nurtured the egos of many whites.

In the 1878 elections the social strategies of the two white factions had differed, but both white factions had flung around contemptuous stereotypes of Black voters and had held Blacks at a distance even as they sought to control their votes. And both factions displayed embarrassment about their own strategies for capturing the Black vote, even as they lambasted their opponents for similar strategies. The negative stigmas and stereotypes established a pervasive component of the political process in Birmingham, continually placing Black voters and leaders at a distinct disadvantage in advancing their community.

EXERCISE OF THE FRANCHISE, 1880–1888

Despite the daunting obstacles to political participation, during the 1870s the African American citizens of Birmingham had voted in local elections and Black political leaders had played a decisive role in victories over the conservative wing of the Democratic Party in the city by supporting a dissident group of Independent Democrats. During the 1880s Blacks stepped up their efforts to influence city government. The white obstruction, and the growth of the Black middle class, had made Black political leaders even more determined.

Black Campaigns and the At-large Election

In the 1870s, Birmingham whites had moved in a sequential way to minimize and marginalize the Black vote and the viability of Black candidates. Their most effective tactic was the at-large election. It diluted the Black vote so effectively that by 1880 no Black had ever been elected to the board of aldermen. The city charter and city ordinances had divided the city into four wards and had provided that eight aldermen would be elected, two to represent each ward. But, to the disadvantage of Blacks, the city charter, based upon an Alabama law enacted in 1874 by the virulently white-supremacist Redeemer Democrats, had also provided that voters from the entire city would vote on all aldermanic candidates from all four wards. Thus, each aldermanic candidate, even though he would represent only one ward if elected, had to run "at large," seeking to win a majority of votes from all four wards combined.

Before 1880 all candidates for aldermen had been white. The common practice had been for each mayoral candidate to publish in the newspapers his own "kite-tail" ticket, a slate of aldermanic candidates, two chosen from each ward, who were running with his endorsement. Each mayoral candidate typically had paper tickets printed up that listed his slate. His supporters could pick up the tickets on election day and cast them as ballots. Many voters simply chose one of the tickets and dropped it in the ballot box, thereby voting for the entire slate. But some voters would take a ticket that matched their preferences fairly closely and then scratch out candidates' names and write in others.

The at-large method of electing aldermen put Blacks at a great disadvantage. By 1880 Blacks were heavily concentrated in the two wards on the far eastern and far western edges of town, where they constituted approximately one-half of the registered voters. But citywide they represented only 29 percent of voters. Moreover, the practice of mayoral candidates printing aldermanic "kite-tail" tickets left out the Black candidates entirely, and made it difficult for them to provide a way for Black voters to cast ballots for them. James Harper had never been able to find a mayoral candidate who would nominate a Black in an aldermanic race, or a Black who would declare himself a nominee.[33]

By 1880, N. R. Fielding, a brickmason, contractor, boardinghouse owner, grocer, and now owner of a small publishing firm, had become even more important than James Harper as a Black political leader in Birmingham. Like Harper before him, Fielding, whom the white newspapers referred to as "Nick" Fielding, continually encountered the negative pressures of the stereotyping of African Americans. Like Harper, Fielding responded with a political initiative, perhaps intentionally striving to challenge the stereotype of Black dependence and lack of civic sense.

In this initiative, he attempted to leverage the spectacular economic development of Birmingham. By 1880 an industrial boom had boosted Birmingham out of depression doldrums, stimulated new construction of stores and houses, and attracted workingmen, many of them Black. Fielding, Harper, and other Black political leaders persuaded many Black newcomers to make their way down to city hall to register to vote in the December 1880 election for aldermen. Black voter registration rose to 192, nearly double the Black registration two years earlier. However, white workingmen had also been moving in and registering to vote, so the Black portion of registered voters had remained quite steady at about 29 percent.[34]

During the fall of 1880 Fielding decided to propose his own name as a candidate for city alderman. Then a prominent Black barber, George W. Evans, added his name. Voters in the Black community took notice, and some probably marveled at the daring of Fielding and Evans. No one was sure how whites might respond. All issues of the *Iron Age* for the year 1880 have been lost, so historians cannot discover whether the Democratic newspaper indulged in its propensity to denigrate any Black who ventured into politics.[35]

Evans, like Fielding and Harper, had arrived in Birmingham with a skilled trade—his was barbering—that could earn him a steady income. He and his wife had also built a large house and took in boarders to pay for it. Altogether Evans accommodated eight single male boarders, several of whom had a skilled trade—including two other barbers—and all of whom were of voting age.[36] Most of Fielding's boarders were young, and they included two women, one a local schoolteacher, who were still in their teens. The Fielding and Evans boardinghouses became centers of social activity for single young people, and it is likely that talk around the boardinghouse tables and in the local barbershops provided some of the impetus for the decision of the two men to run for alderman. Fielding and Evans may well have relied upon the boarders and their networks of friends to do some of the legwork of spreading the word among Black voters.[37]

No record has survived revealing the precise aspirations and conversations that motivated Fielding and Evans. But they had good reason to be disappointed over the meager benefits Blacks had gained despite having helped anti-elite, anti-Democratic Independents win every city election since 1874. James Harper had repeatedly mobilized a decisive bloc of Black votes for the anti-Democratic, anti-elite Independent faction. In every city election since 1874 his efforts and the votes of Black citizens had enabled the Independent faction, which had a lower socioeconomic profile, to defeat the local Democrats. But he had never been recruited as an aldermanic candidate on the Independent ticket, received a city job, or gained control of some plum of city patronage. And he had never been accorded any recognition or prestige among the political leaders of the Independent faction. A major motivation for Fielding and Evans was certainly increasing public support for Black education. At the 1883 Senate hearing Fielding would testify about the deep inadequacy of the Black school. Enhancing public education for Blacks had wide support within the Black community, yet the campaign that Alfred Jackson had waged in 1876 had achieved nothing. Fielding may well have thought that the only way to get greater aldermanic support for the Black school was to put Black men on the board, or at least to demonstrate that Black men could be serious contenders for the board.[38]

Fielding and Evans knew that the at-large voting method made it virtually impossible for them to actually win aldermanic positions. Both men lived in the Second Ward and ran to represent that ward. They were not on any mayoral "kite-tail" tickets, which might have helped them line up votes in other wards. They did not publish their candidacies in the white newspapers. And, as of 1880, there was no local Black newspaper. Consequently they had to rely on word of mouth to seek the support of Black voters in all four wards of the city. And they had to ask their Black supporters to employ the clumsy method of acquiring one of the white tickets, scratching out the white candidates for the Second Ward, and writing in Fielding and Evans. Only those Black voters who had learned to write could carry out this procedure.[39]

Moreover, the Black voters would have to prepare their ballots at the one central polling place in the courthouse. Their scratching and writing would be in full view of an assemblage of white political watchers. The threatening nature of the public voting process had been dramatized in 1878 by former mayor James R. Powell. As part of his effort to discredit and nullify the 1878 election, which he had lost, Powell wrote letters to the editor complaining about bribery. Supporters of his opponent, Thomas Jeffers, countered that Powell people had challenged every Black voter who approached the polling place with a Jeffers ticket in hand. They demanded that the voter prove that he lived inside the city limits. For Black voters the challenges were inconvenient and clearly designed to intimidate them.[40]

On election day in the 1880 contest which Fielding and Evans had entered, approximately 150 Black men voted. The Black candidates persuaded 65 of them to carry out the public scratching-out and writing-in on a ticket for incumbent Jeffers, a ticket probably supplied by James Harper. The 65 write-in votes fell far short of electing the two Black candidates. In fact, even if all 150 Black voters had written in Fielding and Evans, they still would have lost, because a candidate needed more than 200 votes citywide to win.

Incumbent mayor Jeffers easily won reelection, and in most wards his aldermanic "kite-tail" slate also won by large majorities. But in the Second Ward the write-in votes of Blacks placed one incumbent Jeffers aldermanic candidate in jeopardy, narrowing his margin of victory to a mere 16 votes. If Fielding had managed to mobilize 17 more Blacks to vote for him, the incumbent alderman, a popular druggist, would have gone down to defeat.

Even though Fielding and Evans had not come close to achieving election to public office, they had given the Black community greater political presence. The listing of election results in the newspapers labeled the two candidates "colored" and gave them credit for 65 votes. On that day nearly half the Black voters had defied the white aversion to the very idea of Black officeholding, had braved the frowns of white poll watchers, and had cast ballots for Black candidates.[41]

The Lane Regime: An Opening for Blacks in 1882

To the local white political factions, the 1882 mayoral election promised to turn city politics in a new direction. Aspirations for gaining local political power ran high among the white factions and their candidates. It was clear that the Independent regime of the incumbent mayor, Thomas Jeffers, was on the way out, discredited by charges of corruption and favoritism toward utility corporations. But the fading of the old Morris/Jeffers Independent faction meant that Blacks had no obvious faction with which to align.

In November of 1882, Birmingham's Black politicians rented a downtown hall and called a meeting of Black voters to discuss the mayoral election in December. Promoting the meeting by word of mouth, because there was still no Black newspaper, the political leaders, including N. R. Fielding, mobilized a large and enthusiastic turnout. The possibility of behind-the-scenes wheeling and dealing was in the air, but no surviving records indicate who dealt with whom in trying to determine whom they would favor in the election. The meeting no doubt included a good number of the roughly dozen Black professionals—including ministers and teachers—and the fifty or so people in business.

Fielding and other leaders decided to get behind the long-term Conservative Democratic activist Alexander O. Lane, who was supported by the *Iron Age*. This represented a huge shift in strategy. Ever since 1874 the local conservative faction had had no success in city elections, always losing to the Independents. But the Black leadership recognized two problems with sticking with the Independents. First, the Independent faction was waning in power. Second, a new white workingmen's faction, decidedly hostile to Black leaders and Black educational goals, was emerging as the main source of opposition to Conservative Democrats. At the same time, Black leaders regarded Lane as an attractive candidate. The main reason: he was a champion of education. At the 1883 Senate hearings Lane would say that, for Birmingham to attract and retain the high-quality workers—white and Black—crucial to its industrial success, the city must provide higher-quality educational facilities for the children of workingmen of both races. In addition, Lane was well educated, perceptive, and straightforward. When Blacks chose to support him in 1882, they picked the one man among the available candidates who they believed would help them the most. Perhaps Burton Hudson, school principal and top Black property owner, worked in tandem with Fielding by supporting the Lane candidacy behind the scenes. In any event, the Black political leadership displayed instrumental pragmatism.[42]

The Democrats had suffered a long local dry spell, but the Democratic *Iron Age* was not accustomed to relying upon Black votes to win elections. The Democrats no doubt worried about being attacked for relying on Black votes, just as they had so often attacked the Independents. So the *Iron Age* continued to parade stereotypes about Black disposition and ridiculed the November meeting of the Black leadership as a farce.[43]

The Conservative Democrats scored a solid victory in the 1882 election, and the key to the win of Alexander Lane, the Democratic *Iron Age* candidate, turned out to be a heavy Black vote for him. The Lane victory heralded the advent of a Democratic administration that would control city hall throughout the mid-1880s. The Lane regime would be sustained by a broad coalition composed of most Black voters and the "better element" of white voters.

Part of the success of the Lane administration resulted from the leadership qualities of Alexander Lane. In 1882 the young lawyer quickly took charge of city hall. He was attentive and down-to-earth. He was able to take care of himself in rough-and-tumble Birmingham. He brought to the office considerable learning and substantial professional and social standing, and he and his wife were pillars of the Presbyterian Church. The churchgoing elements in Birmingham politics were pleased that Mayor Lane promptly instituted more rigorous enforcement of saloon regulations and imposed stiff fines for drunkenness and violations of the Sunday-closing law. But Lane was no visionary reformer. He realistically saw that prohibition, which some church people advocated, was utterly impractical in Birmingham, and he judiciously steered a firm middle course between the righteous "Puritan" element and the ruder "whiskey ring." In the process he consolidated his political position as a firm and fair city executive.[44]

For African Americans the most positive feature of the Lane administration was his pathbreaking program to upgrade the Birmingham public schools, Black and white. Crucial to this program was the recruitment by Lane and his aldermen of the dynamic superintendent John Herbert Phillips and the support they gave him in creating a new structure and system of school governance. Under it the Black schools made substantial progress, and Black politicians and voters had contributed significantly to it.[45]

Although in 1882 the Black voters became an important component of Mayor Lane's electoral coalition, Lane never offered any Black leader an opportunity to assume some visible or official role in the regime, or to run for alderman on the Lane ticket. Black leaders realized that the only local political organization that might welcome them in any significant role was the county Republican Party organization.

Strengthening Black Leadership:
J. H. Thomason and the Weekly Pilot

In the early summer of 1883, N. R. Fielding made a major step in strengthening local ties with the Republican Party by recruiting John Henry Thomason to move to Birmingham and found, with Fielding's financial support, a newspaper, the *Weekly Pilot*. Fielding and Thomason were well acquainted. Both had lived for several years in Athens, a hundred miles north of Birmingham. Both had strong connections with the Black private school, Trinity Hall, which the American Missionary Association had established in Athens in 1865. Fielding's sister was a talented musician who taught at Trinity Hall, and Thomason had been a star Trinity student, widely regarded as one of the school's most distinguished graduates. Thomason often returned to campus to participate in commencement and play a lead role in organizing alumni activities. Persistent rumors had it that he was always eager to visit campus because he was "crushed" upon Fielding's sister. The first issue of Thomason's *Pilot* listed N. R. Fielding as president of the *Pilot* Publishing Company, publicizing Fielding's financial support and his role in bringing Thomason to Birmingham.[46]

By the time Thomason moved to Birmingham he had developed a strong network of Republican Party connections at local, state, and national levels.

The election year of 1880 had been especially productive and memorable for Thomason as a political leader. He was one of twenty Alabama delegates to the 1880 national Republican convention in Chicago. Many Black southern Republicans, including Thomason, had been distressed at the wavering support they had received from Grant's successor, President Rutherford B. Hayes, and enthusiastically joined the Grant bandwagon. As the *New York Times* observed, the name Grant "is a household word in every lowly Southern cabin." For Blacks, Grant symbolized "safety, freedom, an honest ballot-box, and the complete discomfiture of their oppressors."[47] In the deadlocked Chicago convention, Thomason and the entire Alabama delegation had found themselves thrust into key roles supporting Grant. Thomason was the Alabama representative on the key Committee on Rules and Order of Business, his name listed on the front page of the *New York Times*. Thomason and the other Grant delegates stood firm through thirty-six grueling ballots, usually giving him 306 votes.[48]

Thomason had the satisfaction of reading on the front page of the *New York Times* that "There was something peculiarly impressive in the unfaltering allegiance of the colored delegates from the South. They were voting for the man who had led the armies which had overthrown their oppressors [and] for the man whose election would preserve the liberty which his victory in the field had gained for them." They saw in Grant's name "the safety of their race," and they joined with the general's northern white supporters to present "an unbroken front from morning until night." The 306 had failed to nominate Grant, but they had blocked James G. Blaine, which the *New York Times* considered "a service of no slight magnitude." Thomason had tasted the excitement of a political showdown at the national level, and had the satisfaction of having played an effective role in shaping its outcome.[49]

When Thomason returned to Alabama he discovered that his political endeavors had earned him broad renown. He received symbolic recognition—a medal struck in honor of the "Faithful 306," inscribed with the legend "The Old Guard for Ulysses S. Grant for President." In later years Thomason's friend Charles Hendley, editor of the *Gazette*, helped to keep alive the memory of Thomason's moment of political glory, often referring to him as "the famous republican politician," one of "the old 306 in 1880."[50]

The state and national Republican Party reputation and connections that Thomason brought with him when he moved to Birmingham demonstrated that, in the southern postbellum political realm, more than in the southern postbellum social or economic realms, a highly talented Black man might find opportunity to hold a prestigious position, wield authority in an organization in which both Blacks and whites participated, and achieve a reputation that extended beyond the local community.

Thomason's reputation and connections had helped him launch the *Pilot*, which announced itself as "DEVOTED TO THE INTERESTS OF THE COLORED PEOPLE OF ALABAMA." He declared that they would promote those interests through citizenship: "From slaves of ignorance and the depths of degradation we have become freemen and citizens in all that these terms imply,"[51] In exercising the rights of "freemen and citizens," Thomason no doubt hoped for help from the Republican Party and the federal government, and he hoped his newspaper would become an agent for rallying communal Black political effort.[52]

His paper would be read by many Blacks and even a few whites—sympathetic white Republicans and curious white Democrats. He was able to arrange crucial subsidies from state and national Republican factions who needed his help to mobilize loyal delegates to conventions. And even though no Black could ever get access to the corporation and bank boardrooms, or to the hotel ballrooms where the most prestigious and influential white economic and social elite assembled, Thomason could readily get access to the most dignified public rooms in the city hall and the courthouse for political meetings.

Thomason, however, also confronted limitations that illustrated the vulnerabilities that any Black leader faced in the political realm. In post-Reconstruction Alabama he never had a realistic opportunity to hold any government office at any level. His newspaper could assert his political viewpoints and values, but anything that annoyed white politicians or editors could bring condemnation. Even white politicians who might want his endorsement to help them acquire Black votes would be reluctant to acknowledge or reward his assistance.

The Republican Party and Opportunities for Blacks

In Birmingham the national Republican Party kept a presence through the federal officeholders appointed by Republican presidents to the Post Office, the US District Court, and the US Land Office. These officials also played key roles in the Republican Party apparatus in Jefferson County, and during the early 1880s were willing to work politically with Blacks. To Blacks they seemed by far the most tolerant whites in Birmingham, and federal institutions, particularly the Post Office, were the most reliable and hospitable public agencies.

Under Republican presidents, the Post Office was the agency most likely to appoint African Americans, occasionally hiring them as clerks and letter carriers. Blacks had long looked to such appointments as a litmus test of the regard in which they were held by the national administration. Under President Chester Arthur, Birmingham postmaster Thomas U. Green and his daughter Alice Green had been congenial with Blacks and had always employed one Black postal clerk.[53] In contrast, after Democrat Grover Cleveland won the 1884 presidential election, Thomason and his fellow Black politicos had watched with disappointment as Mayor Lane traveled to Washington, DC, where "The main object of his visit . . . was to prefer charges against Postmaster Green, on the ground of incompetency and partisanship." At Lane's bidding the Cleveland administration replaced Green with a Democratic postmaster who promptly fired the Black mail-clerk. Thereafter, the *Gazette* noted, Birmingham Blacks had "great complaint against the Post Office."[54]

During the late 1870s and early 1880s the county Republican organization had maintained a county executive committee, held conventions, and fielded tickets in several county and state elections, often in cooperation with a coalition of Independents and the Greenback Labor Party (GLP). The Republican and GLP effort had support outside Birmingham among white farmers and miners, both white and African American, who were unhappy with the convict-lease program of the state Democratic regime. But the GLP faded after 1882, even in the minefields, in part because of the difficulty of sustaining a coalition along racial lines. Thomason and his Birmingham friends became frustrated with the Republicans because local white Republican officials, the most amicable whites in town, tried to keep all federal positions and all significant party offices in their own hands, while consigning Blacks to a few insignificant positions such as convention secretary.[55] In January 1884 Thomason noted that "Not a single colored man is now filling any prominent position under the present administration in the state." The 1884 presidential nomination contest was heating up, and Thomason addressed President Chester A. Arthur, who had assumed office in 1881 upon the assassination of President James Garfield. "Come, Mr. President, you must let the colored men have just a little showing or else they may 'kick' against your renomination."[56]

A large faction of white Alabama Republicans who had benefited from Arthur's patronage supported him in 1884, but a sizable "out" faction sought a neutral Alabama delegation to the national convention. Thomason, attending a Republican state executive committee meeting in Montgomery in February of 1884, sized up the factional contest and challenged the custom that whites would hold all important Republican positions.[57]

In March of 1884 local Republican leaders called a Birmingham beat (or precinct) meeting at the Jefferson County courthouse to elect eight delegates to the county Republican convention. Thomason and other Black leaders arranged for a large Black turnout, and as soon as the meeting was convened they elected N. R. Fielding, their top local leader, to the position of chair. They named the Black employment agent, James E. Bush, as secretary. Under that leadership the Black delegates took advantage of the factional split among the whites to elect six Black delegates and two white delegates to the county convention. In several rural beat meetings Blacks were also able to elect predominantly Black slates. Between the beat meetings and the county convention one of the Black Birmingham delegates, Samuel W. Roan, a railroad agent, received an appointment to the position of postal clerk.[58]

The white Republican officeholders had arranged the appointment of Roan as a concession to the newly assertive Blacks, but that was all they were willing to do. In April, when they convened the Republican Jefferson County Convention at the courthouse, the white, pro-Arthur patronage appointees resumed running things in the customary fashion. Sam Thompson, commissioner in the federal court and chairman of the county executive committee, called the proceedings to order and announced that he was appointing a fellow court commissioner, Major W. H. Hunter, to the position of temporary chairman of the convention and was appointing the Black Birmingham delegate, James E. Bush, to the usual Black position of secretary. Alfred B. Jackson, the skilled plasterer who back in 1876 had circulated the first Birmingham Black school petition, jumped to his feet to question the authority of Sam Thompson to appoint a temporary chairman. For chairman, Jackson proposed fellow Black delegate James A. Scott, the attorney and fellow officer of the Magic City Guards. Thompson refused to entertain Jackson's motion, and when Jackson appealed the decision, Thompson refused to consider the appeal.

At that point Thomason rose. His only status in the convention was as reporter for the *Pilot*, but he had a shrewd sense of timing and meeting dynamics, and a reputation that made him a force. Thomason asked loudly whether the delegates agreed to sustain the decision of the white chair. The majority of the delegates, who were Black, shouted no. At once James Scott went forward and asked all who wanted him to preside to stand and be counted, and a majority of the delegates rose. The white chair protested, and a heated discussion ensued, in the course of which Alfred Jackson was recorded as saying, "The colored men intended to have their rights, and if the white men didn't like it they could go back to the democratic party, where they came from." In the end, Scott gained control of the meeting and began to preside over the main business, the election of delegates to the state convention.

Racial and factional lines crossed and tangled, and in the midst of continuing confusion the convention chose the Black chairman, James Scott, for the position of first delegate to the state convention. At that point Sam Thompson, the white chair of the executive committee, had had enough. According to the account published by Thomason in the *Pilot*, Mr. Thompson "arose and asked all of his friends to leave the convention and go to his office and select delegates in peace and quietness." Twelve whites among the sixty-two delegates followed him out but, according to the *Pilot*, "The bolt of Mr. Thompson and his friends did not in the least interfere with the convention." Some whites and most Blacks remained and decided to continue the delegate election.

Factional and racial lines remained confused, but the convention elected a slate of delegates that included three whites and four Blacks, including James Scott, James E. Bush, and Alfred B. Jackson, all of whom had testified before the recent Senate hearing. The convention then decided to replace the whites who had headed the county executive committee with Fielding and Alfred B. Jackson, who were Thomason's close friends and associates.

In the *Pilot*, Thomason declared that the contest had been "local" and not essentially pro- or anti-Arthur. The white *Iron Age* interpreted it differently, calling it entirely a fight for and against Arthur. In fact, the detailed information narrated in both papers showed that the Black-white division had overwhelmed the factional division and that Blacks from both factions had remained, while most whites, also from both factions, had bolted.[59]

Thomason, who had lived in Birmingham less than a year, had continued his connection with the Republican county executive committee in his hometown of Athens. In that committee he held the customary Black office of secretary, and shortly after the turbulent Jefferson County Convention, Thomason took the train north to participate in the Limestone County Republican Convention. There he won election as delegate to the state Republican Convention in Montgomery. The state convention, seeking to patch up factional fights and racial tensions, included him as one of the alternate delegates to the 1884 National Republican Convention, again meeting in Chicago. Thomason saw to it that his activity and honors were carefully recorded in the *Pilot*'s political columns. He was a figure who had to be taken seriously.[60]

Thomason found his second National Republican Convention invigorating, reinforcing his reverence for the national party and his faith in its support of Blacks. He was thrilled when, for the first time in history, a Black man, John R. Lynch of Mississippi, was chosen to preside as temporary chairman. Thomason carried home and reprinted in the *Pilot* an article from the Chicago *Inter-Ocean*. It praised Mr. Lynch as "a most admirable presiding officer . . . his presence commanding," and declared that the entire "colored element" in the convention "deserved and enjoyed not only the respect, but the admiration of all who witnessed the proceedings." Respect for Black politicians was all too rare in Birmingham, and Thomason found it not only personally satisfying, but also meaningful to his readers to report about his experience in a prestigious and powerful national organization.[61]

The Alabama delegation to Chicago had leaned toward renominating President Arthur, and Thomason cast his vote for Arthur. But Thomason became impressed by the surge of enthusiasm that developed for James G. Blaine, who captured the nomination. Thomason told his readers that Blaine had declared, "The Republic must be strong enough to protect the weakest of its citizens in all their rights." Thomason editorialized that Blaine was "a glorious candidate."[62]

Back in Birmingham, Thomason discovered that the Black-dominated county Republican executive committee, chaired by his friend and financial supporter N. R. Fielding, was having trouble. Sam Thompson and the other white federal appointees who had bolted the county convention had organized a separate lily-white county Republican organization and were proceeding to field, under the Republican Party name, candidates for sheriff and other officers in the upcoming county election. With Thomason's support, Fielding's committee counterattacked, calling a mass meeting of county Republicans at the courthouse.[63]

On the appointed day, approximately seventy-five Republicans, most of them Black, gathered in the circuit courtroom, while a number of local white Democrats and a reporter from the white *Iron Age* stood around to observe. Fielding presided over the election of Thomason as chairman. Alfred B. Jackson was elected secretary. The assemblage adopted resolutions declaring the authority of the Fielding executive committee, endorsing Blaine, and denouncing the lily-whites. "Any republican organization which excludes colored men from its membership because of color," a resolution asserted, is "unrepublican" and "contrary to the cardinal principles of the national republican party."[64]

The white *Iron Age* reported the meeting under the headline "REPUBLICAN SURRENDER," emphasizing that "the republican mass meeting" was "almost solidly a negro affair." The Democratic newspaper relished the opportunity to dramatize an image of Black men taking charge of the Republican Party and boldly denouncing the actions of white men. The reporter went into great detail, listing by name many African Americans who played some role in the meeting. He interviewed Fielding, who became "Nick Fielding" in the story. The reporter pointed out that "Eight or ten of the leaders spoke, all asserting a determination to stand for the rights of their race and denouncing the domination of the white and the measures of his political organization, the democratic party."[65]

The *Iron Age* provided a full report of the next meeting of the Black-dominated Republican executive committee, which Fielding, using his credentials as committee chairman, had arranged to hold in the courtroom in city hall. Again the *Iron Age* reduced the chairman to "Nick Fielding" and the secretary to "Bill Jackson," and it listed several other participants, at times explicitly identifying them as "colored." It went into minute detail about a small procedural matter in order to have an excuse to report that at one point "Jim Harper, colored, proposed to 'sorter turn dis thing round a little,'" thus highlighting that Harper, well-hated by many whites, was still around and active politically.

The executive committee sharpened its break with the lily-white Republicans by denouncing the white Republican candidate for sheriff and endorsing a white Independent candidate, R. H. Hagood, who was associated with the Greenback movement outside Birmingham. Thomason endorsed the Independent ticket in the *Pilot*, and he published several campaign statements written and signed by Fielding and Jackson. They appealed to loyal Republican voters "not to be deceived" by the lily-white faction but to vote Independent "to show the white wings of the republican party that we, as colored men, repudiate their secession from the party."[66]

This was daring business. Fielding and Thomason used their positions as executive committee chairman and newspaper editor to play the boldest roles that any Black leaders had ever adopted in an election in Birmingham. They aggressively sought to mobilize a movement of Blacks behind them. Fielding and Thomason were proud and able men, determined to demonstrate that they could take initiative and manage the business of party politics on their own. They were tired of the disrespect they continually experienced, even at the hands of whites who were fellow Republicans, and they defied established Republican leaders. In the process, Fielding and Thomason laid themselves open to retribution from the state and national party organizations. They also jarred the sensibilities of many local whites. They claimed top leadership posts and visibly asserted themselves, just as the white newspapers reported.

Their campaign did not go well. The factional split confused and discouraged a number of Republican voters. Many Black voters in rural communities, deeply loyal to the Republican Party, supported the "straight-out" Republican ticket, despite its lily-white leadership. Moreover, the weakened Greenback-Independent movement could mobilize only a few voters. The Democrats, recognizing the condition of the movement, made particular efforts to woo the farmers and white coal miners who had been inclined to support the Independents.[67]

The Democrats also stirred up white antagonism toward Black demands for rights in the legal system. The *Iron Age* reported that "the negroes say they will support no man for sheriff who will not put them on juries." After Fielding's committee had endorsed R. H. Hagood, the Independent candidate for sheriff, the *Iron Age* claimed that, "when interviewed by the negroes," Hagood had gained their endorsement by giving them to understand that he "would give them their rights or see they got their rights." The Democrats charged that Hagood had promised that if elected he would place Blacks on the jury lists and appoint Black justices of the peace and Black deputies. White voters and newspapers expressed alarm over the alleged promise, and Fielding and his committee suffered the embarrassment of reading in the *Iron Age* a letter signed by Hagood, saying "I now state in the most emphatic manner that I have not promised any one to put negroes on the juries." Hagood gave similarly emphatic denials to assertions that he had promised to appoint Black deputies or justices of the peace.[68]

In early August 1884 the county elections brought a large turnout, but a considerable number of rural Blacks voted the straight Republican lily-white ticket. Moreover, the Democrats succeeded in pulling many formerly Greenback-Independent rural voters, particularly white coal miners out at Pratt Mines, back into the Democratic column. Consequently the Democrats elected their entire county slate, overwhelming both the Republican and the Independent tickets. The Democrats increased their portion of the total county vote from 54 percent in 1882 to 59 percent in 1884.[69]

When Thomason picked up the postelection issue of the white Democratic *Iron Age*, he found the editor rejoicing that "Independentism" and "radicalism" were "stone dead" in Jefferson County because the white people "have plainly said, 'No negro rule in ours.'" And on Friday evening after the election, Thomason, Fielding, Jackson, and other Black leaders had to endure the spectacle of a white Democratic torchlight procession of a thousand marchers. They carried two coffins, labeled "Independentism" and "Republicanism," up and down the streets of Birmingham while a brass band played "the doleful notes of the 'Dead March.'" The procession finally delivered the coffins to a Democratic rally, which "cremated" them in "the most solemn obsequious" manner and celebrated their disappearance with a fireworks display that lit the sky and resounded through the streets.[70]

Birmingham Blacks probably looked forward to Thomason's response to these events in the *Pilot*, but on the Saturday after the election no *Pilot* appeared. The newspaper, only one year and two months old, had been suffering financial difficulty. Neither Thomason nor Fielding left a record of the details of the problem, but Black newspapers were always fragile, struggling along with few subscribers and few advertisers, and often relying on some political subsidy from national candidates, or from the national party. It is possible that Thomason suddenly lost a political subsidy from outside Birmingham, possibly because of retaliation against him by lily-white Republican officeholders. In any case, the *Pilot* had fallen silent, and the Birmingham Black community was abuzz with speculation as to whether Thomason might be able to revive it.[71]

Thomason found that he could not restore the *Pilot* to life, and could not continue to beat the drum for Blaine. Up to his last issue, Thomason had tried to appear optimistic about Blaine's prospects, reassuring his readers that "It will certainly be a 'Cold day in Africa' when this government is given over to the Democracy—at least to the Democracy of *to-day*."[72]

November brought that cold day, and with it dawned the bleak realization that the federal government, which since emancipation had loomed as the final, though sometimes frustratingly quiescent, source of support for Black rights, was now in the hands of a party of avowed white supremacy. Grover Cleveland, the Democratic candidate, had bested Blaine. Gone, at least for the next four years, was the hope that Republicans in the White House and Congress might renew earlier commitments to the principle of equal rights and provide federal support for the rights of African Americans in the South. Gone as well was the federal patronage that had given government jobs to a few Blacks, kept the Post Office and the federal district courts in the hands of relatively friendly white Republicans, and sustained the fragile local Republican organizations.

J. H. Thomason remained in Birmingham for a few months after the collapse of his newspaper and the electoral disappointments. He had to have been pessimistic about the political future. The lack of a Republican administration in Washington would further weaken the Republicans in Birmingham and, without support from Washington, Black Republicans were unlikely to attract white allies. Even white Republicans believed in white supremacy and were apt to withdraw into "lily-white" organizations unless they were allowed to hold all the reins of leadership within the mixed party. Moreover, the 1884 county election seemed to have demonstrated that any attempt to raise such issues as Black service on juries or Black appointment to a few positions as policemen or deputies was futile. In July 1885, Thomason announced that he had changed his address to Booneville, Mississippi.[73]

After Thomason shut down the *Pilot*, N. R. Fielding launched another Black newspaper. It was called the *Magic City*, and its editor was Pastor Isaiah Welch. In late November of 1884, as the next city election approached, Welch, no doubt after consulting Fielding, endorsed the incumbent mayor, Alexander Lane, for reelection. Welch wrote: "The election of Hon. A. O. Lane means good government, good order, general improvement, continuation of good schools, and safety to life and property." The endorsement was motivated primarily by the unprecedented support Lane had given the Black schools, and perhaps also by lack of excitement for the alternative, druggist M. M.

Williams, the workingmen's candidate. Mayor Lane won reelection with a 71 percent majority, and once again a solid Black vote provided an essential component in this overwhelming victory over the workingmen's tickets. It remained to be seen, however, whether the political leaders of the Black community would receive any recognition from the white victors.[74]

End of a Political Career: N. R. Fielding

By the end of 1884, N. R. Fielding had acquired a high profile in Birmingham as a politician. He had been the first Black to run for an office in Birmingham's city government. He ran for alderman twice, in 1880 and 1882. For nine months in 1884 he had served as the chair of the executive committee of the anti-lily-white Republican faction and spokesperson for the county Republican Party. He called and presided over numerous Republican meetings at the courthouse, and issued public statements that were printed over his name in the newspapers. And he had been the driving force behind the creation of two Black newspapers with political missions.

Fielding was especially visible, and potentially vulnerable, because he was more prosperous than the majority of Birmingham whites. He displayed his wealth by building a two-story, thirteen-room house on valuable land at Sixth Avenue and Fifteenth Street.[75] It was tucked away in the far northwestern corner of town, some distance from any white home, but it was just as far from the noise and smoke of the railroads and iron furnaces as were most of the handsome homes of white businessmen. The *Gazette* had called Fielding's house a "splendid residence," worth probably $5,000, the *Gazette* speculated, in a town where the typical residence of a white worker was worth, according to the newspaper, $500.

The name "Nick Fielding" had appeared often in derogatory *Iron Age* stories recounting in disparaging tones the incidents that occurred in political meetings he presided over. Fielding's exercise of political influence and his visible prosperity were out of line with the low status that whites assigned to Blacks and departed from the deferential style that most whites expected to see expressed in Black behavior and Black lifestyle. White political leaders and white newspapers were adept at mobilizing white resentment and attacks against visible Black politicians, often thereby boosting themselves politically.

Despite Fielding's exhausting political work in November 1884, by Christmas he and his family had found time for quiet and privacy. But in the early morning hours of the fourth day after Christmas their holiday calm was shattered when fire broke out in their home. No physical harm came to members of the family, but their house burned to the ground, and all their furniture and clothing were destroyed.

The fire might have been accidental, but the Birmingham correspondent to the *Gazette* felt certain it was not. "It was," he wrote, "the work of an incendiary." Fielding and his neighbors thought so, too. But the record does not indicate any official investigation of possible arson. For the Black community the fire was an alarming event, provoking anxious contemplation about the risks incurred by a Black leader who made himself noticeable. It provided evidence of the danger, including raw physical peril, which was involved in taking on a conspicuous role that was out of line with white-status prescriptions for Blacks.[76]

After the fire, Fielding permanently abandoned politics. The surviving issues of Black newspapers record only two brief low-profile ventures into politics by Fielding after 1884. In 1898 and 1900 he allowed his name to be included on the Jefferson County Republican executive committee which, back in 1884, he had chaired so rebelliously. But after 1884 Fielding undertook no political initiatives, speeches, candidacies, or campaign activities. He disappeared from the political realm.

Fielding did, however, rebuild his fortunes and his home. In subsequent years he remained highly active in the institutions of the Birmingham Black community. The surviving issues of the Black newspapers contain numerous references to his roles during the late 1880s as an officeholder in two Black fraternal associations, the Odd Fellows and the Knights Templar, in other Black lodges, and in the church. He was widely praised for his "conspicuous" success in raising money to support these organizations, and in 1890 he was elected Grand Prelate of the statewide Grand Conclave of Knights Templar, and installed in an elaborate ceremony. By 1892, at about the time that his mother fell into her final illness, Fielding became a minister in the AME Church, and in 1893 he was chosen to address an alumni anniversary at Trinity Hall. He combined his church work with fraternal fundraising and provided crucial support for Tuggle Institute, which established a private Black school at Enon Ridge near Birmingham. By 1903 the Birmingham *Truth*, a Tuggle newspaper, noted that Fielding had relocated to Brighton, Alabama, where he had become "a staunch property owner," and "one of the best known ministers in this State," a man who "knows no such word as failure."[77]

Only in African American Church and fraternal circles had Fielding found a satisfying outlet for his business, rhetorical, organizational, and interpersonal skills. Within the Black community he achieved a level of honor and authority that had been beyond the reach of any Black leader in the political arena of Birmingham's larger community.

End of a Political Career: Isaiah H. Welch

Pastor Isaiah H. Welch had been highly visible from the moment he first arrived in Birmingham in the spring of 1883 to take charge of its largest Black church. The Black community had called upon the eloquent and learned pastor to give key addresses. In October 1883 he had rallied them when the devastating news arrived that the US Supreme Court had ruled the 1875 Civil Rights Act unconstitutional. In November 1883 he had negotiated to gain them a hearing before the Senate committee, and he had led their delegation. That month he had also led a delegation to the railroad commission in Montgomery. He had spoken at many political rallies, particularly during the summer of 1884 when N. R. Fielding was running the anti-lily-white Republican campaign. And when John Henry Thomason had closed down the first Black newspaper, the *Pilot*, it had been Welch who had stepped forward to replace it with the *Magic City*, which in December of 1884 had spoken for the Black community in endorsing Mayor Lane for reelection.

Soon after the December 1884 city election, however, Welch, like his parishioner Fielding, experienced a discouraging setback that dramatized the vulnerabilities of Black leaders. Late in January of 1885 Pastor Welch was visiting friends in Selma, where he had previously served as pastor, when he was rudely arrested, charged with forgery, and forcibly taken by train, in the custody of a sheriff's deputy, back to Birmingham to face trial. They arrived at the Birmingham depot on a Saturday night, and officers swiftly took Welch before a justice of the peace. Several members of Welch's congregation, including N. R. Fielding, obtained a white lawyer to represent the pastor and signed a bond which the attorney posted to obtain Welch's release.

Welch learned that the charges concerned a loan of a hundred dollars made to his church the previous October by a white attorney and justice of the peace, B. M. Allen. Taking out the loan had been authorized at a meeting of the church trustees, and Welch and several of the trustees had signed the note. Two substantial property-owning trustees had been absent from the meeting, and the other trustees had instructed Welch to sign those names to the note, and he had done so. But this shortcut was revealed when the church became tardy in making payments. Allen, the creditor, discovered that some of the names on the note were not actual signatures, and he learned that Pastor Welch was out of town.[78]

Allen was well-known to many Blacks, and he had long been regarded by the Black community as a relatively friendly justice of the peace. But Allen became alarmed and aggressive, mobilizing the law against the pastor. He went so far as to arrange a lien on Welch's newspaper office and, after Welch's arrest, brought Welch to trial for forgery. Ultimately a settlement of the debt by the church along with explanations from the trustees brought an acquittal.[79]

The white *Iron Age* chose to publicize and make sport of the proceedings. The headline read: "A PREACHER'S PEN—He Is Charged with Misusing It—A.M.E. Pastor Arrested for Forgery." The paper printed a full account of the humiliating details of the arrest of the "dignified" pastor and of his undignified return to Birmingham. Black readers could remember that only two months earlier, when Welch had endorsed Mayor Lane for reelection, the *Iron Age* had praised Welch as "a man of education and ability," and had called the *Magic City* "the representative of the intelligence of the colored population of the city." Black readers no doubt knew the answer to the question of whether a white pastor or editor would have been treated with such indignity and legal force over a misunderstanding on a hundred-dollar note.[80]

The Black Selma *Post* and the Huntsville *Gazette* were dismayed by the indignities Welch had suffered. They affirmed that "those who know him best never doubted for a moment his innocence." But the episode had left a blot on Welch's record and soured him on Birmingham, which had already made his life difficult. Back in July of 1884, during the county's hot political campaign, his wife had died quite suddenly of tuberculosis, a disease that continually threatened families in the Birmingham Black community, particularly like Isaiah Welch's, living in the shadow of the Sloss Furnace. Welch was left to raise four boys between the ages of three and ten.[81]

In 1886 Welch discontinued the *Magic City* paper and departed from Birmingham, removing another voice from the ranks of the city's Black political activists. He first relocated to a pastorate in Bowling Green, Kentucky. From there he moved to Harrodsburg, Kentucky, where he founded and served as president of the Wayman Institute, a much-acclaimed preparatory school for Blacks who aspired to a college education. Later he received an appointment as clerk of customs at Pensacola, Florida, where he also pastored a successful AME Church in the Navy yard. Welch became a famous pastor, and several biographies of him appeared in Black biographical anthologies. Each, with slight variations, covered his education, army service, pastorates, and educational leadership. But not one referred to his two influential years in Birmingham.[82]

New Editor, the Surfacing of an Issue, and Retaliation

In 1886, after the departure of Isaiah Welch, a flamboyant new editor, Robert C. O. Benjamin, opened an office in downtown Birmingham and launched the *Negro American*. He also started a law practice that specialized in "collection of debts." He was not a member of N. R. Fielding's network. Benjamin had been born in the West Indies in 1855, studied in England, worked for newspapers in New York, dabbled in teaching and studying law in Kentucky and Tennessee, and had begun writing a biography of the Haitian revolutionary Toussaint Louverture.[83]

In Birmingham, Benjamin wrote under the pseudonym "Cicero" and promised that his newspaper would be "unswervingly for the NEGRO, first, second, and last." The *Negro American* immediately undertook to play an influential role in the 1886 mayoral campaign. Benjamin thrust to the fore a new political issue, proposing that the Black voters of Birmingham should demand recognition in the form of appointment of Blacks to the city's police force. "Wonder how a colored policeman would look in Birmingham?" he asked. "It would look like doing right by the 10,000 colored citizens to appoint one. What say you, Mr. present Mayor, or Mr. future Mayor?" The editor of the *Gazette* had been reading the *Negro American*, and he chimed in, offering Birmingham readers some friendly advice. "As the Magic City is without any representative of its colored citizens in any of the municipal offices it would be a good time now to make terms and secure say a colored policeman, if nothing more."

In the wake of the departure of Fielding from the political fray, Birmingham's Black leaders concluded that the safest strategy for Birmingham Blacks was to support Mayor Lane for reelection. In his second term the mayor had continued to promote improvement of Black schools, and Birmingham's Black leaders appreciated Lane's support. They were also drawn to Benjamin's eloquence and energy, and asked him to preside over a meeting of three hundred Black men at the courthouse. The gathering adopted resolutions and endorsed Lane for reelection. As in the previous campaign, the *Iron Age* printed the Black resolutions. In addition, the newspaper, attempting to insure Black backing for Lane's reelection, commended Benjamin for conducting the Lane meeting "in a most effective manner."[84]

Lane again won overwhelming reelection, running up a two-to-one majority over a "workingman's" candidate, physician J. B. Luckie, who declared that he would "prevent any class or corporations from invading the rights and privileges of another." As historian Henry McKiven Jr. has noted, at the time the definition of a "workingman" was broad, and Luckie's ticket of aldermen candidates included a dentist, a clothing-store owner, a grocer, and two middle-class employees of the L&N Railroad. Lane, however, attracted more skilled white workers than did Luckie. And, once again, the Black vote formed a key part of Lane's coalition, as suggested by the fact that over three-fourths (77 percent) of the Fourth Ward voters, most of whom were Black, supported Lane. In 1886 the support from whites and Blacks gave Lane the largest margin of his three victories in mayoral elections.[85]

Benjamin believed that the Black role in the victory had been substantial enough to deserve tangible reward. No copies of the postelection issues of his *Negro American* have survived, but comments in the *Iron Age* indicate that Benjamin reasserted his request for appointment of some Blacks to the police force and that he also offered the view that Black citizens were made to feel unwelcome in Birmingham because they were not accorded the respect and recognition that went with appointment to government office.

"RACE SEDITION," replied the *Iron Age*. The white editor found the *Negro American*'s statement "turbulent in temper, and in all respects incompatible with judicious conduct in a newspaper." Seizing upon whatever Benjamin had said about Blacks not feeling welcome in a city in which they held no offices, the *Iron Age* blustered: "No newspaper in Birmingham, except the Negro American, is conducted upon the notion that the negro population is unwelcome in the town." The *Iron Age* twisted Benjamin's comment and transformed it into a threat, charging that editor Benjamin "is now engaged in drawing a line which if recognized by the whites will result in disaster, conclusive and exclusive to the negroes."

The *Iron Age* articulated the extent to which most whites regarded Blacks as members of the community. "There is nothing of value in the town to the negroes which the whites did not create," the *Iron Age* declared. "The negroes may go away to the last man, and yet all values will remain, as created by the whites." Renewing threats to Blacks if they got out of place, the editor wrote: "The whites expect to continue to create and just so long, and no longer, as the negroes can enter into the white man's realizations in the relation of useful and beneficial components, very good." The "Negro" would receive "just and fair play" from whites "so long as he does in Rome as the Romans do."

The *Iron Age* had no patience with Black demands for city appointments, especially as police officers. "White men will continue to make laws, national, state and municipal, for both races," declared the editor, and "White officers will continue to judge the laws, and execute them." This declaration came with a threat that undue assertiveness on the part of Blacks would bring dire consequences: "It is greatly to the interest of the negroes that white men be encouraged to continue to make one code for both races," the editor declared. Blacks should be aware that "The evenness of judgment and the impartiality of execution of those laws, will be best promoted by the fewest possible of such outbreaks of temper as that appearing in the last issue of the Negro American."[86]

Benjamin may have offered a response, but there is no record of it. No Black appointments to city positions followed, and Benjamin soon left Birmingham. In April of 1887 the *Gazette* reported that "the Nomadic editor of the NEGRO AMERICAN of Birmingham has taken his departure of the Magic City. . . . The Alabama press is less a very brilliant member." Rumors about Benjamin trickled in for some time. One notice reported that he had retired from journalism because of failing eyesight; another reported that he had died. But a skeptic did "not believe Cicero would do such a thing," and later notices suggested that Benjamin was alive in Texas. Later the *Gazette* reported that the former editor had been heard from in Mexico, and declared that "Benjamin is worth several dead men." What is known is that by 1888 Benjamin had arrived in Los Angeles and in 1890 founded a newspaper, the *California Sentinel,* in San Francisco. In 1900, after moving to Lexington, Kentucky, he was shot in the back by a precinct worker whom Benjamin had accused of intimidating Black voters. Benjamin died, but no charges were brought against his assailant.[87]

Law Enforcement and the Police

Robert C. O. Benjamin, the only Black politician in Birmingham to seek aggressively the appointment of Black policemen, received from the Democratic *Iron Age* some of the most strident denunciations in the history of Birmingham. The verbal attacks on him were more hostile and threatening than the rhetoric directed against any white person, even a notorious criminal. The attacks evidenced the belief of many whites that a central function of policemen and other law enforcement personnel was to use the coercive power of law and courts to control and subordinate Blacks. For law enforcement to control Blacks effectively, whites said, it had to be entirely in the hands of trustworthy whites who could be relied upon to perform that function with fervor and diligence.

During the 1880s, discussions about public order in Birmingham emphasized the threatening dimension of the "child-savage duality" that constituted the prevailing white stereotype of African Americans. The evolving stereotype of African Americans was intensified and made more malevolent by greater emphasis of the image of the Black man as immoral, criminal, and dangerous. In Birmingham the stereotype was powerfully reinforced by rising alarm over a threat to public safety thought to be posed by the "notorious negro resorts" of the saloon/dance-hall/brothel shantytowns—Buzzard Roost and Scratch Ankle.[88] The *Iron Age* spread alarm about the large number of "bloody crimes committed by the drunken and desperate negro thieves and criminals who nightly congregated" in those places, and it warned that both were "resorts and hiding places for the worst Negroes to be found in the South. Escaped convicts, murderers and thieves can always find friends and temporary safety in Buzzard Roost and Scratch Ankle."[89]

Whites viewed the Black "dive" as a "cancerous" sore where antisocial Black behavior and criminality festered, as an "ulcer of drunken crime and licentiousness" that "threatens the peace, the safety, and the good name of the city." In 1889 the *Age-Herald*, the successor to the *Iron Age*, denounced the "dives" of the "Roost" and the "Ankle" as "Deep, Dark, Damnable Dens of Degradation" that were "foul with the presence of prostitutes, thieves and

murderers," and "where vice is flagrant and where evil doers hide and congregate to hatch iniquity." The *Age-Herald* claimed that the crime rate in
Birmingham was high, and the mayor asserted that "the negro saloon is the
source of a large per cent of our crime, and unless it can be properly restrained
by policing, it becomes a pest spot of crime." The *Age-Herald* alleged that it
was from the dives "that burglars sally, and the assassin goes forth to commit
murderous deeds." The dives "afford not only a cover under which crime can
be concocted but a safe retreat and hiding place for the thugs, thieves, and
murderers who commit it."[90] And the paper entertained readers with lurid
stories of "notorious brothel killings." Typical was the story of a Black coal miner
who came into Birmingham to try to get his former partner, who had become
a denizen of a "disreputable resort" known as the "forty room building," to
go with him back to the mining camp. She refused, saying he had never treated
her right, and he shot her fatally and escaped. From such ingredients the white
media concocted a lurid image of a continual "carnival of coon and crime" in
Black "sink holes of sin and violence and prostitution."[91]

The political consequence of this stereotyping of Blacks as having a criminal disposition was the creation of a powerful incentive to prevent Blacks
from attaining any position of authority within city government and above all
to prevent the appointment of any Blacks to the police force. The image of the
criminal Black caused whites to consider it imperative to maintain an all-white
police force which could be relied upon to control Blacks closely. The police,
whites were convinced, must aggressively patrol the Black saloon districts and
accost—and probably arrest—any Black who aroused suspicion by appearing
in a white residential area at an unreasonable hour. And the police and the
courts should be vigilant in bringing to justice any Black suspect.[92]

The complete control of the police and courts by whites put the Black
citizens of Birmingham in continual jeopardy of the most extreme kind. They
knew that the police were quick to resort to violence against Blacks, especially in the saloon shantytowns. "There is more danger of being shot by the
police here than anyone else," complained the Birmingham correspondent to
the *Gazette*. And in 1887 the *Negro American* ran the headline "Our Lawless
Police," and reported: "Another case of unprovoked shooting by the police,"
a case which was "only an example of a common occurrence." The editor
recognized that such occurrences indicated a white disdain for the rights of all
Blacks which rendered every Black citizen vulnerable. "We make this modest

suggestion, he wrote. "Let some of the substantial colored citizens go to the Mayor and lay a complaint before him. Let them inquire into this case, and have an indictment for shooting made out against the policeman who did it, and thus see if under the laws of Alabama there is any protection for a colored man."[93] No record has survived of the outcome, but the correspondent to the *Gazette*, reporting a similar case, concluded that "This is one of the many instances where police and Deputy Sheriffs shoot colored people and go unpunished. There ought to be some law to prevent police shooting colored men as if they were hogs."[94]

A potent legal weapon in the hands of policemen who sought to control Blacks and to mitigate alleged Black criminal tendencies was a law that authorized the arrest of vagrants. This "vagrancy law" was enacted in 1891 at the request of white employers who alleged that Black workers were excessively prone to skipping work and loitering. This key city ordinance defined as a vagrant "Any person having no visible means of support," or who "habitually neglects his employment," or who "habitually loafs and loiters about disreputable places." Occasionally the law was used against whites, primarily white prostitutes, but the vast majority of men arrested for vagrancy were Black. Periodically the police launched anti-vagrancy campaigns, which put any Black man in danger of peremptory arrest if he was not obviously engaged in productive work during regular working hours or if he happened to encounter a policeman in a place that was difficult to explain.[95]

Blacks who found themselves abused by aggressive whites could not hope for effective protection in the courts. In court a Black man's social and political standing rendered him vulnerable. Blacks typically avoided going into court to make a complaint, and they usually appeared in court only when arrested and brought there coercively by policemen. Blacks were painfully aware that any arrest, no matter how arbitrary, put a Black man in a precarious position, because Black testimony carried little weight in court. Just how little weight was made clear during the 1883 Senate hearings in the courthouse when George W. Hewitt, the US congressman from Birmingham, testified that "Of course there are exceptions, and some of the negroes are very truthful, but as a general thing in my practice in court I have found them wholly unreliable as witnesses." He explained: "In a controversy between a negro and a white man," a Black witness "cannot be trusted to tell the truth; he is very certain to be on the side of the negro."[96]

A Black person who was arrested on some minor charge like vagrancy would be brought before the mayor in municipal court, which each year handled hundreds of cases resulting from charges that included not only vagrancy, but also drunkenness, fighting, gambling, and petty theft. The court showed little patience with the excuses of Black defendants. A white newspaper noted that on one typical day in the municipal courtroom "Nearly or quite half of the crowds [of defendants] were charged with no more serious crime than that of getting drunk and deporting themselves in a manner inimical to the peace and good order of society, but that proved to be serious enough to consign the most of them to the street gang, as the saloon keepers had all their money and they had only their muscle left for the city." The street gang was the fate of those who could not pay their fines. The mayor found that most whites managed to raise the money for their fines, but that most convicted Blacks were unable to pay the typical fine of five or ten dollars plus court costs. He typically sentenced them to the street gang for ten to twenty days to work off the fine. The white city fathers calculated that the street gang should average fifty to eighty men—enough to accomplish most of the street cleaning and repairs, thereby saving the taxpayers' money.[97]

The correspondent for the *Gazette* found it "a sad and sickening sight to see a number of human beings tied and chained together," but for Black citizens the clanking and shuffling gang of city convicts, mostly Black, was seen all too frequently on the streets of Birmingham. It was a chilling reminder to any Black man of the disgrace that awaited him if a policeman or judge ruled his conduct "disorderly."[98]

If a Black person were charged with a more serious offense, such as assault or murder, and brought to trial before a jury, only whites would serve on the panel from which the jury would be chosen. This was extremely unsettling, as Pastor Welch and other Black leaders pointed out in an 1883 petition, saying: "We cannot avoid feeling oppressed under the great discrimination made in the selection of jurors." When a Black person was on trial, they said, the exclusion of Black jurors means the deprivation of "the right of trial before a jury of . . . peers."[99]

If an able-bodied Black man were convicted of a serious crime, he would probably be sentenced to hard labor and leased to one of the coal-mining corporations out at Pratt Mines, where he would live in a stockade and dig coal for the corporation. Rumors abounded regarding the terrible conditions and dangers that awaited anyone so unfortunate as to wind up in the convict camps, and reports by white health officials, published in both the Black and the white newspapers, confirmed many of the rumors and inspired new ones.[100]

The combination of charges that most frequently sent Black men to the coal mines was assault and carrying a concealed weapon, which usually brought a sentence of around one hundred days of hard labor in the mines. The matter of concealed weapons presented Blacks with a troublesome dilemma. In Birmingham and in much of the South, many men (60 percent according to an 1897 newspaper estimate) casually and routinely carried a pistol, particularly when going out at night. But policemen would come down hard on any Black man who got into any trouble and was found to be carrying a pistol. Black men found themselves weighing the risk of going out unarmed in the midst of an armed city against the risk that any encounter that made them conspicuous to the police might escalate into a case that could send them to the coal mines if the police found a gun on them.[101]

Black editor John Henry Thomason had shuddered at the "cruelty" of local law enforcement and at the "barbarism" in the convict mines and stockades just four miles from Birmingham. "Is it right and just for the strong and powerful Anglo-Saxon to abuse and oppress his unfortunate colored brother?" he asked. Some whites did wring their hands, but white officials did little, and the convict-lease system persisted.[102]

In short, law enforcement was a component of government that had a profound impact upon Black everyday life. Every Black person knew that he or she must continually beware of city policemen, all of whom were white. Policemen appeared to regard themselves as agents commissioned by white society to see to it that Blacks behaved in a manner commensurate with their lowly economic standing and dishonored social status. The actions of the all-white police, the practices of the courts, the patterns of sentencing and punishment, and above all the exploitation and abuse of convict labor in the Pratt Mines appalled Black spokesmen and editors. Their anger was intense, but they and the Black community they represented found no way inside or outside government to have influence over oppressive law enforcement policies and practices. No Black leaders held positions that allowed them to work within government, and subsequently no Black leader felt it made any sense to follow Benjamin's example by challenging the system of law enforcement though electoral politics.

CHAPTER 9

THE POLITICAL REALM, 1888–1901

Excluding Black Voters

During the mid-1880s, African American politicians in Birmingham had skill-fully contributed to electing an establishment Democrat as mayor for three consecutive terms. They had done so while often paying a high personal cost for their political activities and making no progress in reforming local law enforcement, which was one of their prime goals. But they had succeeded in electing a mayor who would follow through on his campaign promises to im-prove the Birmingham schools, both white and Black. And they had acquired valuable experience which they hoped to use to strengthen their political base. But their aspirations and their political accomplishments in the mid-1880s, coupled with the growing recognition by whites that Birmingham's Blacks were developing a talented and assertive middle class, led to white retalia-tion. White politicians and newspapers escalated the effort to dishonor Black politicians. In 1888 white Democrats unified and adopted a white primary for Birmingham elections.

THE WHITE PRIMARY

In 1888, national politics sparked a revival of the ambitions of Black political leaders in Birmingham. The catalyst was the return of John Henry Thomason from Mississippi. The excitement of another presidential election, and the pos-sibility that the Republican candidate, Benjamin Harrison, might win, induced Thomason to rejoin Fielding and his other Birmingham friends and organize a Frederick Douglass Republican Club on behalf of Harrison. Thomason knew that the Republicans had absolutely no chance to carry Birmingham or Alabama, but he was eager to energize African American voters for the city election that would follow in December, and to set the stage for Birmingham's Blacks benefiting from Republican patronage.[1]

The November results were hardly surprising. After the national election, "Jack Daw," the Black Birmingham correspondent to the *Gazette*, reported: "The Republicans here fought long and well" to turn out the vote for Harrison, "but went down under the present Democratic manner of manipulating the ballots."[2] But the national results thrilled Thomason. He took the lead in organizing a "grand jollification" of local Republicans, and he had the satisfaction of speaking to a large and excited crowd.

Not everyone in the crowd was happy. When Thomason opened the next issue of the *News,* he found a demeaning mockery. An article, "A COLORED POW-WOW," reported that "The colored brothers, who since the election of Harrison considers [*sic*] that their star is once more in the ascendancy, held a meeting of ratification, congratulation and anticipation at Buzzard Roost last night which was characterized, at least by an abundance of enthusiasm, vociferous wind bursts and confident predictions of future political recognition, if not by decorum and the observance of parliamentary rules." The article went on: "There were orators in abundance, each anxious to establish his conspicuousness as a leader of the dusky hosts, and the murky night air was badly ripped up with their excited harangues, which had but little variation, excepting in the use of irrelevant and high sounding words, which neither the speakers or anyone else understood. The burden of their howlings, however, so far as they were confined to language which was intelligible, was that the colored man had long enough submitted to the unjust domination of the white man, and that the rising of Harrison's sun . . . was the auspicious dawning of their day of recognition. That they must demand places on the police force, and other positions where official power would enable them to repay in kind the unjust treatment to which they had been compelled to submit."[3]

Even the most partisan Democratic polemicist would never venture to write such words about a Republican meeting if the participants were all white, as sometimes they were. The wordsmith who described "howlings" and "vociferous wind bursts" of "dusky hosts" was invoking deep-seated stereotypes to portray Blacks as strange and alien beings who must be subordinated lest they acquire positions of authority in city government and undertake retribution against their superiors.

The *News* perceived a threat in the aftermath of Harrison's victory. For the first time since 1875 the Republicans would be in firm control of the presidency and of both houses of Congress. Southern white politicians began to warn about the threat of a new Republican Reconstruction of the South—a coercive intervention that would boost Black political rights and destabilize color boundaries that had been settling back into place. In Birmingham the white leaders of rival factions were preoccupied with such thoughts as they contemplated the upcoming 1888 city election.

Mayor Lane had won admiration throughout the business community for his professional management of city affairs and for his capacity to maintain the loyalty of Black voters. By 1888 the rapidly growing city had three daily newspapers, and two of them—the *Age-Herald* and the *News*, the new and equally pro-business paper—eagerly urged Lane to seek reelection.[4]

Dissent among Democrats, however, had grown. The third daily newspaper, the *Evening Chronicle*, contributed significantly to the discord. The paper had been founded in 1883 by Frank V. Evans, who had worked his way up in life from typesetter to writer to newspaper publisher. Evans had been a protégé of Mayor Lane, serving as an alderman during Lane's first term, then city clerk, and finally city treasurer. But during Lane's final term, mentor and protégé quarreled and broke, and the aldermen took the contract for city printing away from the *Chronicle*. A disgruntled Evans began championing the man who had preceded him as city treasurer, B. Asbury Thompson. He was a carpenter's son who also had worked his way up in life, rising from carpenter to ironworks foreman to city treasurer. He had strong ties with Birmingham's skilled craft unions and the workingmen who had three times opposed Mayor Lane but failed to defeat him.[5]

Four days before the presidential election, Lane announced that he would not run for reelection. He explained that he had to devote himself to resolving the financial difficulties a real estate collapse in 1887 had caused for the Smithfield Land Company, of which he was president. Editor Evans of the *Chronicle* and his candidate for mayor, B. Asbury Thompson, had anticipated this and had a plan ready, which they now implemented. They took advantage of the alarm generated by the Republican victory to stir up talk of creating a white Democratic Party primary to nominate the next mayor and aldermen. The idea caught on rapidly, and Evans lined up prominent Democratic politicians to call a "citizens meeting" to develop a plan to assure "the continued solidarity of the Democracy in this city." One of the key promoters of the primary plan later recalled explicitly that it was designed to provide "relief from free-for-all races in which negro votes were scrambled for."[6]

On one level, the instrumental goal of Evans and Thompson was to deny the Lane faction the benefit of support by Birmingham's Black leaders. On another level, Evans and Thompson sought to take advantage of growing support throughout the white community to reduce or eliminate the influence of Blacks in city politics. Seeking the votes of dishonored Blacks had always been regarded as reprehensible, though sometimes necessary. But this point of view had sharpened as whites recognized that Blacks were rising economically, self-consciously developing a talented and assertive middle class, and becoming more organized and effective in political life. Energetic Black leaders of the caliber of N. R. Fielding, Isaiah Welch, and John Henry Thomason had organized Black voters and made them an electoral force to reckon with. Even though each of those Black leaders had suffered reversals or defeats, the Black voters that they had mobilized had cast the decisive votes in the last three city elections. And now Thomason was back in Birmingham, and there was also a threat that Black Republicans could draw on political assets in Washington for local benefits.

Reinforcing the movement to reduce Black influence was the growing white concern about the threat of the allegedly rampant Black immorality and criminality in local sites like Buzzard Roost and Scratch Ankle. That concern motivated white voters to try to ensure that government, law enforcement, and the police department remained completely under white control. The city had been increasing police patrols in the "Roost" and the "Ankle," and assigning "the best officers in the force" to those beats. The *Age-Herald* reported that "the patrol wagon became a sort of police pendulum that swung through the arc between the Roost and the station house." Whites wanted no Black political presence to undermine vigorous police intervention in the "notorious resorts."[7]

On the appointed evening of the Democrats' meeting, white citizens "filled the criminal court room to utmost capacity." They discussed, amended, and adopted a resolution introduced by Frank Evans. It proposed creating a city Democratic executive committee and arranging a meeting of white citizens in each ward to elect delegates to a city Democratic convention that would nominate candidates for mayor and aldermen. The resolution created what was, in effect, a white Democratic primary election.[8] Frank Evans then used his *Chronicle* to boost the candidacy of B. Asbury Thompson. Within two days the more business-oriented *News* and *Age-Herald* were both endorsing Col. J. F. B. Jackson, a former Confederate colonel who had become a successful railroad contractor and built the South and North Railroad through Birmingham.[9] In the primary election meetings, in which no Blacks could participate, a decisive victory went to Thompson and the workingmen's faction that had never been able to defeat Mayor Lane, largely because of his strong Black support. Thompson polled 62 percent of the votes, Jackson 34 percent, and a minor third candidate 4 percent. The *News* and *Age-Herald* and the business-oriented politicians faced an important decision, which they made quickly. One day after the primary the *News* firmly endorsed Thompson rather than propose an independent movement to challenge Thompson in the general election, where Blacks could vote. The *News* noted that there had been "some bitterness" during the primary election but declared: "Democrats must see to it that the first nominees of a city convention be not defeated."[10]

John Henry Thomason had little time to enjoy the excitement of the Republican national victory because he now had to confront the problem created by the new Democratic white primary. If the Democrats were able to foster enough solidarity among their rival factions to get all or nearly all whites to vote for the Democratic primary winner in the city general election, they would have established a system that could in future exclude Blacks entirely from meaningful participation in the city electoral process. Thomason and the new editor of the *Negro American*, Albert Boyd, realized that they must seek the cooperation of local white Republicans, who had recently sought to bar Blacks from entering a white Republican Club meeting. The two Republican factions agreed to nominate jointly a Republican candidate for mayor and a Republican ticket of aldermen in the city general election. For mayor, they turned to a white Republican, T. G. Hewlett, who was a detective for a railway company. In the recent presidential election, Hewlett campaigned hard for Harrison, and on election-day, according to the *Gazette*, he had "defended the right of the colored man to vote in such a forcible manner that many were allowed to vote who otherwise would have been prevented."[11]

Thomason and Boyd conducted a registration campaign that placed eleven hundred Black voters on the rolls. They turned out to account for nearly one-third (32 percent) of the electorate for the general election. The white Democrats countered by urging all Democrats to register and vote to head off "Republican mis-rule in Birmingham." The Democrats angered Black leaders by launching a vicious antiblack and anti-Republican campaign, invoking the supposed horrors of Black Reconstruction. The *News* declared that "Birmingham will not deliberately commit suicide . . . by turning the city over to Hewlett," who was "supported, in the main, by ignorant colored voters." B. A. Thompson, promised the *News*, would maintain "clean government, honest methods, and white policemen," and would sustain "Birmingham's high credit and fair name, and the general prosperity."[12]

The Birmingham correspondent to the *Gazette* wrote that "The Democrats are using their old time argument viz 'Nigger'—They are doing and saying all they can to stir up the prejudices on account of race." But he also reported that Birmingham Black leaders were not giving up, and that "J. H. Thomason, the old war horse, is busy trying to secure the election of Mr. Hewlett."[13]

On election day in December 1888 Thomason and the Frederick Douglass Club turned out a solid Black vote for Hewlett and the city Republican ticket, giving them 852 votes (equal to 77 percent of the registered Black voters). However, registered whites also turned out well, at a slightly higher rate, giving the Democratic ticket more than a two-thirds majority.[14]

The organizers of the white Democratic primary had won a major victory, proving that they could get almost all whites to support the winner of a tough white Democratic primary fight and then work together for the party ticket at the general election. To perpetuate their success, the white Democrats promptly selected a city Democratic executive committee to conduct the next white primary in 1890. For Thomason, Albert Boyd, and Black voters this outcome was ominous. It might mean that, so long as the white Democrats could sustain support for the white primary system, Blacks would be excluded from meaningful participation in city elections.[15] For African American politicians in Birmingham, this was the turning point toward disfranchisement in 1901.[16]

FALLOUT FROM THE 1888 ELECTIONS

After the elections, the editor of the *Age-Herald*, successor to the *Iron Age*, quickly launched a harsh new attack upon Black suffrage itself. The goals were to emphasize the commitment of southern white Democrats to the political subordination of Black citizens, add to the intimidating effect of the 1888 election, and prepare white citizens for the threat of another Republican intervention from Washington into the South. The editor ran a series of repetitive editorials that forecast a much more conflicted pattern of future race relations unless whites could terminate Black participation in politics. The *Age-Herald* bluntly declared that "the co-habitation of a country by two heterogeneous races in equal numbers, with equal political rights, produces an irrepressible conflict, and that is the condition in the South." Conflict was inevitable because "The whites will not amalgamate or mix socially with the negroes, and will not submit to their political control." Since Blacks did enjoy equal political rights, wherever there was a "nearly equal division of the two races," or, worse, wherever "the blacks have a majority," whites would not tolerate the holding of power by a socially unworthy people.[17]

"The Caucasian and the negro represent the antithetical genera of the human family," asserted the editor. So far whites had upheld supremacy without great difficulty because of Black ignorance and poverty, the editor wrote. But, because Black labor was dependent upon white capital, "as time advances this amicable relation will be the more and more disturbed by the negro's persistent demand for equality and the full enjoyment of those rights which the constitution guarantees him." Indeed, "The political conflict is already upon us and has been emphasized by Harrison's election."[18]

When the editor declared that white and Black "will not amalgamate, and the white man insists on maintaining social and political supremacy," he posed an intractable conflict between social inequality and political equality. He saw the social and the political realms as linked by the reality that, as Blacks advanced educationally and economically, they would increasingly use their political equality to try to establish political control, despite their social inequality. But because Blacks were socially unworthy in the eyes of whites, whites would never tolerate Black political control.

The editor was developing a rationale for proposing that, just as Blacks were excluded from fellowship with whites in the social realm, so they must also be excluded from participation in the political realm. One possible resolution to the conflict that the editor perceived between Blacks' manifest inequality in the social sphere and their possession of formal equal rights in the political sphere would be the removal of Black political rights—that is to say, the complete legal disfranchisement of African Americans. But the editor considered outright disfranchisement too difficult to achieve, particularly in light of the Republican victory in the national election.

In light of that difficulty, the *Age-Herald* editor advocated a "heroic treatment" of the race problem—a plan to set aside exclusive territories for Blacks in the sparsely settled Indian territory in the West and to offer Blacks free lands and free transportation as an inducement to migrate thither, thus creating a "desired segregation." He hoped to resolve the conflict between Black social inequality and Black political equality by radically removing Blacks from the southern body politic. Then the exclusion of Blacks in the social realm would be matched by exclusion of Blacks from the political realm.[19]

In that threatening atmosphere, in March 1889, Thomason took a delegation of Birmingham Black Republicans to attend Benjamin Harrison's inauguration in Washington, DC. After the defeat in the city elections, and the prospect of even higher barriers to Black public life, Thomason and his friends regarded support from Washington as even more critical.

In his inaugural address, President Benjamin Harrison did not speak directly to his Black audience. Instead, he reached out to southern elites and modernizers, hoping to advance simultaneously the growth of the white component of the Southern Republican Party, the enhancement of a protectionist tariff policy, and the development of a solution to the southern race problem. "Is it not quite possible," Harrison asked, "that the farmers and the promoters of the great mining and manufacturing enterprises which have recently been established in the South may yet find that the free ballot of the workingman, without distinction of race, is needed for their defense as well as for his own?" He proposed that, if southern leaders recognized their economic interests, "they would not find it difficult, by friendly instruction and cooperation, to make the Black man their efficient and safe ally, not only in establishing correct principles in our national administration, but in preserving for their local communities the benefits of social order and economical and honest government." He ended his advice, "At least until the good offices of kindness and education have been fairly tried the contrary conclusion can not be plausibly urged."[20]

In Birmingham, the two most influential white newspapers responded to President Harrison's address by intensifying their attacks upon Black suffrage. Rufus Rhodes, who founded the Birmingham *News* and served as its managing editor until his death in 1910, ruled out any accommodation along the lines

suggested by Harrison. "Under nature's laws," Rhodes editorialized, "miscegenation and unity" between "negroes and whites" was "impossible," and
consequently "co-existence, as political and social equals, is also impossible."
The two races, he said, were "as widely separated by every decree of God and
nature as it was possible to make them," and thus the racial "unity and peace"
that Harrison advocated were impossible. "White social and personal relations
and race features and character," said Rhodes, "shape and define political
parties and men's laws can't change the leopard's spots or ethiopian's skin."
Consequently, he concluded, "The chasm between them is only deepened and
widened . . . by every force of government and educational training devised to
bless and lighten and elevate." And "All this talk in the inaugural about political methods of producing inter-race unity in the south, is sheer nonsense."[21]
As for education: "Free schools and Fisk Universities, however great the
alleged good achieved, have dug fathomless chasms between the races."[22]

For days, Rhodes hammered away against Harrison's approach to racial
matters. Turning to Black suffrage, the *News* declared that "it is manifestly
true" that Blacks, "by a large majority," are "unfitted to exercise the privilege
of the suffrage at present." To support his assertion he invoked denigrating
stereotypes. "When the sovereigns of the country, as made so by the Constitution, come under consideration as living in shanties that in the North would
hardly be considered fit to shelter a mule—in a condition of dirt, shiftlessness
and immorality that seems to mark an incapacity for decent civilization," is it
any wonder that "the intelligent minority take measures to nullify the powers
of this great mass of illiterate voters?" Most Blacks "show no ambition to rise,
to better themselves, to acquire property. They lived as their fathers lived,
from hand to mouth. With enough bacon and hominy to satisfy hunger, with
a shanty to shelter them, and a little money occasionally to gladden their souls
with the cup that cheers and lightens the souls of man, they are therewithal
content." They were "jolly, irresponsible and happy-go-lucky," and they were
foolishly superstitious. To replace their ignorance, foolishness, and supersti-
tion, "A century of education will not suffice."[23]

The *News* did not go as far as the *Age-Herald* had by advocating Black em-
igration to western Indian lands to create an apartheid solution. It concentrated
instead on another drastic remedy—complete Black disfranchisement. It had
been "most unwise and cruelly unjust" to "invest ex-slaves with power which
they are and ever will be wholly incapable of exercising." Rehearsing yet again

the concept of profound Black inferiority, as portrayed in the stereotypes of African Americans as shiftless, incompetent, irresponsible, foolish, superstitious, and immoral, the editor assumed that any attentive reader could grasp the impossibility of social equality between Black and white. And to him it was self-evident that the consequent exclusion of Blacks from fellowship in the social realm should be replicated in the political realm. In fact, he called for repeal of the federal constitutional amendments that upheld the Black franchise.[24]

Harrison's timid proposals for addressing racial injustice in the South, coupled with the intensification of local hostility to Black suffrage, dismayed Birmingham's Black political leaders. To make matters worse, in 1889 Harrison appointed as Birmingham postmaster Robert Houston, a young local businessman who had been put forward by a group of lily-white Republicans and their protectionist friends among the white Democrats. He received the vocal support of the *News*. The Harrison administration had passed over the Black leadership in the hope of reinforcing the influence of high-tariff white southerners, particularly the iron industrialists of Birmingham. Economics had trumped any loyalty to Black Republicans. President Harrison further disappointed Blacks by telling a group of southern whites that he would appoint Blacks only to those minor positions which did not involve that "personal contact with and official authority over white citizens . . . which you and your people find so offensive."[25]

African Americans throughout the South denounced Harrison, embarrassing him just enough to lead his postmaster general to exert pressure on major southern postmasters to appoint a few token Black clerks and letter carriers. And so it was that, in October of 1889, Thomason at long last received some tangible reward for his activism. Houston, installed as the Birmingham postmaster, was forced to dismiss two holdover white Democratic letter carriers and to appoint Blacks, including Thomason, in their place. The *Gazette* recognized the importance that many politically interested Blacks attached to the appointment of Thomason even though they would have preferred to have him as postmaster. The editor of the *Gazette* wrote, "His many friends throughout the state will rejoice to hear of the appointment of J. Henry Thomason among the Birmingham letter carriers. . . . Here's to Postmaster Houston—congratulations and a full measure of success" because he had done his duty "bravely."[26]

Thomason had little time to bask in the party recognition he had so long sought, and no opportunity for a calm orientation to his new job. The white

Age-Herald greeted the announcement of Thomason's appointment with a virulent attack on the use of "coon carriers." When Thomason reported to work, he learned that all but one of the six remaining white carriers had resigned in protest, saying they would never serve with Black carriers and would not teach them the routes. The resignations seemed to catch Postmaster Houston by surprise, and he was unable to find experienced replacements. He swiftly appointed three new white carriers and two more Black carriers, including Thomason's friend and political collaborator Albert Boyd, editor of the Birmingham *Negro American* and vice president of Birmingham's Frederick Douglass Republican Club.[27]

For several days, considerable confusion reigned as seven new carriers scrambled to learn the routines of mail sorting and delivery. The white Birmingham *News*, which had sponsored Postmaster Houston, pointed out that it would take several days for the new men to familiarize themselves with their routes. The *News* was confident that "they will perfect themselves as soon as possible."[28] Not so, replied the *Age-Herald*. It made sport of Thomason and Boyd and their fellow Black carriers, labeling them "HOUSTON'S COONS" in front-page headlines. Day after day, it printed elaborate anecdotes that portrayed the "coon carriers" as illiterate and bumbling, incapable of reading addresses or understanding house numbers.[29]

Thomason, a proud man, found his hard-earned position untenable. Within a week he handed in his resignation. Shortly thereafter his fellow Republican activist Albert Boyd joined him. After they were gone from the Post Office, things simmered down, and the other three Black carriers stuck with their jobs and went on to hold them for years. Blacks may well have wondered whether the whole furor had been stirred up to single out and humiliate the two politically prominent Black carriers.[30]

Thomason once again pulled up stakes in Birmingham. Now, he gravitated back to his hometown of Athens. For a man of his ability, the smaller Black community in Athens afforded fewer opportunities, but he threw himself into his duties as president of the alumni organization of Trinity Hall. He continued to participate in northern Alabama Republican politics, addressing the congressional district's Republican Convention in Huntsville in 1892, and serving as an alternate delegate to the Republican National Convention. In 1893 he turned in a new direction, leaving Alabama altogether and taking a job with the Pullman Car Company, "running from St. Louis to Cincinnati." The color line had finally ended the public career of John Henry Thomason, the eloquent editor, renowned politician, and stalwart veteran of General Grant's "Faithful 306" of 1880.[31]

REVERSALS IN MISSISSIPPI AND
WASHINGTON, DC

In 1890, Republicans in Congress launched—as Thomason and his Black friends had hoped, and the Birmingham white editors had feared—an initiative aimed at intervening in the South to support Black voting rights. Republican Senator Henry Cabot Lodge of Massachusetts proposed a federal elections bill, and in July of 1890 the Republicans pushed it through the House of Representatives.[32]

Southern white Democrats denounced the bill, labeling it the "Force Bill," and declared that it was unconstitutional and despotic. In the Senate the southern Democrats slowed the bill down, while in the South they mobilized opposition to it. In Birmingham most white Republicans deserted Lodge on his bill. In July of 1890 former Republican Reconstruction Governor W. H. Smith, who during the past decade had frequently cooperated with Thomason on local Republican matters, came out firmly against the "Force Bill." Smith orchestrated a meeting in Birmingham of several hundred pro-tariff white Republicans to protest the Lodge bill. The meeting passed a memorial to Congress asserting that if the bill became law it would be so hated in the South that, instead of increasing the southern Republican vote, it would decrease it, and intensify race and sectional prejudice.[33]

The gloom that Birmingham's Black politicians felt about prospects for protecting their civil rights deepened in August of 1890 when the news arrived that in neighboring Mississippi the Democrats who advocated disfranchisement of Blacks had called a state constitutional convention that would accomplish that goal. To Charles Hendley of the *Gazette* the Mississippi convention was "the most important current political event in the South" because "its action will define clearly the spirit and purposes not only of the Democratic party of that state, but will be an index to that of the whole south." He wrote that "The Negro . . . looks on with anxious concern" but continues to have hope. "We do not believe that the wisdom of the South will allow any backward step to be taken."[34]

In October, Hendley reported disappointing news. He reprinted the report by the Mississippi convention committee, which laid out the emerging southern hard line that linked denial of Black "social equality" with the proposed repeal of Black political rights. The Mississippi committee asserted that "the white and the negro" were "two distinct races, or types of mankind," which, "though friendly and homogeneous for all business and industrial purposes, are widely separated by race instincts and prejudices in all political and social matters." In such a situation, "the one race or the other must have charge of and control the governments . . . and to do so there will ever be ever-recurring conflicts." Only whites were "capable of conducting and maintaining the government," said the report, "the negro race, even if its people were educated, being wholly unequal to such great responsibility." Consequently, concluded the report, some legal means must be found to restrict and limit African American suffrage.[35]

All too soon it became clear that the Mississippi convention delegates believed that a variety of measures—residence requirements, a poll tax, and a requirement that every voter must convince a registrar that he could read and understand any section of the state constitution—would vastly reduce the Black vote. Apparently the delegates also believed there was a "general understanding" that registrars would routinely pass white illiterates but seldom Black ones. The convention incorporated the disfranchising measures into a new constitution and, wishing to avoid a messy ratification referendum, simply declared the new constitution to be the law of the state of Mississippi.[36]

Editor Hendley hoped that "this business just now down in Mississippi" would awaken Blacks throughout the South to the political danger they faced, and he may have also hoped that Mississippi's demonstration of the intentions of southern white Democrats would spur the congressional Republicans to pass the Lodge bill. But any hope for support from Congress proved short-lived. In the congressional elections of November 1890, the Republicans experienced a disastrous nationwide defeat. They lost half of their seats in the House, along with control of the body, while retaining only a slim majority in the Senate. Many observers regarded the outcome as at least partly a repudiation of the "Force Bill" in the North. In January 1891, when the US Senate, now in a lame-duck session, again took up the Lodge bill, several northern and western Republican senators deserted the measure, depriving it conclusively of the margin it needed for passage. For Thomason and Hendley it was yet another disappointing reversal, and perhaps an even more decisive one than they realized at the moment. In their lifetimes they would never see another serious Republican effort to provide federal support for Black political rights in the South.[37]

FIGHTING BACK IN THE 1890S:
EXPLOITING DIVISIONS AMONG DEMOCRATS

In 1890 the white primary system continued to hold sway in Birmingham. Nobody considered it worthwhile to oppose the Democratic nominees in the general elections. Turnouts were low, and the Democratic victories were almost unanimous. The 1890 mayoral winner was none other than former mayor Alexander O. Lane, who had returned to city politics after reviving the fortunes of his land company. Lane easily figured out how to win in the new white primary system. He took onto his aldermanic ticket and into his administration two key leaders of the workingmen's organization that controlled politics in the First Ward, the site of the Birmingham Rolling Mill. The two were Sylvester Daly, a former rolling-mill puddler who owned the popular Rolling Mill Saloon and who had made it the headquarters of the Irish Democratic Club in the First Ward, and David J. Fox, who had worked in the rolling mill, become a member of the Amalgamated Association of Iron and Steel Workers, and then worked in the L&N Railroad shops before buying a grocery store.

By the end of Mayor Lane's term in 1892, Daly and Fox had led a group of labor and Irish politicians in gaining control of Lane's faction of the Democratic Party in Birmingham. They dominated the Democratic city executive committee and used it to enable Fox to win the next Democratic Primary and then, without a challenge in the general election, replace Lane as mayor. Historian Henry McKiven wrote that, in 1892, "Men of working-class origin had held important positions, elective and appointive in city government, but the election of Fox expressed most forcefully workers' political power." Daly went on to acquire a reputation as the boss of Birmingham politics. When he died of liver ailments in 1901, every aspiring Birmingham politician made a point of attending his funeral at St. Paul's Catholic Church.[38]

Daly and Fox prevailed in 1892, but they did not succeed in unifying the two factions that emerged in the Democratic Party. These factions, known as the "Elements," diverged sharply in their position on a key popular issue—saloon regulation. The faction led by Daly and Fox became known as the "Liberal Element" and opposed strict saloon laws. The other faction was called the "Moral Element" and sought strict saloon regulation. The two factions differed somewhat in their ethnic and class composition. The "Liberal Element" drew strong support from Irish and German ethnic organizations, from Roman Catholics, Jews, and Lutherans, from workingmen, and from smaller businesses. The "Moral Element" was led by evangelical pastors and temperance reformers, and its membership was more elitist, and more oriented toward support of larger businesses than that of the "Liberal Element."

In mobilizing opposition to Fox and Daley, Rufus Rhodes, the editor of the Birmingham *Daily News*, played a key role. A close associate of Rhodes was a wholesale grain dealer, Braxton Comer, who had moved from rural Barbour County in 1890 to take advantage of the cheap railroad rates and commercial activity that Birmingham offered. He may also have anticipated that on his arrival he would immediately be able to join forces with other Birmingham merchants to lobby the Alabama legislature to give the state railroad commission the power to fix a rate structure they viewed as unfavorable. Their lobbying failed in 1891, but Comer continued his efforts, forming an alliance with Rhodes and supporting the "Moral Element." In 1893, Rhodes and Comer cooperated in organizing the Birmingham Commercial Club, which sought to boost Birmingham's industrial and mercantile interests using, when necessary, the instruments of the state and city governments. The "Moral Element" was a convenient vehicle for increasing the civic support for economic development.[39]

From the outset of the Fox administration in January of 1893, the "Moral Element" challenged the new mayor. Among its initiatives was a call for a police commission that would reduce Fox's patronage by removing from him and aldermen the power to appoint the chief of police and police officers. The leaders of the "Moral Element" succeeded in persuading the legislature to give a county judge the power to appoint a five-member police commission, and the judge proceeded to appoint the commission, which, as Fox pointed out, included an officer of a Birmingham street-railway company. Fox and the aldermen countered by passing ordinances that would require the commission to obtain the approval of the mayor before hiring or firing police officers. In March the commission countered by creating its own police force. Mayor Fox, in turn, refused to swear the officers and chief appointed by the commission.

As a consequence of the factional fight over patronage, Birmingham suddenly had two police forces. Eventually, while the Alabama Supreme Court deliberated, the mayor agreed to swear in the commission-appointed officers. The court subsequently ruled for the commission, but Fox kept the issue alive into the election season of 1894. On the one hand, the mayor cast himself as a champion of democracy and opponent of special interests. On the other hand, the reformers represented themselves as the opponents of machine politics and champions of public order.[40]

During 1892, African Americans in Birmingham had continued to find themselves completely shut out of city elections because the Democratic primaries were now the decisive contests. The Reverend Thomas W. Walker, a longtime pastor of Baptist churches in Birmingham, lamented, "We have not been allowed to vote for our choice for mayor. We have usually woke up in the morning to find who was elected the day before."[41] But they had not given up. After the 1892 election, a group of new Black political leaders came forward, and several of them spoke impatiently and assertively. Among them was Reverend Dr. A. J. Warner, pastor of the AME Zion Church, the same church that N. R. Fielding and Thomason had belonged to, and Isaiah Welch had pastored. After Thomason's departure, Warner had emerged as the leading Black Republican operative in Birmingham. In mid-1894 Warner became a delegate and speaker at the Republican congressional district convention, one of Jefferson County's two members on the district Republican executive committee, and a delegate to the county Republican convention. Only about one-fifth of the county delegates were Black. While Warner led the delegation, the most militant Black spokesman was the Reverend H. Seb Doyle, pastor of St. James CME Church and the editor of the *Negro American Press*. At times L. H. Harrison, the editor of a second Black weekly newspaper, the Birmingham *Wide Awake*, rivaled Doyle's intensity.[42]

These Black leaders were troubled by their exclusion from city politics and the obstacles they faced. But they were resourceful. They remembered the decisive role Blacks had played in the elections of the mid-1880s, and watched for some break in the white Democratic unity that would give them a chance to reassert their voice in city politics. The opportunity appeared in 1893 and 1894 during the fight over control of the police force.

In 1893, as the fight deepened, the leaders of the white "Moral Element" organized a "Citizens' Reform Union." It decried machine politics and lax enforcement of saloon laws and declared that its goal was "to secure and sustain faithful, honest and economical government . . . by the enactment and earnest enforcement of proper and wholesome laws for the suppression of vice, disorder and crime of all grades, and to cultivate a healthy popular opinion and sentiment in favor of good morals."[43] The Reform Union and the movement it represented received powerful support from the commercial booster interests organized by Braxton Comer and Rufus Rhodes, and this urban coalition became, in effect, the core of the progressive movement in Alabama.[44]

The white "Citizens" boycotted the 1894 Democratic primary and then, in a departure from the 1892 primary, challenged the primary winner in the general election. They nominated a "Citizens' Reform" ticket headed by James A. Van Hoose, a former Episcopal pastor who had become a successful wholesale grocer (and a natural ally of Comer), and a promoter of civic causes. He had arrived in Birmingham as pastor of the downtown white Episcopal Church and soon took the lead in founding a separate Black Episcopal Mission Church. He served as superintendent for that church, and had raised $7,000 among northern philanthropists to construct a building to house it.[45]

The severity of the political quarrel among whites became obvious to the citizens of Birmingham when Rufus Rhode's Birmingham *Daily News* announced its support for the Citizens' Reform ticket while the other white daily, the *Age-Herald*, backed the Democratic primary winner, as did a white labor-oriented weekly newspaper, the *Independent*.[46] Black leaders seized the moment by deciding to craft an alignment with the proto-progressives. "For the past four years," said Harrison's *Wide Awake*, "the machine has held full sway in the city. . . . The machine is an invention to keep you and I from having any choice as to who shall enforce the laws over you. Vote to knock it into smithereens."[47]

Blacks found a sympathetic ally in Dr. Robert A. Moseley Jr., a local white Republican who had always resisted lily-white tactics, and for years served as chairman of the statewide Republican executive committee. In July of 1894 he founded the Birmingham *Times*, a weekly Republican newspaper. Despite the official high-minded position of the "Moral Reform" faction regarding patronage, Moseley arranged an understanding with the chairman of the Citizens' Reform Committee that, if Blacks and Republicans turned out in large numbers for the Citizens' ticket, and if the Citizens won, then a certain portion of city offices and positions on the city police force would go to Republicans, and Blacks would be appointed to two remunerative but minor positions—poll-tax collector and street-tax collector. In these positions, they would deal only with other African Americans. In light of their previous requests for Black policemen, Black leaders found the proposed allocation of positions disappointing, but hoped they might pave the way for more significant appointments later on.[48]

Pastor A. J. Warner threw himself into the Van Hoose campaign. He organized a committee of Black pastors and skilled workers, rented a major downtown hall, and called a rally of "the Colored People of Birmingham" to boost Van Hoose. According to a hostile account in the white *Age-Herald,* about fifty whites and twelve hundred Blacks, including many Black women, turned out. The first speaker, the Reverend T. W. Walker, emphasized the crucial opportunity for Blacks to break six years of exclusion from local elections. He had gotten tired of primary elections in which "I can't say a word." But, "Bless the Lord," he shouted, in this election, "I think we will have a say who is elected." Van Hoose, though normally a Democrat, had "stepped over the fence and now wants our votes," said Walker. "I thank God somebody had sense enough to bolt, and since somebody gives you a wrench use it. Will you?" And a chorus replied, "Yes, we will."

A Black carpenter, C. C. Caperton, thought African Americans should push beyond voting. Some Alabama cities had appointed Blacks to the police force, he said, "and the sun, moon, nor stars didn't fall." Moreover, he asserted, "If I want to run for alderman in the First ward, why I want to be able to run, and if I don't get elected I won't cry."

Pastor Warner, the Republican Party activist, said that, even though Van Hoose was a Democrat, if he were elected in 1894 with the assistance of Black Republican votes, he might help establish a new pattern that would assure significant Black participation in 1896, and beyond. "Let me tell you how it is," he said. "It's like breaking a young colt. You first put the bridle on and then lead him around; then you rub him behind the ears and down the fetlocks; then you throw an old sack on his back and lead him around some more; then you put the saddle on, tighten up the girth, put your foot in the stirrup, get up in the saddle, and he's ready to ride. That's the way Mr. Van Hoose will be in 1896."[49] Black hopes for developing a long-run political relationship with Van Hoose seemed reasonable in light of Van Hoose's history of helping the Black Episcopal Mission Church.

Most Black speakers emphasized primarily the importance of voting for Van Hoose because he was against the machine and the Democratic white primary system and favored fair elections. Only a few Blacks mentioned concerns with specific government policies or activities. But C. C. Caperton voiced their persistent desire to find evenhanded justice in the mayor's court. "We want a mayor who will give us our rights; not convict a negro and turn a white man loose on the same charge," Caperton said. And Pastor Warner complained that the incumbent Democratic administration had reduced school appropriations, forcing the school board to shorten the school term to eight months and reduce teachers' salaries.

The Reverend H. Seb Doyle, editor of the *Negro American Press*, argued that the Democratic Party itself was the key issue. "No negro can be a democrat," he said. "How can he when the record of the democratic party for 250 years has been strewn with the blood of negro men and the honor of their wives. . . . The democratic party was fostered by slavery and retained itself in power by ballot box stuffing. I hate the democratic party, you hate it, all good men despise it."[50]

The white *Age-Herald* and *Independent*, which were supporting the regular Democratic candidate, roused a furor over the comments of the Black speakers, and soon they had the unhappy experience of reading in Rhodes's *News*, which was supporting the Citizens' ticket, that some Citizen leaders were uncomfortable with the Black remarks, and denied any responsibility for them. Meanwhile, Democratic speakers invoked yet again the "horrors of reconstruction" and of "negro domination." They warned that, if the Citizens won with the aid of Black votes, Blacks would demand "ridiculous" privileges, such as appointment of Republican judges and even Black policemen.[51]

Black politicians wrestled with intractable dilemmas. As leaders of a community whose achievements and aspirations were rising, they had to speak assertively. But they faced nearly uniform disdain for Blacks and apprehension over Black aspirations among whites. White politicians could denounce Black political opinions with impunity. And denouncing Blacks played so well with white voters that it boosted the fortunes of the white politicians who did it the most dramatically.

Black political leaders and pastors made a concerted effort to register Black voters, but they learned that, as soon as Blacks signed their name and address on the registration list, the tax collector of the Democratic administration took down the addresses and showed up at their residences, demanding that they pay the annual city-street tax of three dollars. The white Democratic *Age-Herald* announced, perhaps in an effort to deter some Blacks from registering, "It is difficult to locate the residence of the negro except during elections, when he comes forward and registers for the purpose of voting. . . . why should he not be called on for street tax?" Despite such deterrents, by election day 2,018 Blacks had placed their names on the registration list, thereby accounting for 36 percent of the total registered electorate—an impressive figure because Blacks comprised 39 percent of the city population.[52]

The white Democrats mobilized their traditional supporters, especially the members of the German and Irish communities who favored the pro-saloon position of the regular Democrats. But the lax saloon policies had alienated many evangelical Protestant whites, and on election day the white vote split down the middle, approximately 1,000 to the regular Democrats and 1,000 to the progressive Citizens' Reformers. About 1,300 Blacks went to the polls and voted solidly for the Citizens, giving them a two-to-one margin of victory, with a total Citizen vote of 2,300 to a regular Democratic vote of 1,022.[53]

Black leaders rejoiced. For the first time in eight years their votes had been decisive. The Republican *Times* proclaimed: "THE MACHINE IS NOW CRUSHED. . . . The tide has turned, . . . the people in their might have arisen and dealt a death blow forever to machine Democracy." The *Times* reminded Mayor-Elect Van Hoose that the Republicans expected some recognition for their contribution to his victory: "We trust that you will give us a NON-PARTISAN administration." Black and Republican leaders looked forward eagerly to the first meeting of the Van Hoose administration, when new city officers would be elected.[54]

Disappointment arrived swiftly. The Citizens refused to acknowledge the contribution of Blacks and Republicans to the progressive victory. The Birmingham *Daily News* claimed that only 900 (rather than 1,300) Blacks had gone to the polls, and that 300 Black votes had been "thrown out for one reason or another." Van Hoose, the paper claimed, had received a large majority of the white Democratic vote. The *Times* responded by demonstrating the inaccuracy of that analysis. The *Times* editor concluded: "Van Hoose could not be Mayor today had not the anti-Democratic vote been cast for him. We call now upon Mayor Van Hoose to keep his promise of a NON-PARTISAN administration."[55]

At the first meeting of the administration, the Citizens reneged on every patronage promise to the Republicans and African Americans. The Democratic *Independent* reported gleefully that after the meeting Dr. Moseley, the Republican leader who had received and had relied upon the Citizens' promises, ranted loudly on the street corner outside city hall while "pumping air and pounding the sidewalk with his cane. He lacked for language to do the subject justice."[56]

That was not the case. In the next issue of the *Times*, Moseley declared that "Reform Democracy" like that of Van Hoose had proved to be so treacherous and deceitful that "there is no help for her." So, he said, "let her die between now and 1896 and we will bury all the little good that remains with her bones." Republicans, Black and white, should expect nothing from the Van Hoose administration, he warned, but should work hard for the next two years to prepare for a straight-out Republican effort in the 1896 mayoral election.[57]

During the next two years, no Blacks received recognition or appointments from the Van Hoose administration. Moreover, Blacks suffered a sharp setback in fighting for equity in education allocations. Budget cutting by Van Hoose, coupled with depression-driven reduction in tax revenues, lowered the Black/white ratio of school expenditures per school-age child to below one-third.[58] Black frustration and disenchantment were profound, and two years later Pastor A. J. Warner was still reminding people that in the 1894 election Blacks had voted in a body for the Citizens, had "commanded the situation," and had "elected a ticket," only to experience "much disappointment."[59]

The election of 1896 began as a replay of the 1894 contest between Citizens and Democrats. Once again, the Democrats held a white primary, and the Citizens then challenged the Democratic nominee, entering their own ticket in the city general election. It appeared likely that the Republicans would back the candidate of the progressive Citizens. But Black disillusionment with the Citizens led to a significant defection from the coalition that had elected Van Hoose.

In 1896, Pastor Warner was still the leading local Black Republican in Birmingham. He had attended the 1896 Republican National Convention as an official delegate and was named a McKinley presidential elector from Alabama. Warner remained so upset over the betrayal by the Citizens that he refused to support their ticket. Instead, in 1896 he threw his support to the Democratic nominee for mayor, Frank V. Evans. "I know and like the man," he said, "and believe him to be friendly to the colored race."[60]

At the same time, another Black Republican, William R. Pettiford, who was rising as a political leader in Birmingham, made a very different decision. Before stepping into Republican politics, Pettiford had established himself as a prominent figure in the Black religious and business community. In 1883, as a young pastor at the First Baptist Church, he had helped to found the Negro Ministers' Association. Through the years he had continued to promote co-operation among Black churches, often using a bicycle to get to meetings at churches in different sections of town. Pettiford had also taken a lead in civic activities. He had become a leader in statewide Baptist activities, serving as financial secretary for the State Baptist Convention and as financial agent of Selma University, a private Black school. He had also developed ties with Booker T. Washington and Tuskegee Institute, and in 1892 he was the major speaker at the laying of the cornerstone of a new building at Tuskegee.[61]

Pettiford had meanwhile forged a significant business career. In 1890 he founded the Alabama Penny Savings Bank. He raised $50,000 capital stock by selling shares at $25 each. The bank succeeded and became a vital promoter of growth in the Black business community. Part of the bank's success stemmed from Pettiford's ability to rally churches behind it, placing key pastors on the board of directors, and arranging to have committees of laymen from each church as sponsors of the bank. Also crucial to the success of the bank had been the appointment of Burton H. Hudson, the successful businessman who had raised funds for Birmingham's first Black school, to the position of bank cashier. As cashier Hudson was the bank's chief operations officer, and his penetrating judgment of people and investments helped the bank to thrive and to stand as a symbol of Black economic advancement. Hudson was also the largest shareholder in the bank.[62]

Until 1889, Pettiford, like Hudson, had carefully avoided electoral or partisan politics. But after 1889 he had become a Republican activist, striving to find ways for Blacks to overcome "the contempt that is shown for us as a part of the body politic." One of the ways he pursued that goal after founding his bank was cultivation of the white business leaders who had launched a progressive movement within Birmingham and organized the "Citizens' Reform" ticket.[63]

By the time of the 1896 election, Pettiford was edging ahead of A. J. Warner as a Republican leader, and when Warner switched from the Citizens to the Democrats, Pettiford broke with him and supported the Citizens' Reform ticket and their candidate for mayor, Christian F. Enslen. The white Republican leader R. A. Moseley, despite his unhappiness over the treachery of the Citizens in 1894, joined him and again supported the Citizens. The Birmingham Republicans were giving the strategy of forming a coalition with the progressives another chance, having concluded that it was the better of two unpromising options. And they may well have hoped to gain access to the administration of the president elect, McKinley.[64]

On election day 1896, approximately two-thirds of the Black voters stood by Pettiford and the Citizens, but one-third followed Warner and switched to the Democrats. It was enough to bring victory to Evans and the regular Democrats. Unsurprisingly, Evans extended no recognition and no appointments to Blacks.[65]

The 1896 Democratic victory terminated the Citizens' revolt. From 1896 through 1910 the white Democratic primary system resumed its complete sway over municipal elections. The saloon issue continued to produce a major cleavage in local politics, but the disputes were fought out within the white primaries. The general elections became uncontested and perfunctory.[66]

In the hotly contested elections of 1894 and 1896, Black voters had given the victors their margins of victory, but the outcome was that Blacks found themselves completely shut out of city politics. The exercise of the franchise by Black citizens in Birmingham elections had essentially ended until the last decades of the twentieth century.

DISFRANCHISEMENT

After 1896 the white primary system effectively prevented Birmingham's Black citizens from exercising their right to vote in city elections, but they could participate and influence Alabama elections. However, during the late 1890s, W. R. Pettiford and his political colleagues found the political air filled with white proposals to call a constitutional convention to disfranchise Blacks in Alabama state elections.

The possibility of such a convention had been discussed in Alabama since the state of Mississippi had adopted what was called the "Second Mississippi Plan" in 1890. The "First Mississippi Plan" was the mobilization of violent whites, beginning in 1875, to suppress Black voting. The Second reinforced the First by enacting a poll tax and a literacy test along with a provision that allowed registrars discretion to make exemptions, thereby allowing poor whites to cast ballots. In 1890, Alabama's governor, Thomas Seay, proposed calling a statewide convention to consider following Mississippi's example.

Support for adopting a version of the Second Mississippi in Alabama was slow to grow because all of the major political parties and factions often sought the support of Black voters, who remained numerous and politically active throughout the 1890s. Most white voters in Alabama were Democrats but, as in Birmingham, the party experienced severe factional disputes in which one or more of the contending groups might seek out Black voters even though most of them were Republicans. Black Republicans were often open to temporary alliances with Democratic factions, especially because their own party was weakened by its racial split into two factions, white and Black. The dominant faction of the two tended to be the "lily-whites," led in Birmingham by R. A. Moseley, and this group received the lion's share of federal patronage during the years when Republicans controlled the presidency (1889–93 and 1897–1901). Further intensifying the competition for Black voters in the 1890s was the challenge to the Democrats by a third major party—the Populists. In 1892, and especially during the depression of 1893–97, the Populists drew many away from the Democratic Party in rural and small-town Alabama. The Populist vote was always weak in Birmingham, but in the national elections of 1892 and 1894 the party attracted significant support from miners outside the city in Jefferson County.[67]

The strength of the Populists was an especially important factor in slowing the movement to disfranchise Blacks. Populist leaders worried that a system of disfranchisement of Blacks on the basis of income or literacy, unless carefully constructed and monitored, might disfranchise a significant number of its supporters. But the Populist threat waned quickly after Democratic victories in 1896 state elections and the beginning of economic recovery, and the upward movement of farm prices, in 1897. In addition, President William McKinley seemed to remove any possibility that his Republican administration might intervene. In his 1897 inaugural address and annual messages in 1897 and 1898 he said nothing about any threats to democracy in the South or any need for federal intervention. On December 16, 1898, he traveled to Tuskegee to visit Booker T. Washington and his institute. He praised the institute for seeking "to cultivate and promote an amicable relationship between the two races," and not "attempting the unattainable."[68]

With the potential problems of Populism and federal power eased, the Alabama Democratic Party endorsed the movement for a disfranchising convention in early 1899. The feeble state Republican Party and its newspaper, the Birmingham *Times*, officially opposed the disfranchisement movement, but even this newspaper made concessions to the mounting antiblack sentiment.[69] For example, in 1899 the *Times* opposed Black officeholding and in doing so employed an ugly metaphor. There was no question as to the legal right of an African American to hold office, said the *Times*, "Nor is there any question of the legal right of a man afflicted with some great physical deformity to be a candidate for the Presidency." But, "Our sense of propriety and the fitness of things revolts against the idea, and while we pity the misfortune of the individual we expect him to so far respect public sentiment as not to force himself into an obnoxious position."[70] The *Times* acknowledged that there were a "few examples in this state of offices filled by colored men with conspicuous ability, but this does not alter the sentiment against the practice." The real objection, said the *Times*, "is not against the individual but against the whole race of which he is part," because "Every sentiment of the white race revolts at the idea of positions of authority being filled by the sons of Ham."[71]

As the white Republican allies made concessions to white denigration of African Americans, white Democratic opponents grew bolder and more explicit about their racist intentions. In 1900, for example, the *News* observed that a petition to Congress concerning lynching had not stimulated Republican partisans in Congress to attack the South, as would have been the case in the 1870s and 1880s. The *News* concluded: "Our northern neighbors have learned to take a rational view of such matters as lynchings, negro disfranchisement and the like. They are, in fact, rapidly coming over to the Southern way of thinking on these subjects. They are perceiving that negro enfranchisement has been the curse of the race, and that what Southern white men do is what Northern white men would also do, should like conditions prevail in the North."[72]

After debates in state elections, in December of 1900 the state legislature set an election on the question of whether to call a state convention. From that point onward, Black leaders no doubt had the sense of being swept out to sea by powerful currents against which they were virtually helpless. Black leaders found it difficult to exert any influence on the creation of the state convention. At the election, voters recorded a yes or no on the issue of holding a constitutional convention, and then designated delegates to the convention in the event that the yes votes prevailed. The frustrated Black leaders in Birmingham mobilized a large Black "no" vote, but they knew the proposition would carry. The delegations to the convention then became crucial, but it became clear that the many Black voters would have little chance to have an impact on their makeup. The Democratic Party called local and county conventions to nominate party slates of delegates. The Republicans did likewise, but the Black and Republican vote would be much smaller, and it was inevitable that the entire Democratic slate would be swept in and the entire Republican slate excluded.[73]

That is what happened. When the convention assembled, there was not a single Black delegate. The only minority voices would be those of 7 white Populist and 6 white Republican delegates from the Northern Alabama hill country. They would be overwhelmed by the voices of 141 regular white Democrats and one independent white Democrat. The only way to access the convention formally was through petition. W. R. Pettiford joined with 14 other Alabama Black leaders, led by Booker T. Washington of Tuskegee Institute, in taking that route. In their petition the Black leaders pointed out that their race was at the mercy of the convention and asked that the delegates leave "the Negro some humble share in choosing those who shall rule over him." Other Black activists in Alabama added their protests, including suggestions that the Washington group had been too cautious, discussions of the possibility of mass exodus of Blacks from the state, and at least one hint of race war.[74]

The protests, the moderate as well as the more radical, had no effect. The Democratic convention delegates proceeded to adopt a suffrage plan that incorporated discriminatory registration procedures, literacy and property requirements, and a poll tax. Judging by the experience of other southern states that had already adopted such measures, it was obvious that the suffrage provisions would disfranchise most Blacks and probably a good many poorer whites.[75]

The last chance to block the disfranchising constitution was a statewide ratification election called by the convention. Black leaders organized a Birmingham meeting of one hundred Black Republicans in September to formulate plans to fight against ratification. But most of the people who showed up recognized that they were powerless to defeat ratification, and the meeting decided to concentrate on raising funds for a legal challenge to the constitution and taking it all the way to the US Supreme Court if necessary.[76]

The white Democrats mounted a campaign for ratification. Most Birmingham white political leaders supported ratification. After the 1894 and 1896 demonstrations of the potential of Black power at the polls, the Democrats were ready to move beyond the white primary to strict disfranchisement. The *News, Age-Herald,* and Birmingham *Labor Advocate* weighed in heavily. They hailed "suffrage reform" as a progressive step to purify the electoral process. The *News* proclaimed that "White men must not be compelled any longer in this progressive State to steal ballots from negroes, to place themselves upon an equality with the negro by pretending to give him the right of suffrage and then sneaking it from him."[77]

Birmingham Blacks could register their unhappiness on election day, and many did so, but many others, considering the matter hopeless, stayed away from the polls. On election day the *Age-Herald* reported that "The negroes were on hand in large numbers voting in every case against ratification," and noted Democrats were pointing with alarm to a large Black turnout against the constitution "as a stimulus to the white man to support it." The Black turnout in Birmingham was actually small, indicating the discouragement of Blacks in the face of the disfranchisement juggernaut. In the city of Birmingham 3,974 votes were cast for the constitution, but only 721 votes against. Thus the "no" vote, not all of which was Black, was less than half the 1,300 Black votes cast in the 1894 mayoral election, and the "no" percentage of 15 percent was about half the usual 30 percent that Black votes had comprised of the city electorate.[78]

Even with the poor turnout of Black voters in Birmingham, in Jefferson County there was some potential for biracial opposition, across class lines, to disfranchisement. In rural Jefferson County white coal miners and farmers had developed serious doubts about the new suffrage plan. They feared that the new constitution would disfranchise many working-class whites, and their heavy "no" vote made the county result surprisingly close, with 8,088 votes (57 percent) for ratification and 6,160 votes (43 percent) against. Moreover, in Alabama as a whole many poorer whites, suspicious that the suffrage plan would disfranchise them as well as Blacks, voted "no."[79]

A biracial coalition against disfranchisement, however, faced the problem of a large vote of Blacks in the southern Black Belt counties *for* ratification. The massive "yes" majorities of the Black Belt counties carried the constitution in the statewide tally. It was widely known that most of the Black "yes" votes of the Black Belt were fraudulent, manufactured by white Democratic election officials to carry the state for disfranchisement. But Republicans and Blacks who pointed this out received little notice—another discouraging indicator of how low their political fortunes had sunk.[80]

For most African Americans in Birmingham, and Alabama generally, the Constitution of 1901 ended their voting. From 1898 through 1901 in Birmingham, approximately one thousand Blacks had been paying their annual poll tax of $1.50, but after 1902, when payment of the poll tax became prerequisite for voting, typically fewer than fifty Birmingham Blacks paid it. Most Birmingham whites rejoiced that, at last, the entire state had created legal rules that subordinated Blacks as fully in the political realm as had the more informal but robust methods that had long subordinated Blacks in the social and economic realms. White postbellum efforts to reconstruct race had finally produced a powerful reconvergence of boundaries of color in all realms of life. They thus raised the fourth pillar of Jim Crow—disfranchisement of Black voters.[81]

The process of creating the four pillars had extended over Birmingham's first generation, and was broad in scope and deeply emotional. There is good reason to think that social experience was fundamentally the same throughout the urban areas of the New South, and cities elsewhere in the nation during the twentieth century. The social breadth and psychological intensity of the process revealed in Birmingham may help explain why racist ideas, practices, and policies have continued to be so powerful, even into the current century.

HISTORIANS AND THE INTERPLAY OF
CLASS, RACE, AND CASTE

Birmingham's first generation of white elites and less privileged whites mani-fested intense racism and cooperated in implementing a wide range of segre-gationist practices and policies. This emphasis on social pressures, which ex-tended far beyond the realm of politics, differs from the way in which C. Vann Woodward and some other historians of the New South have analyzed the sources of segregation in the roles and interplay of class and race.

Woodward's *Strange Career of Jim Crow*, first published in 1955, was thin in its analysis of the economic class issues involved in the rise of Jim Crow. Woodward provided little discussion of the elements of segregation with sig-nificant economic dimensions—notably, school segregation, labor segmen-tation, and urban residential segregation. This was surprising because his 1951 book, *Origins of the New South*, had provided discussions of economic life that established him as the South's most distinguished "Beardian" histo-rian—meaning a historian who followed Charles Beard in concentrating upon economic issues and economic interest groups and upon how such issues and groups shaped politics.[1]

Strange Career incorporated only one Beardian construction, albeit an important one, in its narrative of the political battles during the 1890s over dis-franchisement. In his analysis of these battles, Woodward focused on the roles of the two main contending camps—the conservative plantation elites and the populist agrarians—and attended to their economic interests, identities, and goals. He saw the sharp political/economic conflict between white elites and white non-elites, including populists, as having caused non-elite whites to suffer deep frustration and lash out aggressively.[2] Woodward also suggested that elite whites cynically used propaganda to provoke the non-elites to direct their aggression irrationally onto Black scapegoats rather than toward the white elite, who had caused the frustration. Thus Woodward flirted with social-psychological frustration/aggression theory, using it to imply that a false consciousness induced by deep frustration had confused non-elite whites. He thereby shifted ultimate blame for the rising racism of the 1890s onto the white elite. At the same time, however, he acknowledged the role of non-elite energy.[3]

In *Strange Career,* Woodward structured his 1890s political stories primarily to highlight disfranchisement issues and their consequences. As a consequence he omitted all economic groups that were not directly involved in disfranchisement, including the economic interest groups which had played significant roles in constructing segregation at the local level. In his retrospective 1988 essay about "*Strange Career* Critics," Woodward admitted that he had neglected the urban aspect of segregation and acknowledged as well that segregation had been "essentially an urban, not a rural, phenomenon." In this essay, Woodward suggested an expansion of his interpretative scope to include the cities. In so doing, he noted and endorsed the scholarship of other historians, including Howard Rabinowitz, John W. Cell, and J. Morgan Kousser.

In announcing his neglect of urban segregation, Woodward attributed his interpretive shift in his 1988 essay partly to the findings of Howard Rabinowitz. In his 1978 book, *Race Relations in the Urban South, 1865–1890,* Rabinowitz had shown that urban Piedmont centers had invented segregation. And he pointed to an intensification of segregation after 1890, a timing consistent with Woodward's *Strange Career* paradigm. In the 1988 essay, Woodward wrote "that more segregation, both de facto and de jure, existed earlier in the nineteenth century than I had originally allowed," but he continued to stress the significance of the 1890s in the rise of Jim Crow. He added: "I fondly believe that most of my critics now concede that toward the end of the century an escalation in white fanaticism resulted in a rigidity and universality of the enforcement of discriminatory law that was a sufficient change to mark a new era in race relations."[4]

Rabinowitz, however, had not explained the politics of segregation in a Beardian fashion—in other words, as an elite white response to a populistic political challenge from non-elites. Rabinowitz never suggested that the intensification of segregation was a maneuver to enhance elite power and hegemony. He explained it as a united response by whites of all classes to a new pattern of resistance to white supremacy by a more assertive generation of Blacks, one not been born under slavery.[5] Nonetheless, in 1988 Woodward continued to embrace a "Beardian" take on political developments in the 1890s, even though by implication these political developments included the experiences of the Piedmont cities.

In explaining urban segregation in the 1890s, Woodard turned for support to John W. Cell, author of *The Highest State of White Supremacy,* a comparative study of segregation in South Africa and the American South, and to J. Morgan Kousser, author of a powerful 1974 study of suffrage restriction, *The Shaping of Southern Politics: Suffrage Restriction and the Establishment of the One-Party South, 1880–1910.*

Like Rabinowitz, Cell argued that "segregation was primarily an urban phenomenon." It had developed in the "modern" sector of society, he wrote, and not in the "traditional" or rural or agrarian sector. And "it was linked in significant ways to the early, formative industrial growth of the region." After examining briefly the conditions in cities, Cell proposed that urban Blacks posed a more substantial threat to white supremacy than did rural Blacks. Blacks in cities "were better educated, better organized politically, and more 'uppity.'" In response, southern inland cities "invented and tested most of the various devices . . . that were to be fused into the legal system of segregation across the South." Jim Crow, Cell concluded, "was not a rural 'redneck'"; instead he was "a city slicker."[6] In explaining Cell's approach, Woodward wrote: "On the forces behind change in race relations, Cell agrees with J. Morgan Kousser (as I have come to) that privileged, rather than underprivileged, whites were mainly responsible and that their ends were primarily political."[7]

Kousser had demonstrated in *The Shaping of Southern Politics* that in most of the South the state campaigns to disfranchise Blacks had been led by "Democrats, usually from the Black Belt and always socioeconomically privileged." The Democratic leaders were mostly affluent, well educated, and connected with large planters. Kousser saw the events of the 1890s as perhaps less decisive than had Woodward. In Kousser's view, the conclusive disfranchising constitutional conventions and constitutional amendments represented the culminating episodes of a sequential process that had begun during Reconstruction and that had stretched across several decades. In that long process, southern white Democrats, loath to see socially unworthy Blacks exercising any political power and also eager to handicap voters who typically opposed them, had enacted state legislation that had systematically and cumulatively decreased voting participation by Blacks and oppositional whites, weakening them politically and setting them up for further debilitating suffrage restrictions. The post-1890 constitutional conventions and amendments had been "largely anticlimactic," Kousser wrote.[8]

Woodward, however, portrayed the 1890s as a decisive "turning point" in racial history, and assigned responsibility to "privileged" whites in language that reached beyond the two precisely defined 1890s spheres—disfranchisement and school allocations—in which Kousser had demonstrated the agency of privileged whites. In Woodward's 1988 reformulation, he saw privileged whites as having produced the "new era in race relations."[9]

Woodward seemed to gravitate toward Cell's expansive argument that the rise of segregation was related to "the formation of the Southern capitalist power elite," to "the New South's strategy of capitalist development," and to "the political consolidation of the power elite in the Democratic Party."[10] In posing this "power elite" thesis, Cell had, in effect, combined Kousser's demonstration that elite Black Belt planters controlled the statewide (and largely rural) disfranchisement movement with Rabinowitz's demonstration that urban Piedmont centers invented segregation. Conflating the findings, Cell leapt to the conclusion that a privileged political elite, responding to "the internal political challenge of populism," had created segregation to establish and fortify its hegemonic political power.[11]

Woodward had some reservations, but he bought into much of Cell's argument. He noted that Cell fully agreed with his view that race relations and segregation had been politically constructed. Woodward wrote that, "In explaining the new racial order in the agrarian South, Cell concludes that 'economic determinism will not work. On that, as with so many of his conclusions, Woodward is absolutely right.'" Woodward observed with approval that Cell "concludes that in the long run, the new order of race relations was 'not economically determined,' was 'not based on economic but on political grounds,' and that 'it grew directly out of political responses to circumstances [the Populist revolt] that were mainly political.'" Thus, Woodward found that Cell agreed with him on a central interpretation: the 1890s intensification of racism had been largely a conservative *political* response to the political threat of Populism.[12]

Cell and Woodward united in support of the view that the upsurge in racism was politically constructed. In the process, however, they created a confused and improbable scenario. They failed to locate their prime suspects, elite rural white planters, at the scene of the crime—the Piedmont cities that invented segregation. Further, they provided no concrete evidence regarding the nuts and bolts of the creation of urban segregation. They offered no analysis of urban political, economic, or social issues, no analysis of the urban interest groups who struggled with the issues, no analysis of the strategies formulated by urban interest groups, and no analysis of the outcomes of these struggles. More specifically Cell and Woodward failed to narrate the creation of any urban system of segregation which generated a political struggle whose resolution in some way reinforced the hegemonic power of the plantation elite, or, for that matter, of any elite. In formulating a power-elite paradigm, Cell never took the necessary first steps in making a power-elite theme credible—identifying some specific power elite members and locating them in the cities of the Southern Piedmont.

The history of Birmingham in the late nineteenth century may clarify how interest groups in urban Birmingham interacted in the social, economic, and political realms as whites invented systems of separation and control to defeat or contain the aspirations of Blacks. In Birmingham far more was involved than a clash of class interests. Race, therefore, should not be seen as merely a function of class. To subsume race under class would result in portraying only one fundamental component of racism and racial prejudice—the instrumental component—and to neglect almost completely the socioemotional component. To be sure, white elites often had venal, instrumental motives, including on occasion the advance of their economic interests by deliberately dividing Blacks and working-class whites along racial lines. But the history of segregation, broadly defined, in Birmingham suggests that the motivations of white elites were heavily socio-emotional as well. The socioemotional sources of racism cut across class lines and had a powerful influence on the development of segregation in Birmingham during its initial decades.[13]

Close attention to the influence of socio-emotional factors on the development of Jim Crow can be found in the work of W. E. B. Du Bois. To be sure, Du Bois made it clear that in his view slavery, along with the economic exploitation associated with it, was the root cause of race prejudice. "The income of the Cotton Kingdom based on Black slavery," he wrote, "caused the passionate belief in Negro inferiority and the determination to enforce it even by arms."[14] But Du Bois also believed that far more than the opportunities for profit created by slavery were involved in creating and sustaining Jim Crow. In *Dusk of Dawn*, Du Bois proposed that, in America,

> . . . instead of a horizontal division of classes by race, there was a vertical fissure, a complete separation of classes by race, cutting square across the economic layers. Even if on one side [of] this color line, the dark masses were overwhelmingly workers, with but an embryonic capitalist class, nevertheless the split between white and black workers was greater than that between white workers and capitalists; and this split depended not simply on economic exploitation but on a racial folk-lore grounded on centuries of instinct, habit and thought and implemented by the conditioned reflex of visible color.[15]

Thus, for Du Bois it was necessary to go beyond "economic exploitation" to explain fully the rigidity and longevity of racial segregation in America. To convey a sense of the scope and staying power of segregation, and the complexity of the noneconomic forces shaping its development, Du Bois at times invoked the term "caste" to characterize American segregation and "castes" to describe the segregated group and the group doing the segregating.

In 1935, in *Black Reconstruction in America*, Du Bois wrote that in the wake of emancipation "caste has been revived in a modern civilized land" although "it was supposed to be a relic of barbarism and existent only in Asia." However, he went on, "it has grown up and has been carefully nurtured and put on a legal basis with religious and moral sanctions in the South." He explained that segregation involved not just separation of the races and "domination of blacks by white officials." It was also the construction of "a determined psychology of caste." Du Bois explained:

> In every possible way it was impressed and advertised that the white was superior and the Negro an inferior race. This inferiority must be publicly acknowledged and submitted to. Titles of courtesy were denied colored men and women. Certain signs of servility and usages amounting to public and

personal insult were insisted upon. The most educated and deserving black man was compelled to occupy a place beneath the lowest and least deserving of the whites. Public institutions, like parks and libraries, either denied all accommodations to the blacks or gave them inferior facilities.[16]

Five years later, in 1940, in *Dusk of Dawn* Du Bois addressed the psychological complexity and weight of a system that could be described as a "caste" system. "It is difficult," he wrote, "to let others see the full psychological meaning of caste segregation" and "to think through a method and approach and accommodation between castes." Those who would advocate on behalf of the "entombed" caste must face the difficulty that, "no matter how successful the outside advocacy is, it remains impotent and unsuccessful until it actually succeeds in freeing and making articulate the submerged caste."[17]

Du Bois may have regarded the term "caste" as useful in dramatizing the scope of the social barriers faced by American Blacks, but he did not invoke the term to advance social analysis. He regarded it as lacking an "economic foundation" and a clear operational definition. He expressed those views in 1937, between the appearance of *Black Reconstruction* and *Dusk of Dawn*, after John Dollard published a book bearing the title *Caste and Class in a Southern Town*.[18]

Dollard presented an unusually rich historical record of the habits and protocols that governed the everyday lives of Blacks and whites in Indianola, Mississippi, during the 1930s, at the height of the Jim Crow system. His close knowledge of psychological theories and concepts enabled him to formulate his questions and his findings with unusual rigor, but his definition of "caste" was rather thin, and perhaps largely an afterthought to increase the visibility of the book. The term had, of course, originally referred to the extremely rigid and well-documented Indian caste system, but Dollard adopted the vague definition of caste proposed by sociologist W. Lloyd Warner: "A theoretical arrangement of the people of the given group in an order in which the privileges, duties, obligations, opportunities, etc., are unequally distributed between the groups which are considered to be higher and lower." Warner recognized that this definition "also describes class," so he added to his definition the provision that caste was an "organization" in which "marriage between two or more groups is not sanctioned and where there is no opportunity for members of the lower groups to rise into the upper groups or of the members of the upper to fall into the lower ones."[19]

The additional provision superficially justified Dollard's use of "caste" to describe Jim Crow, but the definition was still weak, providing little guidance as to how one might compare caste systems across cultures or analyze the deep historical sources of Jim Crow. The imprecision and ahistorical abstraction of the terminology are the reasons why this book has not employed caste as an analytical paradigm.

Du Bois saw an additional problem with the caste terminology. In 1937 it seemed to him that it might be possible to focus reform energies into an attack on the economic structures maintaining segregation. But, to Du Bois, the approach that Dollard had followed seemed to create "a timeless symbiosis that collapsed class and even race into the absolute of caste," in the words of historian David Levering Lewis, Du Bois's leading biographer. Lewis went on to explain that emphasizing caste "threatened to freeze the American race problem into hierarchical immutability."[20] This concern seems less compelling today than it did in the late 1930s. Then, both of the two major political parties ignored the realities of Jim Crow, and their leaders generally welcomed excuses to avoid discussing race. Today, however, characterizing Jim Crow as a means of imposing or reinforcing a caste system could find a large receptive audience. In the process, invoking the concept of caste might well be an effective way to dramatize how socio-emotional factors and economic class interests have intersected and sustained racial discrimination in the United States.

APPENDIX

Social Psychology, Color Lines, and the Blumer Model

This book has drawn on research in the broad field of social psychology to develop an interpretative framework and has adapted a model that sociologist Herbert Blumer began to devise during the late 1950s to understand racial color lines.[1] Blumer's model featured a color line consisting of criteria, rules, and images to govern interactions between Blacks and whites. A color line, wrote Blumer, "defines the approach of each racial group to the other," limiting "the degree of access to each other" and outlining "respective modes of conduct toward each other."[2]

Blumer developed this model within the context of a group-oriented sociological approach called "symbolic interactionism." This approach asserted that individual people define themselves and generate the meanings they see in the world through a process of interaction with others in human groups. Blumer rejected the "realistic" view that things in the world had an intrinsic meaning that was part of their objective makeup. He rejected as well the psychodynamic view that the meaning that a person attributed to a thing in the world arose from the psychological organization or conflicts within the person's own mind. Blumer argued instead that meaning arose through individual interactions and discussion with people in human groups. Individuals gravitated toward human groups in which they and other group members could "fit their activities to one another," shaping their own conduct in response to group influence. Such "articulation of lines of action" would give rise to collective group agreement upon "joint action."[3] In recent decades Lawrence

Bobo, a prominent sociologist who studies the social psychology of race relations, has drawn attention to the value of Blumer's theoretical foundation for group-level, as opposed to an individual-level, analysis. Historians, however, have only rarely cited Blumer's analysis, let alone employed it.[4]

Blumer presented his model of the color line between whites and Blacks in the United States graphically as three circular and concentric color lines, one for each of three realms of life—social, economic, and political. A small inner circle, the "bull's eye" of the figure, represented the inner bastion of social separation and exclusion. A slightly larger concentric circle surrounded it, representing the color line of economic disadvantage and subordination. That line in turn was surrounded by a still larger circle—the color line of political discrimination, which denied Blacks basic civic and political rights and segregated them in public accommodations. Within this series of concentric bastions, said Blumer, "Outer portions . . . may . . . be given up only to hold steadfast to inner citadels."

In Blumer's model, the white defense of the *inner social color line* was emotionally more intense than was the white defense of the two outer color lines. Whites who were convinced "that the Negro [was] alien and different" imposed rigorous inner-circle rules that excluded Blacks from fellowship with whites at any familial or close social level, and forbade sexual approaches by Black males toward white females. To implement social exclusion, whites enforced an entire protocol of social rules. For example, Blacks should not eat with whites, nor approach their front doors. Blacks should always address whites with titles of respect like "Mister" and should always show deference. The rules of the social "inner circle" denied African Americans admission "into intimate and private circles, represented by social sets, cliques, private clubs, friendship sets, family circles, courtship, and marriage."[5]

In developing his model, Blumer took an innovative group-level approach, incorporating both sociology and psychology, to the study of race prejudice. On the one hand, Blumer posited a sociological or "instrumental" component of prejudice, which has been the component most consistently emphasized by historians. In Blumer's framework, within the practical material and political arenas of society, whites used prejudice as an "instrument" to help them achieve white domination and Black subordination. Their instrumental motivation was to take advantage of Blacks economically and politically. Through control over ownership of property, assignment of groups to

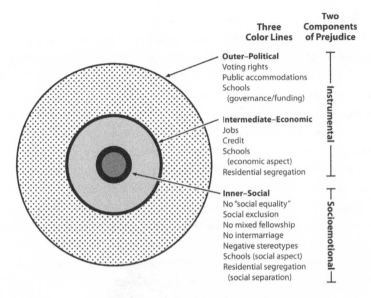

Blumer's Three-Color-Line Model

occupations, and political positions and decisions, Blumer argued, the white slave owners of the Old South implemented domination and achieved "hierarchical ordering and positioning." With regard to his three-color-line model, Blumer combined the two outer lines—the political and economic—into the instrumental component of prejudice.

On the other hand, Blumer posited a psychological component of the prejudice members of one social group developed toward another group or groups—a component driven by powerful emotions. In a kind of shorthand, Blumer referred to this component as "socioemotional." The boundary around this component was the inner social color line—what he called the "inner citadel." This citadel, this social core of segregation, protected the status and fervently held images of the in-group, and enforced the exclusion of the out-group. Blumer postulated that in a racialized social order the members of the dominant group would collectively form a superior self-image of their own racial group and ardently, even joyously, identify with it. At the same time they would create an emotionally malevolent image of the racial out-group. Dominant in-group members insisted that access to social intimacy with their members should be restricted to fellow in-group members. They welcomed the "socioemotional embrace" of fellow in-group members, but they experienced emotional "recoil" against out-group members, expressed by a wide range of emotions, including disgust and hatred. The members of the in-group systematically excluded all members of the dishonored out-group from social fellowship, thereby making an emotionally intense moral commitment to the assumption that the subordinate out-group was alien and socially inferior in traits, capabilities, and typical behavior. In the socioemotional component, Blumer saw psychological motivations that were separate from and independent of the political and economic motivations of the instrumental component. Socio-emotional prejudice arose from emotionally intense identification with the in-group and emotionally intense dishonoring of the out-group.

Blumer thus conceived of the two components of prejudice—the instrumental and the socio-emotional—as quasi-autonomous, arising independently from different motivations through different processes. But the inner citadel anchored and energized the entire system, and in-group members were eager to invoke the values and boundary principles of the socio-emotional inner circle even in the more instrumental intermediate and outer circles. In Blumer's theoretical and experimental model the two components, which were deeply rooted, coequal, and interlinked, formed the foundations upon which groups built prejudice.[6]

Blumer's color line—consisting of criteria, rules, and images—functioned like an interaction boundary, as cultural anthropologist Fredrik Barth defined such a boundary in 1969. Barth focused on the behavior of groups along cultural boundaries and argued that an ethnic group was subjectively generated not only by the people inside the group but also by oppositional people outside the group, people who were actively differentiating themselves from the group and often seeking to subordinate the group. In 1976 the social psychologists Marilynn B. Brewer and Donald T. Campbell elaborated Barth's approach, which had stressed the importance of what he called criteria of membership and rules of interaction in defining boundaries. Brewer and Campbell added the concept of stereotypes. They, along with many other social psychologists, defined stereotypes as images or expectancies or judgmental sets of beliefs about the personal attributes, the personality traits, and the typical behaviors of members of the out-group. By 1981 social psychologists had, in the words of social psychologist Thomas F. Pettigrew, "fashioned" the "concept of stereotype" into a valuable tool in the analysis of prejudice and intergroup conflict and also into "a significant explanatory mediator between individual and social phenomena."[7]

One of the psychologists most influential in developing an understanding of the role of stereotyping was Henri Tajfel. In his "social identity theory" he emphasized the group process of creating, embracing, and enhancing "social stereotypes." Such stereotypes were significant, he argued, because they were "shared" and acted upon by large numbers of people inside an in-group. He concluded that the content of the typical stereotype was influenced less by actual qualities of the out-group than by the function of helping in-group members explain and justify their patterns of interaction with the out-group. Tajfel argued that his experiments revealed a fundamental human tendency— a deep-seated human propensity to identify quickly and strongly with groups, and, on the basis of that identification, to discriminate in favor of the in-group, even if primarily social standing or prestige is involved. The mere perception of belonging to a group in the presence of an out-group, even if assignment to the groups was overtly randomized, was sufficient, Tajfel found, to provoke an individual to become competitive about the relative status of the groups and accordingly to discriminate in favor of the in-group with which the individual identified.[8]

Tajfel argued that the content of stereotypes was influenced also by several fundamental human biases of perception. Tajfel saw stereotyping as part of the useful, universal, and necessary human mental activity of processing and categorizing the chaotic welter of incoming perceptions about the complex world. But the normal categorizing process could have perverse consequences, said Tajfel, partly because all humans are prone to certain universal perceptual biases that continually work inside the minds of individual human beings. As Tajfel and his colleagues developed their group-oriented theory, they showed how the individual-level cognitive biases shaped the group-level process of stereotyping.

One fundamental bias was the "accentuation effect." In experiments Tajfel found that if he asked subjects to judge the relative lengths of eight lines that differed from each other by a constant ratio the subjects made quite accurate judgments. But if he separated the very same lines into two separate groups, experimental subjects tended to exaggerate the differences in the lengths of the lines in one group as compared with the lines in the other group, and also to exaggerate the similarity of the lengths of lines within each of the groups. In technical terms, the perceivers consistently accentuated differences between categories and accentuated similarities within categories.

Mistakes about lines could seem inconsequential. But if perceivers in the social world looked at *people* who had been categorized into *groups*, the accentuation became more robust. The accentuation effect was significant in experiments where subjects looked at collections of photographs of people identified as belonging to either one or another of two groups. The effect became stronger when the subjects were assigned to membership in one of the groups, and then became even stronger when people themselves voluntarily identified with an in-group and embraced its criteria of group membership as personally important. Then categorization was conducted "overwhelmingly with reference to *self*," so that people classified others "on the basis of their similarities and differences to *self*." People accentuated similarities between self and fellow in-groupers and accentuated differences between self and out-groupers. People also stereotyped themselves, exaggerating the extent to which they themselves matched the defining positive characteristics of the in-group image.[9]

In addition to the accentuation effect, some social psychologists identified what they regarded as a deep human bias toward "dispositional attribution." In this perceptual bias, an observer believes that another person's actions directly express his or her inner personality traits—traits that grow intrinsically out of the person's interior psychic disposition. Typically, the observer exaggerates the role of internal personality traits in shaping the actor's behavior, failing to see the crucial force of external pressures upon the actor's behavior. The observer underestimates pressures from the social structures around the actor and ignores the powerful constraints they may impose. For example, observers often attribute the nurturing behavior of women to an intrinsic feminine disposition toward nurturing, and they neglect to take into account the power of social expectations and social roles in fostering women's nurturing actions. The bias toward erroneously attributing behavior to internal disposition has been termed "the fundamental attribution error."[10]

When people have categorized themselves as an in-group in contrast to a specific out-group, then dispositional bias takes a perverse twist that Thomas F. Pettigrew has called the "*ultimate* attribution error" (emphasis mine). An in-group perceiver who sees *negative* behavior on the part of an out-group member will believe it was caused by inherent internal negative dispositional traits of out-group members. But if an in-grouper sees *positive* behavior on the part of an out-group member, he will explain it by referring to external situational factors.[11] Furthermore, in-group members who are in an advantageous position may engage in what social psychologists have called "detachment," ignoring, dismissing, and detaching themselves from the misfortunes of a disadvantaged out-group. Detachment enables people who are well-off to deny any sense of personal responsibility for the sharp disparities in living standards. It leads them to believe, for example, that differences in work ethic, inner discipline, and effort account for the disparities, and that the out-group has deserved its unfortunate condition.[12]

In the 1980s and 1990s Lawrence Bobo assessed Blumer's theoretical formulations and made it clear that Blumer's approach was consistent in many ways with Tajfel's Social Identity Theory.[13] In essence, Blumer's theory, which emphasized the consensual process of stereotyping, provided analytical context for understanding Tajfel's findings. Blumer had emphasized the role of an intense communal process of public discussion in which in-group elites and non-elites would interact to create a "collective image of the subordinate group," generate in-group consensus about the image, which could be regarded as a stereotype, and thereby foster solidarity and mutual commitment to the in-group's values and interests. Blumer acknowledged that a dominant racial in-group would include a wide variety of individual members. But, said Blumer, "all are led, by virtue of sharing the sense of group position," to construct and to agree upon a common defining image of the subordinated out-group. The sense of group position "transcends the feelings of the individual members of the dominant group, giving such members a common orientation that is not otherwise to be found in separate feelings and views."

The creation of a "collective image" of the subordinated out-group would be a public process. "Leaders, prestige bearers, officials, group agents, dominant individuals and ordinary laymen present to one another characterizations of the subordinate group and express their feelings and ideas on the relations," wrote Blumer. "Through talk, tales, stories, gossip, anecdotes, messages, pronouncements, news accounts, orations, sermons, preachments and the like definitions are presented and feelings are expressed." In such public discussion "major influence" will be exercised by individuals and by "interest" groups "who have the public ear," and who "are felt to have standing, prestige, authority, and power." But non-elites will be involved and their views and contributions will shape the emerging consensual stereotype.

In such a "vast and complex interaction," wrote Blumer, different "feelings" and "separate views" would "run against one another, modify each other, incite one another . . . , stimulate each other, feed on each other, intensify each other and emerge in new patterns." If the interaction "becomes increasingly circular and reinforcing, devoid of serious inner opposition," then currents of feeling polarize, "grow, fuse and become strengthened." Thus "a collective image of the subordinate group is formed and a sense of group position is set."

The process might be disrupted if some in-group constituencies persistently oppose the emerging collective image. But such internal opposition can be avoided if the group fosters collaborative interaction between its leaders and its other members so as to defuse and eliminate any disagreement that might arise from differences in perspective or class interest. If conflict is averted, in-groupers of all classes could converge upon a consensual "*abstract image* of the subordinate racial group," and the group would become "defined as if it were an entity, or whole."

Groups also engage in self-stereotyping, Blumer pointed out. "To characterize another racial group is, by opposition, to define one's own group," said Blumer. He explained that, when an "unlettered individual with low status in the dominant racial group" compares himself with members of the subordinate group, he often has "a sense of group position common to that of the elite of his group." His identification with the in-group self-stereotype makes him feel superior to even the elite of the out-group. An effective way for any in-group member to demonstrate his commitment to the in-group and to reinforce his good standing within it is to publicly affirm his endorsement of the dominant image of the out-group. On the other hand, any in-grouper who rejects the consensual image may "risk a feeling of self-alienation" and "face the possibility of ostracism."[14]

Blumer's theory of prejudice and stereotyping originally lacked the support of rigorous laboratory experiments. But during the 1990s and early 2000s social psychologists enhanced the appeal of Blumer's approach by using what they called "communication analysis" to test and confirm key components of Blumer's delineation of a collective process by which an in-group constructed "consensual stereotypes." Among the findings was that most people sense a need to validate their own subjective beliefs through reality testing but also believe that fellow in-groupers are the best people to perform the validating function. In experiments, when a set of in-groupers were told that a set of fellow in-groupers, meeting in a separate room, had validated a specific negative image of the out-group, the first set of in-groupers endorsed the specific image more wholeheartedly, and they intensified their perception that all members of the out-group homogeneously corresponded to the image. Accordingly, they reinforced their negative behavior toward out-groupers.[15]

Communication experiments also indicated that, during a process of talking about the out-group, in-group members gradually altered their stereotype to make it more consensual, more tightly defined around a few central traits, and thus more abbreviated, concise, simplified, exaggerated, and polarized. The experimenters concluded that typically, when in-groupers discussed an image, they sharpened it by omitting details that detracted from or qualified the essence of the image and by exaggerating details that contributed to it. Also, as in-groupers talked together, they gained more confidence that their shared image had been confirmed to be objectively valid, rather than a subjective opinion. The psychologists called this the "accentuation effect."[16]

These experiments demonstrated the human susceptibility to certain biases and the ways those biases function in the creation and sustaining of stereotypes. In turn, these experiments confirmed the significance of Blumer's socio-emotional component of prejudice—in other words, the component associated with images of racial identification and of "inclusion and exclusion." Blumer saw collectively constructed in-group stereotypes of the out-group to be central expressions of the crucial in-group "feeling that the subordinate race is intrinsically different and alien." He emphasized the power of stereotypes to create the "feeling of superiority" that causes the in-group to "place the subordinate people *below,*" and also "the feeling of alienation" that places the out-group *"beyond."* And Blumer stressed that prejudice as a sense of group position depended upon "a scheme of racial identification," a scheme that must involve "an image or a conception of one's own racial group and of another racial group." Thus, he wrote: "A basic understanding of race prejudice must be sought in the process by which racial groups form images of themselves and of others."[17]

The interdisciplinary work of understanding the psychology of color lines and group dynamics has, I believe, great potential for expanding the historical understanding of the segregation of African Americans. What this understanding requires is the establishment of linkages between the societal and the individual levels of explanation. This crucial task is largely unaccomplished, as historian Thomas Holt pointed out in 1995. Holt aptly described the intellectual challenge as "'the levels problem,' that is, the problem of establishing the continuity between behavioral explanations sited at the individual level of human experience and those at the level of society and social forces."[18] This book suggests that social psychological theory and experimentation may offer historians valuable assistance in responding to that challenge.

NOTES

EDITOR'S PREFACE

1. Carl V. Harris, *Political Power in Birmingham, 1871–1921* (Knoxville: University of Tennessee Press, 1977), "Reforms in Governmental Control of Negroes in Birmingham, Alabama, 1890–1920," *Journal of Southern History* 38 (November 1972): 567–600. In the Wisconsin PhD program, Carl's mentors were, in chronological order, William Hesseltine, Richard Current, and J. Rogers Hollingsworth. Carl also worked extensively with Allan Bogue and Eric Lampard.

2. Carl V. Harris, "Right Fork or Left Fork? The Section-Party Alignments of Southern Democrats in Congress, 1873–1897," in *Journal of Southern History* 42 (November 1976): 471–506. The essay was reprinted by John B. Boles and Bethany Johnson in their *Origins of the New South, 1877–1913, Fifty Years Later: The Continuing Influence of a Historical Classic* (Baton Rouge: Louisiana State University Press, 2003), 59–95. A new essay by Harris, "Redeemers vs. Agrarians?" accompanied the reprint of "Right Fork or Left Fork."

3. Carl V. Harris, "Stability and Change in Discrimination against Black Public Schools: Birmingham, Alabama, 1871–1931," *Journal of Southern History* 51 (August 1985): 375–416.

INTRODUCTION: THE SOCIAL HISTORY OF JIM CROW

1. A convenient source for *The Souls of Black Folk* (1903) is *W. E. B. Du Bois: Writings* (New York: Library of America, 1996), 347–547. The long quotation is from "The Forethought," 359. The generational reference is from "Of the Sons of Master and Man," 481. In this book I refer to the Jim Crow system of segregation as not only the segregation imposed by statues or other forms of legal regulation but also the segregation resulting from the racial boundaries created and defended by private individuals, groups, and institutions.

2. C. Vann Woodward, "*Strange Career* Critics: Long May They Persevere," *Journal of American History* 75 (December 1988): 857–60.

3. Birmingham was probably the first city of the New South for which founding boosters invoked the nickname "Magic City." But promoters of other southern cities and towns followed suit, most notably Roanoke, Virginia; Middlesborough, Kentucky; and Kingsport, Tennessee. See Carl V. Harris, *Political Power in Birmingham,* 11–38; and Rand Dotson, *Roanoke, Virginia, 1882–1912: Magic City of the New South* (Knoxville: University of Tennessee Press, 2007), xx and 266n61.

4. For an explanatory discussion of the research in social psychology by Herbert Blumer, other sociologists, cultural anthropologists, and psychologists, see the appendix to this book.

5. Du Bois, "Of the Sons of Master and Man," in *The Souls of Black Folk.* For the essay, see his *Writings* 475–92, and for the quotation, 489.

6. The quotation is from C. Vann Woodward, *Thinking Back: The Perils of Writing History* (Baton Rouge: Louisiana State University Press, 1986), 82–83. Woodward developed his interpretations most fully in *The Strange Career of Jim Crow.* After the appearance of the book in 1955, it went through several revised and expanded editions. Unless otherwise noted, the citation in this book will be to the 1974 edition, which was reprinted in a commemorative volume in 2002 with an afterword by William S. McFeely. The citation is *The Strange Career of Jim Crow* (3rd rev. ed., New York: Oxford University Press, 1974 and 2002).

7. See Grace Elizabeth Hale, *Making Whiteness: The Culture of Segregation in the South, 1890–1940* (New York: Pantheon, 1998). She provides evocative descriptions of specific sites at which Blacks and whites encountered each other and at which the culture of segregation was formed—for example, passenger trains, railroad depots, retail stores, gas stations, lynching sites, and southern homes with Black servants. But Hale's account seldom deals with schools, churches, occupational patterns, workplaces, patterns of residential segregation, political officials, political campaigns, government institutions, or government policies.

8. For analysis of drawing "the color line" in Durham during the late nineteenth century, see Leslie Brown, *Upbuilding Black Durham: Gender, Class, and Black Community Development in the Jim Crow South* (Chapel Hill: University of North Carolina Press, 2008), 1–80. On page 39, Brown noted that, by the 1880s, "even without laws, Durham was more segregated than older cities like Charleston and Wilmington."

9. Glenda Elizabeth Gilmore, *Gender and Jim Crow: Women and he Politics of White Supremacy in North Carolina, 1896–1920* (Chapel Hill: University of North Carolina Press, 1996).

10. Dotson, *Roanoke, Virginia,* 67, 105–52, 171, and 202–5.

11. Howard N. Rabinowitz, *Race Relations in the Urban South, 1865–1890* (New York: Oxford University Press, 1978). See also Rabinowitz, "More than the Woodward Thesis: Assessing the Strange Career of Jim Crow," *Journal of American History* 75 (December 1988): 842–56.

12. Woodward, "*Strange Career* Critics," 857–60; John W. Cell, *The Highest Stage of White Supremacy: The Origins of Segregation in South Africa and the American South* (Cambridge, UK: Cambridge University Press, 1982), esp. 133–34 and 175–76.

13. Rabinowitz, *Race Relations in the Urban South,* quotations from pages xv and 333.

1. CITY OF OPPORTUNITIES AND BOUNDARIES

1. Harris, *Political Power in Birmingham,* 12–18.

2. *Congressional Record,* 47 Cong., 1 sess., 5430.

3. Alfred H. Kelly," The Congressional Controversy over School Segregation, 1867–1875," *American Historical Review* 64 (April 1959): 537–63; Bertram Wyatt-Brown, "The Civil Rights Act of 1875," *Western Political Quarterly* 18 (December 1965): 763–75. A majority of Republicans supported the mixed-school clause only on a few procedural votes. Regarding southern segregation of classrooms, the single exception of New Orleans proved the rule. New Orleans had long had a relatively affluent and assertive free Black community. Even before the Civil War free Blacks had transformed a Catholic school into a de facto public school. During Reconstruction, pressure from this community produced, historian Walter Stern writes, "The desegregation of at least twenty-one of the city's schools between 1871 and 1879," making "them the nation's closest approximations of the common school ideal." Stern explains that, "For a brief moment, these schools were *public* not simply because taxpayers funded them but because they were places where all members of the community came together." See Walter C. Stern, *Race and Education in New Orleans: Creating the Segregated City, 1764–1960* (Baton Rouge: Louisiana State University Press, 2018), 3–4, 16–17, and 36–41. See also Louis R. Harlan, "Desegregation in New Orleans Public Schools during Reconstruction," *American Historical Review* 67 (April 1961): 663–75, and Eric Foner, *Reconstruction: America's Unfinished Revolution, 1863–1877* (New York: Harper & Row, 1988), 366–67 and 546–47.

4. Daniel W. Crofts, "The Black Response to the Blair Education Bill," *Journal of Southern History* 37 (February 1971): 42–43; Hilary Green, *Educational Reconstruction: African American Schools in the Urban South, 1865–1890* (New York: Fordham University Press, 2016), 189–95.

5. The entire Blair-Welch episode is recorded in US Congress, Senate, *Report of the Committee of the Senate Upon the Relations Between Labor and Capital, and Testimony Taken by the Committee,* 4 vols. (Washington, DC: GPO, 1885), vol. 4: 403–4, 455–56 (hereafter, US Congress, *Labor and Capital*). Several times the stenographer wrongly spelled Welch's last name "Welsh."

6. Montgomery *Advertiser*, rpt. in Birmingham *Iron Age*, July 9, 1874.

7. Crofts, "The Black Response to the Blair Education Bill," 41–65.

8. US Congress, *Labor and Capital* 4: 372–73.

9. Horace Talbert, *The Sons of Allen* (Xenia, OH: Aldine Press, 1906), 130; Charles Spencer Smith, *A History of the African Methodist Episcopal Church* (1922; rpt. New York: Johnson Reprint Corp., 1968), 72, 90; "Rev. Isiah H. Welch, D.D." in G. F. Richings, *Album of Negro Educators* (1900), babel.hathitrust.org/cgi/pt?id=uiug.30112077158019&view=1up&seq=20&q1=Welch.

10. Talbert, *The Sons of Allen*, 130; Smith, *A History of the African Methodist Episcopal Church*, 72, 90; "Rev. Isiah H. Welch, D. D." in Richings, *Album of Negro Educators; Advertiser*, rpt. in *Iron Age*, July 9, 1874.

11. Despite their dislike of institutional separation and state control, Black leaders generally supported passage of Blair's education bill, which they regarded as the most promising post-Reconstruction initiative of the Republican Party designed to intervene positively in race relations in the South. After Blair returned to Washington, he reintroduced his education bill, and he did so again and in several succeeding congresses. Three times he pushed it through the Senate, but he never could get the House to pass it. In 1890, the measure finally died, primarily over disagreement regarding control of the allocations. Most Black leaders were profoundly disappointed by its death. It signaled an end to serious federal initiatives to boost the rights and welfare of southern Blacks. In the early twentieth century no less a figure than W. E. B. Du Bois sought to revive the

Blair idea of federal aid to common schools, but to no avail. See Crofts, "The Black Response to the Blair Education Bill," 42–43.

12. Huntsville *Gazette,* July 26, 1884; US Congress, *Labor and Capital* 4: 372.

13. US Census, *Tenth Census, 1880,* vol. 1: *Population of the United States,* 380; vol. 19: *Social Statistics of Cities,* part 2: 205; US Congress, *Labor and Capital* 4: 373–76.

14. Map 1 has been traced from the map of Birmingham on the Index page of a map book produced in 1888 by the Sanborn Map and Publishing Company. The Sanborn Company created complex large-scale maps depicting the sections of cities and the size, shape, and construction of residential, commercial, and industrial structures. The maps were designed to provide fire insurance companies with information from which they could estimate fire risks so as to calculate insurance rates. See "Sanborn Fire Insurance Maps," www.lib.berkeley.edu/EART /sanborn_union_list. The Birmingham Sanborn maps are available on microfilm from ProQuest Information and Learning, 300 North Zeeb Road, Ann Arbor, MI 48103. See also www.loc.gov /collections/sanborn-maps/?all=true&fa=location:alabama%7Clocation:birmingham.

15. Harris, *Political Power in Birmingham,* 12–17.

16. The descriptions in this chapter and chapter 5 rely on tabulations of locations from the Birmingham *City Directory,* 1883; on the Business Directory published on pages 259 to 284 of the *City Directory;* on descriptive material published on pages 2–51 of the *City Directory;* on the *Map of the City of Birmingham Alabama and Suburbs,* drawn for the Elyton Land Company by H. Schoel (Elyton Land Co., 1888); on maps drawn in 1885 by the Sanborn Map and Publishing Company; on travelers' descriptions published in the Birmingham *Iron Age,* January 5, 1881, August 17, September 28, October 5, 19, November 2, 1882, and March 22, July 26, 1883, and in the Birmingham *Semi-Weekly Review,* December 19, 1883; on accounts of local conditions published in the *Iron Age,* September 1, 15, 1881, January 19, May 18, June 1, August 17, 24, December 14, 1882, and January 10, 1884, in the Birmingham *Weekly Pilot,* August 18, September 1, and October 6, 1883, and in the *Negro American,* October 9, 1886; and on descriptions in Ethel Armes, *The Story of Coal and Iron in Alabama* (Birmingham, 1910), 284–85; and Martha Mitchell Bigelow, "Birmingham: Biography of a City of the New South," PhD diss., University of Chicago, 1946, 11, 25–26, 55–70. Also helpful on the appearance of some buildings is a large panoramic map of Birmingham drawn in 1885 by landscape artist Henry Wellge. However, Wellge strove for attractive images that would please Birmingham boosters. See Wellge, *Panoramic Map of Birmingham, Alabama, 1885* (Milwaukee: Norris, Wellge & Co., 1885). The map is part of a collection of city and town maps at the Library of Congress, www.loc.gov/collections/?q=City+and+Town+maps.

17. Romeo, "Our Limestone Letter," *Gazette,* February 3, 1883; *Iron Age,* March 22, 1883.

18. *Iron Age,* September 28, December 14, 1882, March 22, July 26, 1883, March 27, June 1, 1884; *Pilot,* October 6, 1883; *Birmingham City Directory, 1883.*

19. *Birmingham City Directory, 1883; Iron Age,* January 10, 1884, September 10, 1885; Jefferson *Independent,* December 10, 1881; *Pilot,* August 18, 1883.

20. *Gazette,* June 13, 1885; *Iron Age,* March 22, 1883, March 19, 1885.

21. *Pilot,* August 18, 1883; *Gazette,* July 26, 1884; US Congress, *Labor and Capital* 4: 373.

22. In some churches, segregation was a departure from antebellum practice. Birmingham had not existed before the Civil War, but in the surrounding Jones Valley many white churches had incorporated slaves as subordinate members, requiring them to sit in the rear of the church or in

a balcony, and preventing them from participating in worship or church governance. But after emancipation, many Blacks of Jones Valley had taken the initiative to leave the white churches and establish their own Black churches. They wished to break free from white circumscription, to worship as they desired, to govern their church life themselves, and to make the churches the central social institutions of their communities. Once Blacks established separate churches, white churches began excluding Blacks, began endorsing church segregation, and began enforcing it rigorously. See Wilson Fallin Jr., *The African American Church in Birmingham, Alabama, 1815–1963: A Shelter in the Storm* (New York: Garland, 1997), 5–17.

23. US Congress, *Labor and Capital* 4: 326–27, 372–73; *Birmingham City Directory, 1883*.

24. US Congress, *Labor and Capital* 4: 326–27, 372–73. One minor exception to the pattern of sharp church segregation was alluded to by Black Pastor Isaiah Welch. He reported that he had heard that the priest of the local Catholic Church had extended an invitation to "colored Catholics" to unite with the whites in worship. At that time very few Black Catholics would have lived in Birmingham.

25. Wyatt-Brown, "The Civil Rights Act of 1875," 766.

26. The black business corner is identified on sheet 4B of the Sanborn 1885 map of Birmingham, which explicitly labels the "Negro" businesses. See also *Birmingham City Directory, 1883*.

27. Paul Worthman, "Working Class Mobility in Birmingham, Alabama, 1880–1914," in Tamara K. Hareven, ed., *Anonymous Americans* (Englewood Cliffs, NJ: Prentice Hall, 1971), 176–78.

28. The first issue of the *Pilot* that survives was August 18, 1883. See also issues of September 1, 1883, February 23, April 5, June 21, 1884; see also Thomason's testimony in US Congress, *Labor and Capital* 4: 396–99.

29. *Pilot*, August 18, 1883.

30. *Pilot*, August 18, 1883, October 27, 1883, January 12, 26, 1884.

31. *Pilot*, August 18, 1883; US Congress, *Labor and Capital* 4: 396.

32. *Gazette*, April 28, 1883, August 30, 1884, May 1, July 10, August 21, 1886, November 5, 19, 1887, May 10, 1890. The founding date of 1879 for the *Gazette* comes from Irvine Garland Penn, *The Afro-American Press and Its Editors* (Springfield, MA: Wiley and Co., 1891), 286.

33. *Iron Age*, October 11, 1888; Assessment of Taxes on Real Estate and Personal Property in the County of Jefferson, 1875, 1876, 1877; Tax Assessment Block Books, 1893, Birmingham County Courthouse.

34. *Iron Age*, October 11, 1888; *Birmingham City Directory, 1884:* 277; Assessment of Taxes on Real Estate and Personal Property in the County of Jefferson, 1875, 1876, 1877, Tax Assessment Block Books, 1893, Birmingham County Courthouse; Concise Form of the Amount of Taxes Due by each Tax Payer of Jefferson County, Ala., for Tax Year 1884, available on microfilm, Birmingham Public Library.

35. *Iron Age*, October 11, 1888.

36. Wellge, *Panoramic Map of Birmingham*, 1885; Map of Birmingham, Sanborn Map and Publishing Co., 1888.

37. *Iron Age*, September 12, 1887, and October 11, 1888.

38. *Iron Age*, September 12, 1887.

39. *Pilot*, August 18, 1883, January 19, 1884; *Gazette*, June 20, 1885; *Iron Age*, November 9, 1887. *Birmingham City Directory, 1883:* 48–49; US Congress, *Labor and Capital* 4: 375.

40. *Pilot*, August 18, 1883, January 19, 1884; *Birmingham City Directory, 1883:* 48–49; US Congress, *Labor and Capital* 4: 375.

41. *Iron Age,* October 5, 1882, March 27, 1884, September 30, 1886; *Birmingham City Directory, 1883.*

42. *Birmingham City Directory,* 1883.

43. Harris, *Political Power in Birmingham,* 35.

44. US Congress, *Labor and Capital* 4: 282–87, 388–89.

2. TRANSITION TO THE NEW SOUTH: RECONSTRUCTING BOUNDARIES

1. George Fredrickson, "White Images of Black Slaves in the Old South," in his *The Arrogance of Race: Historical Perspectives on Slavery, Racism, and Social Inequality* (Middletown, CT: Wesleyan University Press, 1988), 206–15. See also Fredrickson, *The Black Image in the White Mind: The Debate on Afro-American Character and Destiny, 1817–1914* (Middletown, CT: Wesleyan University Press, 1971), 52–55.

2. Herbert Blumer, "Race Prejudice as a Sense of Group Position," *Pacific Sociological Review* 1 (1958): 6. For a detailed discussion of the ways in which Herbert Blumer and social psychologists have described and analyzed stereotypes and their role in shaping and reshaping racial boundaries, see the appendix to this book.

3. *Register* qtd. in *Tuskaloosa Blade,* March 11, 1875.

4. *Register* qtd. in *Blade,* March 11, 1875; *Iron Age,* September 3, 17, 1874; *Blade,* August 27, 1874.

5. *Register* qtd. in *Blade,* March 11, 1875.

6. *Register* qtd. in *Blade,* March 11, 1875.

7. *Iron Age,* September 3, 1874.

8. Randolph had strong political connections with Birmingham, and in 1880 he would move to Birmingham. He turned against the local Democrats and published an independent newspaper, the Birmingham *True Issue.* See the *True Issue,* June 19, 1880. On Randolph's career, see Allen W. Trelease, *White Terror: The Ku Klux Klan Conspiracy and Southern Reconstruction* (New York: Harper and Row, 1971), 84–87, 253–60; Robert K. Bell, "Reconstruction in Tuscaloosa County," MA thesis, University of Alabama, 1933; Gladys Ward, "Life of Ryland Randolph," MA thesis, University of Alabama, 1932; Walter L. Fleming, *Civil War and Reconstruction in Alabama* (New York: Columbia University Press, 1905); Sarah Woolfolk Wiggins, "The Life of Ryland Randolph as Seen through His Letters to John W. DuBose," *Alabama Historical Quarterly* 30 (Fall–Winter 1968): 145–80; Sarah Van V. Woolfolk, "The Political Cartoons of the Tuskaloosa *Independent Monitor* and *Tuskaloosa Blade,*" *Alabama Historical Quarterly* 27 (Fall–Winter, 1965): 140–165; Mike Daniel, "The Arrest and Trial of Ryland Randolph, April–May, 1868," *Alabama Historical Quarterly* 40 (Fall–Winter, 1978): 127–43.

9. Bell, "Reconstruction in Tuscaloosa," 9, 40; Wiggins, "Life of Ryland Randolph," 164; Trelease, *White Terror,* 84; Fleming, *Civil War and Reconstruction,* 662n2, 666, 577; Woolfolk, "Political Cartoons," 141; Ward, "Life of Ryland Randolph," 9.

10. Randolph wrote to Walter Fleming, "I well remember those notices in *The Monitor,* for they were concocted and posted by my own hand—disguised of course." Fleming, *Civil War*

and Reconstruction, 677, 678n1, 679n2; Trelease, *White Terror,* 86, 257–58; Bell, "Reconstruction in Tuscaloosa," 43.

11. Trelease, *White Terror,* 84. For a discussion of the kind of spite that Randolph brought to the process of reconstructing the stereotyping of African Americans around a central image of the personality, the inner disposition, and the character traits of Blacks, see the appendix.

12. Ward, "Life of Ryland Randolph," 43–49.

13. Randolph Memoirs, Samford University, Special Collections, Birmingham, qtd. in Daniel, "Arrest and Trial of Ryland Randolph," 86–88; Ward, "Life of Ryland Randolph," 8.

14. Daniel, "Arrest and Trial of Ryland Randolph," 127–43; Randolph letter to DuBose, qtd. in Wiggins, "Life of Ryland Randolph," 166; *Monitor* qtd. in Daniel, "Arrest and Trial of Ryland Randolph," 129–30.

15. Woolfolk, "Political Cartoons," 154–53; Ward, "Life of Ryland Randolph," 27–29; Bell, "Reconstruction in Tuscaloosa County," 31–33. At the time Randolph acknowledged only that the woodcut cartoon had been fashioned in the *Monitor* office, but later historian Walter L. Fleming, who had talked with Randolph and received many letters from him, wrote that "The wood-cut from which this picture was printed was fashioned by Randolph himself in *The Monitor* office." See Fleming, "Introduction," in J. C. Lester and D. L. Wilson, *Ku Klux Klan: Its Origin, Growth and Development,* introd. and notes by Walter L. Fleming (New York: Neale Publishing Co., 1905), 42.

16. Woolfolk, "Political Cartoons," 153; Ward, "Life of Ryland Randolph," 29. The woodcut has been reprinted in countless history textbooks as a graphic illustration of southern white hostility to Radical Reconstruction. See, for example, cartoon dated September 1, 1868, Foner, *Reconstruction,* among the illustrations following 386.

17. *Blade,* October 2, 1873; see also October 9, 1873, January 8, 15, 29, February 12, 1874. *Iron Age,* February 19, 1874. Fleming, *Civil War and Reconstruction,* 611–17, 660–69. Daniel, "Arrest and Trial of Ryland Randolph," 127–43; *Iron Age,* April 16, September 24, 1874.

18. *Blade,* January 23, 1873, November 28, 1872.

19. *Blade,* January 23, 1873, December 10, 1874.

20. *Blade,* October 2, 9, November 27, December 11, 1873, January 15, February 26, 1874; *Iron Age,* February 19, 26, March 19, April 23, August 27, October 15, 1874, September 9, 1875, August 23, 1876. Ezra J. Warner, *Generals in Gray: Lives of the Confederate Commanders* (1959; rpt. Baton Rouge: Louisiana State University Press, 1989), 160–61.

21. *Iron Age,* March 19, 26, April 9, 16, 23, 1874; *Blade,* October 2, 1873.

22. *Iron Age,* March 19, April 23, July 23, 1874, September 25, October 30, 1878; US Census, *Tenth Census, 1880,* Jefferson County, Manuscript Population Schedules, vol. 11, E.D. 75, sheet 26, line 26; *True Issue,* July 17, 1880, Jefferson County, Tax Assessment Book, 1874, 1875; *Independent,* September 1, November 10, 1877.

23. *Iron Age,* April 23, 1874.

24. *Iron Age,* April 23, 1874, December 16, 1875; US Census, *Eighth Census, 1860,* Manuscript Slave Schedules, Jefferson County; US Census, *Eighth Census, 1860, Population,* (Washington: GPO, 1864), 8; US Census, *Ninth Census, 1870, Population,* 80; Roger Ransom and Richard Sutch, *One Kind of Freedom: The Economic Consequences of Emancipation* (Cambridge, UK: Cambridge University Press, 1977), 6, 44–50, 232–36.

25. *Iron Age,* February 19, April 23, September 24, 1874.

26. *Iron Age,* April 4, 1877, February 19, April 23, September 24, 1874, April 22, October 10, 28, 1875, June 5, 1878; *Blade,* February 19, 1874.

27. *Iron Age,* April 23, August 27, 1874, May 20, 1875, July 19, August 23, 1876; *Blade,* October 9, 1873. The local Grange was the Oakland Grange.

28. *Iron Age,* September 20, 1876.

29. Thomas McAdory Owen, *History of Alabama and Dictionary of Alabama Biography* (Chicago: S. J. Clarke Publishing Co., 1921), vol. 3: 685–86; John Witherspoon DuBose, *Jefferson County and Birmingham, Alabama: Historical and Biographical* (1887; rpt. Easley, SC: Southern Historical Press, 1976), 316; Eutaw *Whig and Observer,* July 25, 1878; Jefferson County Tax Assessment List, 1874; *Iron Age,* August 17, 1874, January 13, 27, 1876, July 10, 1878.

30. *Iron Age,* April 23, 1874.

31. *Iron Age,* August 17, 1875, November 1, 1874; *Blade,* December 10, 1874.

32. *Iron Age,* October 28, 1875, June 5, 1878.

33. *Iron Age,* April 23, 1874; *Montgomery Weekly Advertiser,* July 17, 1877. To the white ingroup, core personality deficiencies had produced the misfortunes of African Americans. For white farmers this explanation could serve the function which social psychologists have labeled "detachment." See the appendix to this book.

34. Letter from New York *Tribune* special correspondent E. V. Smalley, qtd. in *Weekly Advertiser,* July 17, 1877. The correspondent was indulging in what psychologists call "dispositional attribution," one of the perceptual biases that psychologists regard as commonly influencing the construction or elaboration of stereotypes. See the appendix to this book.

35. *Iron Age,* July 19, 1876.

36. *Iron Age,* June 25, 1874, quoting with approval an editorial in the Memphis *Appeal.*

37. See chapter 1 of this book.

38. US Congress, *Labor and Capital* 4: 50.

39. US Congress, *Labor and Capital* 4: 50–51.

40. US Congress, *Labor and Capital* 4: 40, 48–50.

41. US Congress, *Labor and Capital* 4: 40, 42–48.

42. US Congress, *Labor and Capital* 4: 150–54.

43. US Congress, *Labor and Capital* 4: 282–87, 388–89.

44. US Congress, *Labor and Capital* 4: 287–90.

45. Armes, *The Story of Coal and Iron in Alabama,* 272–74.

46. US Congress, *Labor and Capital* 4: 481–83.

47. US Congress, *Labor and Capital* 4: 270.

48. US Congress, *Labor and Capital* 4: 268.

49. US Congress, *Labor and Capital* 4: 271.

50. US Congress, *Labor and Capital* 4: 271.

51. US Congress, *Labor and Capital* 4: 269–72.

52. US Congress, *Labor and Capital* 4: 68–69, 78–85.

53. US Congress, *Labor and Capital* 4: 67, 68, 70, 74–75.

54. US Congress, *Labor and Capital* 4: 70–75, 79–85.

55. US Congress, *Labor and Capital* 4: 71.

56. US Congress, *Labor and Capital* 4: 67–74.

57. US Congress, *Labor and Capital* 4: 70–72, 90.

3. PROTOCOLS, SANCTIONS, AND MOB TERROR

1. For a discussion of research in social psychology that assists in understanding the power of prejudice and stereotyping, see the appendix to this book.

2. The 1865 legislation marked a distinct toughening of the law. In 1852, Alabama had established interracial sex as a crime, but not a felony. In 1856, the state explicitly banned interracial marriages and made presiding at an interracial marriage ceremony a felony. In its 1865 legislation, the state continued the felony status of officiating at an interracial marriage but also made participation in an interracial sexual relationship a felony. For superb analysis of the complicated contests that followed in the courts into the 1880s over the status of this legislation under both state and federal constitutions, see Julie Novkov, *Racial Union: Law, Intimacy, and the White State in Alabama, 1865–1954* (Ann Arbor: University of Michigan Press, 2008), 29–67. Novkov traces "the legal system's endorsement of a deeply rooted state interest in white families as the fundamental unit of state structure." The endorsement, Novkov concludes, "sent a message to blacks about the centrality of the normative white family structure" (40).

3. Edward Ayers, *The Promise of the New South: Life After Reconstruction* (New York: Oxford University Press, 1992), 156–59.

4. *Pilot*, August 18–November 1, 1883.

5. Except where otherwise noted, the account of the Houston case is based on the *Iron Age*, November 29, 1883. The issues of the *Pilot* for these weeks have not survived.

6. *Iron Age*, November 29, 1883; *Gazette*, December 1, 1883.

7. *Gazette*, December 1, 1883.

8. *Iron Age*, November 29, 1883.

9. *Iron Age*, December 6, 1883, July 16, 1885. Unless otherwise noted, the account of the Posey case is based upon *Iron Age*, December 6, 1882; *Gazette*, December 8, 1883; Birmingham *Semi-Weekly Review*, December 5, 8, 12, 1883.

10. *Pilot*, July 26, 1884.

11. *Iron Age*, December 6, 1883.

12. *Pilot*, May 31, 1884; see also *Gazette*, December 8, 1883.

13. Mobile *Register* qtd. in *Gazette*, December 8, 1883.

14. *Pilot*, January 12, 1884. The precise involvement and motivations of Governor Edward O'Neal are unknown, although it is reasonable to suppose that he believed lynch mobs damaged the national reputation of the New South and disrupted labor relations as well assaulting the rule of law. Since the 1840s he had practiced law in Florence, located on the Tennessee River in northern Alabama. After the Civil War, he became active in Democratic politics, playing an important role in Alabama's 1875 constitutional convention during which he sought to promote major increases in federal funding for education. In 1882 and 1884 he won election as governor as a supporter of commercial and industrial development. Emmet O'Neal, his son and law partner after the Civil War, had a similar social and economic orientation, taking a leadership role in calling for disfranchisement in 1901 and supporting corporate interests when he served as gover-

nor of Alabama from 1911 to 1915. It is intriguing that in May 1919 ex-governor Emmet O'Neal attended a national anti-lynching conference in New York which, based on the research of the NAACP, urged people "to oppose with all their power the recurrence of the crime and shame of mob lynching." On Edward A. O'Neal, see Malcolm Cook McMillan, *Constitutional Development in Alabama, 1798–1901: A Study in Politics, the Negro, and Sectionalism* (Chapel Hill: University of North Carolina Press, 1955), 190n7, 191, 206, and 107n127. On Emmet O'Neal, see Harris, *Political Power in Birmingham,* 83–84, 110, and 138; Glenn Feldman, *The Disfranchisement Myth: Poor Whites and Suffrage Restriction in Alabama* (Athens: University of Georgia Press, 2005), 68–70; and George B. Tindall, *The Emergence of the New South, 1913–1945* (Baton Rouge: Louisiana State University Press, 1967), 173.

15. *Iron Age,* July 16, 1885; *Pilot,* May 31, 1884; *Iron Age,* June 19, December 18, 1884; *Gazette,* January 12, 26, 1884.

16. *Iron Age,* August 28, 1884. The identities of the alleged mob members are unknown.

17. *Pilot,* July 26, 1884; *Iron Age,* July 31, 1884; *Gazette,* August 2, 1884.

18. See chapter 6 of this book. The "rabid hostility" of the white miners toward Black miners is emphasized in the brief description of this episode by historian Daniel Letwin in *The Challenge of Interracial Unionism: Alabama Coal Miners, 1878–1921* (Chapel Hill: University of North Carolina Press, 1998), 31 and 36–37.

19. Birmingham *Age-Herald,* January 13, 1889.

20. *Age-Herald,* January 14, 1889.

21. *Age-Herald,* January 14, 1889; Birmingham *News,* January 18, 1889.

22. *News,* January 14, 1889.

23. *News,* January 14, 15, 1889; *Age-Herald,* January 13, 1889.

24. *News,* January 14, 1889; *Age-Herald,* January 15, 1889.

25. *News,* January 14, 15, 1889.

26. *Age-Herald,* January 15, 1889.

27. *News,* January 15, 1889.

28. *News,* January 17, 18, 1889; *Age-Herald,* January 17, 18, 1889.

29. *News,* January 18, 19, 1889; *Age-Herald,* January 19, 20, 1889; *Alabama Sentinel,* January 26, 1889.

30. *Age-Herald,* January 20, 27, 1889.

31. *Alabama Sentinel,* February 1, 1889.

32. *News,* January 18, 19, 1889; *Age-Herald,* January 19, 20, 1889; November 29, 1890; *Alabama Sentinel,* January 26, 1889.

33. *Age-Herald,* October 6, 1890.

34. Gunnar Myrdal, *An American Dilemma: The Negro Problem and Modern Democracy* (New York: Harper and Row, 1944), 60–61, 587.

35. Myrdal, *An American Dilemma,* 590–91.

36. Myrdal, *An American Dilemma,* 589–91, 575.

37. For discussion of the permission extended to white men to exploit Black women, see Blumer, "Race Prejudice as a Sense of Group-Position," 4–5; Lawrence Bobo, "Prejudice as Group Position: Microfoundations of a Sociological Approach to Racism and Race Relations," *Journal of Social Issues,* 55 (1999): 447–49, 454–57.

38. *Pilot,* November 3, 1883; US Congress, *Labor and Capital* 4: 373.

39. Hale, *Making Whiteness,* 32.

40. Brown, *Upbuilding Black Durham,* 86.

41. *Negro American,* October 29, 1887.

42. US Congress, *Labor and Capital* 4: 455.

43. *Age-Herald,* March 10, 15, 1889. Beale had been appearing before Birmingham courts at least as early as June of 1884. See *Iron Age,* June 19, 1884.

44. Many whites did deplore the existence of the "Dens of Degradation," condemning them as a menace to the family morals of the entire community, particularly because the occasional discovery there of married white men spread disgrace through prominent households. Periodically the white newspapers would conduct a spectacular exposé and campaign to shut down the "dives," but such campaigns were short-lived, and soon the Black brothels were again busy while the police and courts and most white citizens looked the other way. *Age-Herald,* March 15, 1889; February 19, April 1, 1891, July 29, 1894; *News,* November 11, 1896, August 10, 15, 16, 1900.

45. *Negro American,* May 12, 1894.

46. C. Vann Woodward, *Tom Watson: Agrarian Rebel* (New York, Oxford University Press, 1963), 239–43.

47. *Negro American,* May 26, 1894.

4. SCHOOL SEGREGATION

1. *Independent,* November 10, December 22, 1877.

2. Kelly, "The Congressional Controversy over School Segregation," 537–63, quotations 547, 549, 555; Wyatt-Brown, "The Civil Rights Act of 1875," 763–75.

3. *Iron Age,* July 9, 1874, rpt. from the *Advertiser.*

4. Kelly, "The Congressional Controversy over School Segregation," 539.

5. Quotations from Wyatt-Brown, "The Civil Rights Act of 1875," 765; Kelly, "The Congressional Controversy over School Segregation," 549, 553.

6. Kelly, "The Congressional Controversy over School Segregation," 553, 554, 558; Wyatt-Brown, "The Civil Rights Act of 1875," 769. The presumption was that there was no provision in the US Constitution that compelled a state to provide educational programs.

7. Kelly, "The Congressional Controversy over School Segregation," 562–63; Wyatt-Brown, "The Civil Rights Act of 1875," 773–75; and Camille Walsh, *Racial Taxation: Schools, Segregation, and Taxpayer Citizenship, 1869–1973* (Chapel Hill: University of North Carolina Press, 2018), 15–34.

8. Constitution of Alabama, 1875, Article XII, Section 1; McMillan, *Constitutional Development in Alabama,* 206.

9. This conclusion in consistent in a very general way with C. Vann Woodward's view that school segregation "appeared early and widely" during Reconstruction. He described this as the "most conspicuous" type of early segregation, and that it "took place promptly and prevailed continuously." Ten pages later, however, he also wrote: "More than a decade was to pass after Redemption before the first Jim Crow law was to appear upon the law books of a Southern state, and more than two decades before the older states of the seaboard were to adopt such laws," Apparently he did not see any conflict between the second conclusion and the extensive adoption

of segregationist public policies that had begun during the 1870s. Woodward, *The Strange Career of Jim Crow*, 24 and 34.

10. US Census, 1880, Manuscript Population Schedules, Jefferson County, E.D. 74; Birmingham, Board of Education, *Annual Report, 1887*, 39–42.

11. Bigelow, "Birmingham," 219–22; Birmingham, Board of Education, *Annual Report, 1887*, 39–42.

12. Bigelow, "Birmingham," 219–22; Birmingham, Board of Education, *Annual Report, 1887*, 39–42; Birmingham, Board of Aldermen, Minutes, B, 29 (December 20, 23, 1873), 41–43 (February 4, 1874), 69 (April 10, 1874), 93 (July 15, 1874), 152–53 (January 20, 1875); *Iron Age*, March 5, April 23, July 30, 1874.

13. Birmingham, Aldermen, Minutes, B, 29 (December 23, 1873), B, 41, 43, (February 4, 1874), B, 93 (July 15, 1874), B, 152–53 (January 20, 1875), B, 412–13 (October 4, 1876); Alabama, Department of Education, *Annual Report, 1876*, 22–35; *Iron Age*, July 16, 1874. In 1874–75 the school authorities had received some assistance from the philanthropic Peabody Educational Fund, but the bulk of the annual salary money came from regular city revenue. Birmingham, Board of Aldermen, Minutes, B, 43 (February 4, 1874), 70 (April 10, 1874), 107 (August 19, 1874), 111 (September 2, 1874), 113 (September 11, 1874), 119 (October 7, 1874), 151–52 (January 20, 1875), 208–10 (August 4, 1875), 222 (September 6, 1875), 263 (January 5, 1876), 293 (March 1, 1876), 404 (September 6, 1876); Birmingham, Board of Education, *Annual Report, 1887*, 39; Alabama, Department of Education, *Annual Report, 1875*, 52, 69, 110–11; *Iron Age*, July 30, 1874.

14. Alabama, Department of Education, *Annual Report, 1876*, 22–35; Birmingham, Board of Mayor and Aldermen, Minutes, B, 412–13 (October 4, 1876).

15. Alabama, Department of Education, *Annual Report, 1876*, 22–35; Birmingham, Board of Mayor and Aldermen, Minutes, B, 412–13 (October 4, 1876).

16. Birmingham, Board of Aldermen, Minutes, B, 401 (September 6, 1876); US Census, 1880, Manuscript Population Schedules, Jefferson County, Alabama, Enumeration District 74, Sheet 14; US Congress, *Labor and Capital* 4: 388–89.

17. Peter Kolchin, *First Freedom: The Responses of Alabama's Blacks to Emancipation and Reconstruction* (Westport, CT: Greenwood Press, 1972), 95.

18. Kolchin, *First Freedom*, 95; Alabama, *Constitution of 1875*, Article XII, Section 1; Birmingham, Board of Aldermen, Minutes, B, 401 (September 6, 1876).

19. Birmingham, Board of Aldermen, Minutes, B, 401 (September 6, 1876); US Census, 1880, Manuscript Population Schedules, Jefferson County, E.D. 74; *Birmingham City Directory, 1883*.

20. *Iron Age*, September 13, 1876.

21. Birmingham, Board of Aldermen, Minutes, B, 412–13 (October 4, 1876); Alabama, Department of Education, *Annual Report, 1878*, data on 1876–77 school year, xlvii–lvii.

22. Birmingham, Board of Aldermen, Minutes, B, 412–13 (October 4, 1876). US Congress, *Labor and Capital* 4: 388–89. Reports of later political meetings in Birmingham indicate that Jackson was assertive and at times confrontational. See the *Pilot*, April 5, 1884, and *Iron Age*, April 10, 1884.

23. Birmingham, Board of Mayor and Aldermen, Minutes, B, 412–13 (October 4, 1876). Alabama, Department of Education, *Annual Report, 1875*, 110–11, and *1876*, 22–35. The Peabody Education Fund required that schools had to raise from public revenues between three to four

times as much money as the fund provided. Earle H. West, "The Peabody Education Fund and Negro Education, 1867–1880," *Journal of Education Quarterly* 6 (Summer 1966): 3–21.

24. Assessment of Taxes on Real Estate and Personal Property in the County of Jefferson, for 1876, tax list available in Birmingham Public Library. See US Census, 1880, Manuscript Population Schedules, Jefferson County. The only tax paid by Birmingham Blacks was a state poll tax of $1.50 per adult male between ages twenty-one and forty-five, a tax instituted under Republican Reconstruction to support the state school fund. The revenue from the poll tax did not go into the city treasury; rather it was collected under the authority of the state and then was incorporated into the annual state school fund. Birmingham Black poll-tax payments did not amount to much. The poll tax was not a requirement for voting, and in the past two years it had not been collected rigorously, partly because of clerical errors that had been found in the state law. See Horace Mann Bond, *Negro Education in Alabama: A Study in Cotton and Steel* (New York, Atheneum, 1939, 1969), 148–49; Assessment of Taxes on Real and Personal Property in the County of Jefferson for 1874, 1875, 1876; and Birmingham, Department of Education, *Annual Report, 1887*, 39–42.

25. For the nation as a whole, historian Camille Walsh has described how "techniques of separate taxation structures" facilitated "segregation and inequality" and suggests that their origins were in the South in the nineteenth century. She observes: "The customary practice of racially labeling tax monies and diverting the bulk of tax funds overwhelmingly to all-white schools continued well into the twentieth century." Walsh, *Racial Taxation*, 33 and 175.

26. Alabama, Department of Education, *Annual Report, 1878*, xlvii–lvii; Birmingham, Board of Aldermen, Minutes, B, 431 (December 20, 1876), 453 (February 21, 1877), 648–49 (December 4, 1878); *Independent*, February 10, 24, 1877.

27. Alabama, Department of Education, *Annual Report, 1879*, 18–109; 1880, 19.

28. Alabama, Department of Education, *Annual Report, 1879*, 27, 30.

29. Alabama, Department of Education, *Annual Report, 1879*, 27, 30.

30. Birmingham, Minutes, C, 34–35 (July 13, 1880), 43–44 (August 25, 1880); Alabama, Department of Education, *Annual Report, 1880, 1881*; US Census, 1880, Manuscript Population Schedules, Jefferson County.

31. Fallin, *The African American Church in Birmingham*, 87–88.

32. Information about Hudson has been drawn from *Gazette*, June 13, August 15, 1885, January 15, 1887; Birmingham *Negro American*, October 9, 29, 1887; Birmingham *Truth*, September 17, 1903; *Iron Age*, May 25, 1882; US Census, 1900, Manuscript Population Schedules, Jefferson County, Alabama; Jefferson County, "Concise Form . . . Taxes Due, 1884."

33. Jefferson County, "Concise Form . . . Taxes Due, 1884." Dividing the state tax due for each taxpayer by the 1884 state tax rate of .0065 reveals the assessed valuation.

34. Harris, "Stability and Change," 382. On James Harper's political role, see chapter 8 of this book.

35. *Iron Age*, May 25, 1882; Birmingham, Minutes, C, 46 (September 1, 1880).

36. *Iron Age*, May 25, July 20, 1882; *Gazette*, May 27, 1882.

37. Wadsworth was a close associate of Henry F. DeBardeleben. Wadsworth was secretary-treasurer and manager of the Alice Furnace and trustee in charge of all of DeBardeleben's industrial interests in the Birmingham District. US Congress, *Labor and Capital* 4: 461–63; Armes, *The Story of Coal and Iron in Alabama*, 250, 287, 306; Birmingham, Minutes, C, 303–4 (September 5, 1882).

38. *Gazette*, October 14, 1882.

39. DuBose Report from New Orleans *Times Democrat*, rpt. in *Iron Age*, September 4, 1884; *Independent*, December 11, 1880; *Iron Age*, November 23, 30, December 7, 14, 1882.

40. *Iron Age*, November 23, 30, December 7, 14, 1882; December 4, 1884; November 25, December 2, 9, 1886. *News*, November 28, 1888. *Gazette*, November 10, 1888. US Congress, *Labor and Capital* 4: 389.

41. Elizabeth Mason Ware, "John Herbert Phillips, Educator," MA thesis, Birmingham-Southern College, 1937, 2–9.

42. Birmingham, Board of Education, *Annual Report, 1887*, 39–41, 45; David B. Tyack, *The One Best System: A History of American Urban Education* (Cambridge, MA: Harvard University Press, 1974), 5.

43. Harris, "Stability and Change," 382.

44. US Congress, *Labor and Capital* 4: 368; Birmingham Board of Education, *Annual Report, 1887*, 42–44.

45. Board of Education, Minutes 1: 50 (October 30, 1885); *Annual Report, 1887*, 29, 37.

46. Board of Education, *Annual Report, 1887*, 36–37; *Annual Report, 1907*, 87.

47. Board of Education, Minutes 1: 184 (November 5, 1889); "Report of the Committee on Public Health" in Minutes 1: 267, (December 1, 1891); *Annual Report, 1887*, 36; *Annual Report, 1891*, 7, 11–12, 39; *Annual Report, 1907*, 86–88, 93; *News*, January 23, March 28, 1889.

48. Board of Education, Minutes 1: 68–69 (October 12, 1886), 130 (n.d.), 184 (November 5, 1889), 253 (June 27, 1891), 254–55 (July 10, 1891); *Annual Report, 1887*, 37; *Annual Report, 1891*, 11–12, 39. *Iron Age*, November 11, 1886, November 2, 1887; *Age-Herald*, December 6, 1889; *Alabama Sentinel*, June 2, 1888.

49. Alabama, Department of Education, *Annual Report, 1881–1882*, 45–48.

50. Board of Education, *Annual Report, 1887*, 7, 29.

51. Board of Education, *Annual Report, 1891*, 7, 11, 12, 39.

52. In 1911 the southern secretary of the National Child Labor Committee, A. J. McKelway, reported that Phillips and other southern educators asserted that "the Negro school buildings compare as favorably with average Negro homes as the white school buildings do with white people's homes," and that, in fact, the African American schools were "generally the best looking buildings in the Negro sections of the city." See McKelway, "Conservation of Childhood," *Survey* 27: 1526 (January 6, 1912); See also Board of Education, Minutes 1: 131 (September 7, 1888); *Annual Report, 1902*, 19; *Annual Report, 1887*, 37; *Annual Report, 1891*, 70.

53. John Herbert Phillips, "School Economics," typescript, Birmingham Board of Education Research Department, n.d.

54. Board of Education, *Annual Report, 1891*, 44–45.

55. *News*, February 19, 23, 24, 26, March 12, 17, September 25, 1897; Harris, *Political Power in Birmingham*, 101–3; Harris, "Stability and Change," 382.

56. *News*, September 14, 1897.

57. Birmingham *State-Herald*, December 3, 1896.

58. Birmingham *Labor Advocate*, October 2, 16, 30, 1897; *News*, September 25, 28, October 11, 1897.

59. *Labor Advocate*, September 25, 1897; Paul B. Worthman, "Black Workers and Labor Unions in Birmingham, Alabama, 1897–1904," *Labor History* 10 (Summer 1969): 375–80.

60. *Labor Advocate,* September 25, 1897.
61. Birmingham, Board of Education, *Annual Report, 1899,* 30.

5. URBAN RESIDENTIAL SEGREGATION

An early version of this chapter, which included an outline of what became the central argument of this book, was presented as Carl W. Harris, "The Social Core of Jim Crow," at the annual meeting of the Southern Historical Society, Atlanta, on November 4, 2005.

1. In antebellum southern cities, slaves had lived in walled compounds behind the residences of their masters, and such compounds had not been segregated in one part of town, but instead spread throughout. See Richard Wade, *Slavery in the Cities: The South 1820–1860* (New York: Oxford University Press, 1964), 61.

2. See John Kellogg, "Negro Urban Clusters in the Postbellum South," *Geographical Review* 67 (1977): 310–21; and Rabinowitz, *Race Relations in the Urban South,* 18–30, 97–100. Regarding the heavy migration of Blacks into southern cities, Kellogg found that, in southern cities with more than 4,000 people in 1870, the black population had increased by an average of 80 percent over 1860 levels, whereas the white population had increased by only 13 percent. Rabinowitz showed that between 1860 and 1870 the Black percentage of population in Nashville had increased from 23 percent to 38 percent, in Atlanta from 20 percent to 46 percent, and in Richmond from 38 percent to 45 percent. See Rabinowitz, *Race Relations in the Urban South,* 19.

3. See Woodward, *The Strange Career of Jim Crow* (2nd rev. ed., New York: Oxford University Press, 1966), 13–15, 32, and 100. When Woodward first published this book in 1955 he relied entirely on anecdotal evidence, which he did not analyze. Woodward, *The Strange Career of Jim Crow* (New York: Oxford University Press, 1955); 24–25, 86. In 1966, he invoked antebellum evidence in Wade, *Slavery in the Cities,* to support the postbellum argument that the urban South was very slow to segregate housing.

4. After the turn of the century, however, southern cities began to experiment with racial zoning. See Randolph Hohle, *Racism in the Neoliberal Era: A Meta History of Elite White Power* (New York: Routledge, 2018), 141–43. Hohle's characterization of residential patterns in the late nineteenth century resembles Woodward's. Hohle writes that a "checkerboard pattern captures how blacks and whites lived side by side in southern urban areas" (141).

5. *Birmingham City Directory, 1883.*
6. US Congress, *Labor and Capital* 4: 286.
7. Map 2 contains the symbol "•" for every black household and the symbol "×" for every white household for which the *Birmingham City Directory, 1883,* provided a definite street address. The symbols indicate approximate rather than precise household locations, in part because often the addresses in the city directory were approximate. As of 1883 only the downtown business district had a system of street numbers. In the residential areas a typical address was only approximate, following, for example, the form "res ss 6th alley, bet 17th and 18th sts" (*Birmingham City Directory, 1883:* 197). Some residents, Black and white, were listed without street addresses. They could not be included in map 2, but nothing indicates that their absence distorted the picture of the city's overall residential configuration. The plotting of the household addresses was informed by contin-

uous consultation with Wellge's *Panoramic Map of Birmingham, Alabama, 1885.* The plotting of households was informed also by consultation with a set of maps published in 1885 and 1888 by the Sanborn Map and Publishing Company. Across large portions of the blocks east of Welch's church the Sanborn mapmakers typically wrote "Negro dwellings," "Negro shanties," or "Negro Quarters." Along many alleys they drew small structures that they likewise labeled "Negro shanties."

8. Woodward, *The Strange Career of Jim Crow* (1966), 14–15, 32, 42–43.

9. *Birmingham City Directory, 1883.*

10. Harris, *Political Power in Birmingham,* 155, 180. Birmingham, *Annual Reports of the Officers of the City Government, 1889,* "Report of the City Engineer," 72–83; "Report of the Street Commissioner," 97–102.

11. Streetlight locations tabulated from Birmingham, Minutes of the Mayor and Board of Aldermen.

12. Birmingham maps, Sanborn Map and Publishing Co., 1885, 1888, 1891.

13. *Age-Herald,* March 23, 1889.

14. Birmingham *City Directory, 1883,* "White Department" and "Colored Department." See the testimony of furnace owner James W. Sloss in US Congress, *Labor and Capital* 4: 286–87. See also Paige McWilliams, Introduction, *We've Come This Far By Faith: Black Migration to Birmingham, 1900–1940,* Oral History Project, University of Alabama at Birmingham (Birmingham: Sloss Furnaces National Historic Landmark, 1988), 2–3; Sloss Furnaces National Historic Landmark, *Like It Ain't Never Passed: Remembering Life in Sloss Quarters, 1930s–1950s* (Birmingham: Sloss Furnaces National Historic Landmark, 1985). See also John A. Fitch, "The Human Side of Large Outputs: Steel and Steel Workers in Six American States: IV, Birmingham District: Labor Conservation," in *Survey,* January 6, 1912: 1537–39; US Congress, *Labor and Capital* 4: 286.

15. W. David Lewis, *Sloss Furnaces and the Rise of the Birmingham District: An Industrial Epic* (Tuscaloosa: University of Alabama Press, 1994), 307, 423; Fitch, "The Human Side of Large Outputs," 1532, 1537–39; US Congress, *Labor and Capital* 4: 286; *Birmingham City Directory, 1883.*

16. Assessment of Taxes on Real Estate and Personal Property in the County of Jefferson for 1875, Precincts 1–21; for 1876, Precincts 1–22; for 1877, Precincts 1–24; Tax Assessment Block Books, 1893, Birmingham County Courthouse; Lewis, *Sloss Furnaces and the Rise of the Birmingham District,* 307.

17. In 1883 among Black male heads of households with alley addresses, 47 percent listed their occupation as simply "laborer," 7 percent as skilled laborer, and 27 percent as having no specific occupation. Among the alley dwellers who gave occupations, less than one-fifth listed a specific domestic occupation. See *Birmingham City Directory, 1883,* "Colored Department."

18. *Birmingham City Directory, 1883,* "Colored Department."

19. Rabinowitz, *Race Relations in the Urban South,* 105–12. The face block was a unit that Karl E. Taeuber and Alma F. Taeuber employed in their pathbreaking monograph, *Negroes in Cities: Residential Segregation and Neighborhood Change* (Chicago: Aldine Publishing Co., 1965). The linear "face block" is a relatively small unit, in contrast to such larger units as wards or census tracts, and using face blocks tends to increase the resulting quantitative indication of the degree of segregation. See Douglas S. Massey and Nancy A. Denton, *American Apartheid: Segregation and the Making of the Underclass* (Cambridge, MA: Harvard University Press, 1993), 62–67.

20. "Street Directory" in *Birmingham City Directory, 1883:* 17–85. In 1978 historian Howard Rabinowitz pioneered the use of face-block maps for southern cities in *Race Relations in the Urban South*. Rabinowitz found that "the great majority of linear blocks" in Atlanta and Richmond "were either all-white or all-black," or at least 90 percent one way or the other, and he concluded that by 1891 "segregation was firmly established" (105–12).

21. *Birmingham City Directory, 1891,* including the "Street Directory" on 17–85. The 465-page alphabetical list of Black and white residents and their addresses included the abbreviation "al" to indicate alley locations. A systematic reading of every name and address permitted identification of the alley dwellers of Birmingham and rectified their exclusion from the "Street Directory." With some variations, the *Atlanta City Directory, 1891,* had limitations and distortions similar to those in the 1891 Birmingham directory. As a result, Rabinowitz's map of face-block segregation presented an exaggerated image of separation. Atlanta's white residential areas did not have as many alleys as did those in Birmingham, but Rabinowitz's map, which did not systematically indicate alleys, underrepresented Black alley dwellers, particularly in Black residential clusters where developers had packed many cabins into alleys. *Atlanta City Directory, 1891;* Hughes Litho. Co., *Bird's eye view of Atlanta, Fulton Co., State capital, Georgia,* drawn by Aug. Koch (n.p.: Saunders and Kline, ca. 1892), www.loc.gov/resource/g3924a.pm001220/?r=-0.11,-0.06,1.253,0.729,0. The Atlanta street grid had not been laid out as systematically as the Birmingham grid, and some white residential areas did not contain many alleys and did not develop the back-alley pattern of Black housing prominent in Birmingham. The 1891 Atlanta street directory did list each alley by name and indicate its location, but, with two small exceptions, it did not list the occupants of the alleys.

22. Tabulated from *Birmingham City Directory, 1891,* alphabetical section. The business-and-government district contained the blocks inside a boundary line that started at the intersection of First Avenue and Eighteenth Street and that ran along Eighteenth Street, Fourth Avenue, Twenty-Second Street, Second Avenue, Twenty-Third Street down to its intersection with First Avenue, and then west along First Avenue back to Eighteenth Street. The prime residential district did not include any of the blocks inside the business-and-government district, but it did surround them, and spread to embrace all remaining blocks inside First Avenue, Eighth Avenue, Sixteenth Street, and Twenty-Fourth Street, except one block of the eastern Black residential cluster that lay west of Twenty-Fourth Street.

23. Using a chi-square test applied to actual and "expected" frequencies with which people of each race lived in each type of location, the author found a high statistical relationship between race and space in the Birmingham data.

24. Birmingham Map, Sanborn Map and Publishing Co., 1891.

25. Birmingham Map, Sanborn Map and Publishing Co., 1891.

26. Woodward, *The Strange Career of Jim Crow* (1966), 14–15, 32, 42–43.

27. *Birmingham City Directory, 1891.*

28. Wade, *Slavery in the Cities,* 61.

29. David M. Katzman, *Seven Days a Week: Women and Domestic Service in Industrializing America* (New York: Oxford University Press, 1978), 200–201.

30. *Age-Herald,* August 9, 1916.

31. *Birmingham City Directory, 1883, 1884, 1891.*

32. *Birmingham City Directory, 1891.*

33. Birmingham, *Annual Reports of the Officers of the City Government, 1889, 1890, 1891, 1897, 1898, 1899, 1901,* with special attention to the reports of the city engineer.

34. Report of City Engineer Julian Kendrick, in Birmingham, *Annual Reports of the Officers of the City Government, 1898,* 41–50.

35. Birmingham, *Annual Reports, 1889–91, 1897–1901.*

36. Harris, *Political Power in Birmingham,* 104–6.

37. After 1885, 33 percent of the costs could be assessed directly to adjacent property owners; after 1891, 50 percent; and after 1895, 100 percent. Harris, *Political Power in Birmingham,* 176–77.

38. Harris, *Political Power in Birmingham,* 176–77. For the best history of the operation of special-assessment taxation in a nineteenth-century American city, see Robin L. Einhorn, *Property Rules: Political Economy in Chicago, 1833–1872* (Chicago: University of Chicago Press, 2001).

39. Harris, *Political Power in Birmingham,* 176–77.

40. Harris, *Political Power in Birmingham,* 176–80.

41. *Age-Herald,* December 22, 1901.

6. THE ECONOMIC REALM: WORK AND PROPERTY

1. US Congress, *Labor and Capital* 4: 403–4.

2. US Congress, *Labor and Capital* 4: 374–75, 361.

3. Gavin Wright, *Old South, New South: Revolutions in the Southern Economy Since the Civil War* (New York: Basic Books, 1986), 158 and 177 on segregation.

4. Jefferson County, "Concise Form . . . Taxes Due," 1884.

5. US Congress, *Labor and Capital* 4: 403–4.

6. Jefferson County, "Concise Form . . . Taxes Due," 1884.

7. US Congress, *Labor and Capital* 4: 403–4; Wright, *Old South, New South,* 177–95.

8. Data from the *Birmingham City Directory* and from the US manuscript census for Birmingham were first analyzed by Worthman in "Working Class Mobility in Birmingham"; see esp. 176–79, tables 1 and 2.

9. Worthman, "Working Class Mobility in Birmingham," 176–79.

10. On the importance of prior on-the-job experience, see Wright, *Old South, New South,* 177–95.

11. Worthman, "Working Class Mobility in Birmingham," 178–79, table 2.

12. *Pilot,* August 18, September 8, 1883; *Gazette,* March 4, 1882; US Congress, *Labor and Capital* 4: 380–83.

13. US Congress, *Labor and Capital* 4: 399–404, 388–92; *Birmingham City Directory, 1883;* Worthman, "Working Class Mobility in Birmingham," 178.

14. Worthman, "Working Class Mobility in Birmingham," 176–79.

15. *Birmingham City Directory, 1883:* 259; *Gazette,* February 3, 1883, April 28, August 9, 1884, June 13, 1885, May 1, 1886; *Pilot,* August 18, 1883, January 12, February 2, 9, 1884; Worthman, "Working Class Mobility in Birmingham," 176–79.

16. *Birmingham City Directory, 1884–85, 1886, 1887;* Worthman, "Working Class Mobility in Birmingham," 176–79.

17. Worthman, "Working Class Mobility in Birmingham," 178–79, table 2. US Census, *Thirteenth Census, 1910*, vol. 4: *Population*, 538–39; *Fourteenth Census, 1920*, vol. 4: *Population*, 1060–62; *Fifteenth Census, 1930, Occupation Statistics*, 121–23.

18. US Congress, *Labor and Capital* 4: 284–85, 288, 367; Worthman, "Working Class Mobility in Birmingham," 175–80, 192.

19. US Congress, *Labor and Capital* 4: 284–85, 288.

20. Worthman, "Working Class Mobility in Birmingham," 175–80, 192; US Congress, *Labor and Capital* 4: 367.

21. Worthman, "Working Class Mobility in Birmingham," 176, 178, 192.

22. US Congress, *Labor and Capital* 4: 284–85, 366–67, 406–7, 440–43; *Gazette*, April 29, July 8, 1882; *Iron Age*, July 17, 1884; *Birmingham City Directory, 1883*.

23. US Congress, *Labor and Capital* 4: 284–85, 366–67, 406–7, 410, 430, 435, 437–42.

24. US Congress, *Labor and Capital* 4: 284–85, 366–67, 406–7, 410, 430, 435, 437–42.

25. *Iron Age*, October 4, 25, December 20, 1883.

26. US Congress, *Labor and Capital* 4: 427–42; *Iron Age*, July 17, 1884.

27. For suggestions of the influence of slavery models and experience on the use of convict labor in Birmingham coal mines, see W. David Lewis, "The Emergence of Birmingham as a Case Study of Continuity Between the Antebellum Planter Class and Industrialization in the "New South," *Agricultural History* 68 (Spring 1994): 72, 75–76; and Lewis, *Sloss Furnaces and the Rise of the Birmingham District*, 18–19, 22–23, 30–31, 33–34, 82–86, 89–91, 192, 214, 243, 475–77, 479, 481–82, and 488. For analysis of the economic and social strategies of the employers of convict labor, see Alex Lichtenstein, *Twice the Work of Free Labor: The Political Economy of Convict Labor in the New South* (London: Verso, 1996). Lichtenstein draws primarily on Georgia sources but presents a good discussion of the employers of convict laborers in the Birmingham area during the 1880s and 1890s (91–95).

28. Mary Ellen Curtin, *Black Prisoners and Their World, Alabama, 1865–1900* (Charlottesville: University of Virginia, 2000), 70. Curtin finds that the conditions at New Castle were especially brutal for county prisoners (95–96, 148ff.). For an excellent discussion of female prisoners in Alabama, see Curtin, *Black Prisoners*, 113–39. Douglas A. Blackmon relies heavily on Curtin's research but provides additional details on convict leasing in Alabama and other states during the 1880s and 1890s. See Blackmon's *Slavery by Another Name: The Re-Enslavement of Black Americans from the Civil War to World War II* (2008; New York: Anchor Books, 2009), 58–113. See, also, Michelle Alexander, *The New Jim Crow: Mass Incarceration in the Age of Colorblindness* (New York: New Press, 2020), 38–40. For analysis of convict leasing in Georgia with special attention to the intersection of issues of race, gender, and class, see Sarah Haley, *No Mercy Here: Gender, Punishment, and the Making of Jim Crow Modernity* (Chapel Hill: University of North Carolina Press, 2016).

29. Reports by Dr. Jerome Cochrane, state health officer, and Dr. J. B. Gaston, president of the Alabama Board of Health, regarding the New Castle Prison near Pratt Mines, as seen at an inspection, March 10, 1882. Published in *Iron Age*, November 23, 1882.

30. Curtin, *Black Prisoners*, 120–22.

31. *Pilot*, August 25, 1883.

32. US Congress, *Labor and Capital* 4: 427–42; *Iron Age*, July 17, 1884. Some unusually strong and skilled convicts did get a wage of 40 cents per ton for mining more coal than required by their

quota. On the leasing and subleasing of convicts by the Pratt Mines, see Curtin, *Black Prisoners*, 73–78, 86–88. On the growth of the convict leasing system in the mines during the 1880s and 1890s, see Curtin, *Black Prisoners*, 130–31, 197–98, 206–7; and Alex Lichtenstein, *Twice the Work of Free Labor*, 91–93.

33. US Congress, *Labor and Capital* 4: 427–42; *Iron Age*, July 17, 1884. On the training of black miners, see Curtin, *Black Prisoners*, 73–74.

34. US Congress, *Labor and Capital* 4: 284–85, 300, 366–67, 406–7, 436–43; US Census, *Thirteenth Census, 1910*, vol. 4: *Population*, 538–39.

35. Henry M. McKiven Jr., *Iron and Steel: Class, Race, and Community in Birmingham, Alabama, 1875–1920* (Chapel Hill: University of North Carolina Press, 1995).

36. Daniel Letwin, "Interracial Unionism, Gender, and 'Social Equality' in the Alabama Coalfields, 1878–1908," *Journal of Southern History* 61 (August 1995): 522; Letwin, *The Challenge of Interracial Unionism*, 131.

37. Worthman, "Black Workers and Labor Unions," 375–407.

38. Letwin, *The Challenge of Interracial Unionism*, 131.

39. Letwin, "Interracial Unionism, Gender, and Social Equality," 522, 538, 542, 548–49, and Letwin, *The Challenge of Interracial Unionism*, 80–83. In discussing the racism of white workers through the prism of social psychology, I have not followed the lead of David Roediger, a pioneer in "whiteness" studies. He applied the Freudian concept of projection to suggest that white industrial workers projected their anxieties about the new industrial discipline onto Blacks, thereby generating a negative Black stereotype and fostering racism. The notion of "projection" had been given its original formulation in Theodor Adorno's *Authoritarian Personality*, a postwar product of the Frankfurt School of Social Research. The Frankfurt School conducted intensive individual-level analysis of the "psychodynamics" of conflict inside particularly intolerant and maladjusted personalities, and it suggested that such personalities projected unwanted traits onto minorities. Roediger, however, applied the individual-level concept of projection to an entire social group (northern white workers) and did not incorporate the Frankfurt School's most widely accepted findings—that many personality types exist, that different personality types vary enormously in the ways they respond to societal-level anxieties and to racist ideologies, and that irrational projection is not a ubiquitous and universal mechanism, but rather that projection is characteristic of a small fraction of extremely intolerant personality types, such as the authoritarian personality. See David R. Roediger, *The Wages of Whiteness: Race and the Making of the American Working Class* (rev. ed., New York: Verso, 2007); Theodor W. Adorno et al., *The Authoritarian Personality* (New York: Harper, 1950). Although the individual-level psychodynamic approach proved not to be the most productive path forward in rigorous social psychology, modern culture has assimilated popularized versions of projection.

40. For a close study of the white and Black mine workers, their organization, their employers, and their communities from the 1908 strike through World War I and another major strike in 1920, see Brian Kelly, *Race, Class, and Power in the Alabama Coalfields, 1908–1921* (Urbana: University of Illinois Press, 2001). In this history of that strike and its aftermath, Kelly emphasizes the powerful role of employers in exacerbating race conflict in the coal mines of Birmingham.

41. *Labor Advocate*, April 18, 1906.

42. *Birmingham City Directory, 1883*; US Congress, *Labor and Capital* 4: 388; *Pilot*, June 7, 1884.

43. US Congress, *Labor and Capital* 4: 361, 374–75, 400.

44. US Congress, *Labor and Capital* 4: 133–34; see also the testimony of Henry J. Evans, 171–72.

45. McKiven, *Iron and Steel*, 23–53; Worthman, "Working Class Mobility in Birmingham," 176–78.

46. Edna Bonacich, "A Theory of Ethnic Antagonism: The Split Labor Market," *American Sociological Review* 37 (October 1972): 547–59. For discussions of how this theory helps explain labor conditions in the New South, see George Fredrickson, *White Supremacy: A Comparative Study in American and South African History* (New York: Oxford University Press, 1981), 212–16, and Wright, *Old South, New South*, 177–95.

47. Worthman, "Working Class Mobility in Birmingham," 194–95, tables 9 and 10. The persistence percentages are from Worthman's pooled 1880 and 1890 samples. Even the small mobility percentages reported by Worthman exaggerated the actual degree of upward occupational movement, since most Blacks and whites who came to Birmingham, like the working population in most nineteenth-century American industrial communities, were highly transient, staying only a few weeks or months or years and then moving *away* rather than moving *up*. Only a minority—about 43 percent of Blacks and 34 percent of whites—stayed as long as ten years. Also see Wright, *Old South, New South*, 177–95.

48. Wright, *Old South, New South*, 158, 177–97. C. Vann Woodward, in *The Strange Career of Jim Crow*, included one paragraph on labor segregation before the adoption of legislation by South Carolina in 1915 that prescribed "the segregation of employees and their working conditions." In two brief sentences he acknowledged the themes of urban struggle between Black and white laborers, of job segmentation, of exclusion of Blacks from skilled jobs, and of subordination of Black labor. "In most instances," he noted correctly, "segregation in employment was established without the aid of statute." Woodward was very well aware of the struggles of black males who were laborers. Four years earlier, in *Origins of the New South*, he identified "white labor's determination to draw a color line of its own," an economic color line designed "to relegate the Negro to the less desirable unskilled jobs, and to exclude the Negro entirely from some industries." He counted "fifty strikes against the employment of Negro labor in the period from 1882 to 1900" as evidence of this determination. Woodward, *The Strange Career of Jim Crow*, 98; Woodward, *Origins of the New South, 1877–1913* (Baton Rouge: Louisiana State University Press, 1951), 222.

49. US Congress, *Labor and Capital* 4: 282–89.

50. The 1883 *City Directory* listed 350 black women in the explicit menial service occupations of servant, cook, domestic, or washerwoman, but its enumeration excluded Black married women and young Black single women whom the *directory* regarded as part of the households of their husbands or fathers. The same patterns prevailed in other cities of the New South. For an excellent description of the household work of African American women in the late-nineteenth century, see Tera W. Hunter, *To 'Joy My Freedom: Southern Black Women's Lives and Labors after the Civil War* (Cambridge, MA: Harvard University Press, 1997), 50–65.

51. US Congress, *Labor and Capital* 4: 105.

52. There is a view that whites allowed Black servant women to participate in the private home life of white families because there the women servants interacted only with white women, not with white men. See Ayers, *The Promise of the New South*, 140. Ayers's interpretation fits neatly with his larger generalization that "the history of segregation shows a clear connection to

gender; the more closely linked to sexuality, the more likely was a place to be segregated." But his interpretation seems to overlook evidence that in white homes Black women all too often encountered sexually aggressive white men.

53. On Margaret Ketcham Ward, see Douglas Southall Freeman, *The South to Posterity: An Introduction to the Writings of Confederate History* (New York: Charles Scribner's Sons, 1939), 120–23.

54. US Congress, *Labor and Capital* 4: 318.

55. US Congress, *Labor and Capital* 4: 343.

56. US Congress, *Labor and Capital* 4: 345.

57. US Congress, *Labor and Capital* 4: 343.

58. US Congress, *Labor and Capital* 4: 346.

59. US Congress, *Labor and Capital* 4: 343–46.

60. *Birmingham City Directory, 1883.*

61. *Birmingham City Directory, 1883.*

62. US Census, 1880, Manuscript Schedules, Jefferson County, p. 501C; US Congress, *Labor and Capital* 4: 402–5; *Birmingham City Directory, 1883:* 260–61; *Pilot,* August 25, September 15, October 6, 27, 1883, January 12, March 29, 1884; *Gazette,* April 28, 1883.

63. *Birmingham City Directory, 1883; Pilot,* August 18, October 6, 27, 1883, January 12, February 2, 1884.

64. *Pilot,* August 18–November 1, 1883; January 12, 26, and February 2, 9, 1884; *Birmingham City Directory, 1883:* 259; and Worthman, "Working Class Mobility in Birmingham," 176–78.

65. *Gazette,* February 27, March 13, 1887; *Birmingham City Directory, 1887.*

7. THE ECONOMIC REALM: SOCIAL SPACE

1. C. Vann Woodward defined segregation as "physical distance, not social distance—physical separation of people for reasons of race." Chapter 5 and this chapter discuss types of racial segregation that might seem to fit Woodward's definition because of their spatial dimension. But these chapters stress that these types of segregation had a lot to do with social distance in that they involved the efforts of whites to establish and defend social distance between whites and Blacks. Woodward, *The Strange Career of Jim Crow,* xi.

2. US Congress, *Labor and Capital* 4: 367, 269, 272.

3. US Congress, *Labor and Capital* 4: 165.

4. *Pilot,* August 18, 1883–January 19, 1884.

5. *Pilot,* August 18, 1883–January 19, 1884.

6. *Pilot,* August 18, 1883–January 19, 1884.

7. *Negro American,* November 19, 1887.

8. Birmingham *City Directory,* 1883.

9. Exceptions occurred. One single Black woman, a teacher, received the title "Miss," but a second Black woman teacher did not. Three married Black women received the title "Mrs.," for no apparent reason. Women who lived in households headed by men were not separately listed in the directory. Almost all of the listed women were widows, single adult boarders, owners of businesses, or keepers of boardinghouses. None were listed as keeping house. Altogether women comprised only one-eighth of the listed individuals.

10. Birmingham *City Directory,* 1883; *Pilot,* August 18, 1883.

11. Perhaps in some cases women who were part of a non-English-speaking culture had not been aware that they should include a title when they responded to the directory canvasser, but not all of the exceptions fit that explanation.

12. Birmingham *City Directory,* 1883. Lurid newspaper accounts confirmed the occupations of these women and of the madams. See *Iron Age,* March 8, 1883; June 5, October 16, December 25, 1884.

13. Woodward heavily emphasized the experimental and sometimes surprisingly tolerant racial practices on railroad facilities. See *The Strange Career of Jim Crow,* 23–28, 38–40, and 97.

14. Ayers, *The Promise of the New South,* 137–46; Blair L. M. Kelley, *Right to Ride: Streetcar Boycotts and African American Citizenship in the Era of Plessy v. Ferguson* (Chapel Hill: University of North Carolina Press, 2010), 33–49.

15. Otto H. Olsen, ed., *The Thin Disguise: Turning Point in Negro History.* Plessy v. Ferguson: *A Documentary Presentation (1864–1896)* (New York: Humanities Press for A.I.M.S. 1967), 52–121; Ayers, *The Promise of the New South,* 139–40.

16. US Congress, *Labor and Capital* 4: 456–58.

17. *Pilot,* November 3, 1883. For an excellent summary of Harlan's dissenting opinion, see Steve Luxenberg, *Separate: The Story of* PLESSY V. FERGUSON, *and America's Journal from Slavery to Segregation"* (New York: W. W. Norton, 2019), 351–55.

18. US Congress, *Labor and Capital* 4: 457.

19. US Congress, *Labor and Capital* 4: 457, 382; see also *Pilot,* May 24, 31, June 21, 1884.

20. Kelley, *Right to Ride,* 43–44.

21. US Congress, *Labor and Capital* 4: 361–472, *Iron Age,* November 15, 1883.

22. On the 1891 enactment, including the support of it by Populists, see Sheldon Hackney, *Populism to Progressivism in Alabama* (Princeton, NJ: Princeton University Press, 1969), 43–47.

23. Woodward, *The Strange Career of Jim Crow,* 23–28, 38–40, 97.

24. Michael Perman, *Struggle for Mastery: Disfranchisement in the South, 1888–1908* (Chapel Hill: University of North Carolina Press, 2001), 245–48 and 256–58.

8. THE POLITICAL REALM, 1871–1888: ORGANIZING AND VOTING

1. The best account of this history of disfranchisement in the South is J. Morgan Kousser, *Colorblind Injustice: Minority Voting Rights and the Undoing of the Second Reconstruction* (Chapel Hill: University of North Carolina Press, 1999), esp. 12–68. Kousser argues that instrumental partisan strategies were among the most important drivers of nineteenth-century discrimination. The difference between his argument and the one advanced by this book, which places greater weight on socio-emotional factors, is a matter of emphasis.

2. Michael W. Fitzgerald, *Reconstruction in Alabama: From Civil War to Redemption in the Cotton South* (Baton Rouge: Louisiana State University Press, 2017), 334. In contrast with Fitzgerald, C. Vann Woodward concluded that during Reconstruction "As a rule . . . Negroes were not aggressive in pressing their rights," and after Reconstruction "the Negro became confused and politically apathetic." Woodward, *The Strange Career of Jim Crow,* 28 and 59.

3. US Census, 1880, Manuscript Schedules, Jefferson County, Enumeration District 72, Sheet 17; *Iron Age,* December 6, 1876, August 15, 1877; Jefferson County, Tax Assessment List, 1874.

4. *Iron Age*, December 6, 1876, August 7, 15, 1877.

5. *Independent*, November 18, 25, December 2, 9, 1876; *Iron Age*, November 1, 5, 22, December 6, 1876.

6. *Iron Age*, July 2, December 10, 17, 1874, September 9, 23, October 14, 1875; Armes, *The Story of Coal and Iron in Alabama*, 227–28, 253–54; Henry M. Caldwell, *History of the Elyton Land Company and Birmingham, Ala.* (Birmingham, 1892), 8–12.

7. *Iron Age*, December 10, 17, 1874, December 6, 1876; *Independent*, December 2, 1876.

8. *Iron Age*, December 10, 17, 1874.

9. *Iron Age*, December 10, 17, 1874, January 7, October 14, 1875.

10. *Iron Age*, November 15, 1876; *Independent*, November 18, 1876.

11. *Iron Age*, December 10, 17, 1874, February 3, 10, 24, December 6, 1876, March 28, October 24, 1877; *Independent* December 2, 1876.

12. *Independent*, December 9, 1876, November 30, 1878; *Iron Age*, December 6, 1876, August 7, 15, 1877.

13. *Iron Age*, December 6, 1876.

14. *Iron Age*, December 6, 1876; *Independent*, December 9, 1876; November 30, 1878.

15. *Iron Age*, February 3, 10, 24, March 23, November 15, 22, December 6, 1876; and March 28, August 15, October 24, December 12, 1877.

16. *Iron Age*, December 6, 1876, March 28, October 17, 1877; *Independent*, March 24, May 5, 1877; Birmingham, Board of Aldermen, Minutes, B, 441, 442, 464, 527 (1877); Armes, *The Story of Coal and Iron in Alabama*, 298–99; Caldwell, *History of the Elyton Land Company*, 12.

17. *Independent*, July 7, August 11, 18, 1877; *Iron Age*, July 7, 18, August 8, 1877.

18. *Independent*, July 7, August 11, 18, and 25, 1877, September 1, 1877; *Iron Age*, July 7, 18, August 8, 1877; DuBose, *Jefferson County and Birmingham*, 204–5.

19. *Independent*, August 18, 25, September 1, 1877.

20. *Iron Age*, July 3, 1878; *Independent*, August 11, 1877, September 1, 1877; Kenneth S. Greenberg, *Masters and Statesmen: The Political Culture of American Slavery* (Baltimore: Johns Hopkins University Press, 1988), 23–41.

21. US Census, 1880, Manuscript Schedules, Jefferson County, Alabama.

22. *Independent*, October 20, November 10, 17, 1877; *Iron Age*, October 24, November 7, 21, 1877.

23. *Independent*, December 2, 1876, August 18, November 10, 1877.

24. *Iron Age*, November 7 and 21, 1877; *Independent*, November 10 and 17, 1877.

25. *Iron Age*, December 6, 1876, November 7, 1877; Jefferson County Tax Assessment List, 1877; Armes, *The Story of Coal and Iron in Alabama*, 250–73; US Congress, *Labor and Capital* 4: 278; US Census, 1880, Manuscript Schedules, Jefferson County; Birmingham *City Directory, 1883*. To attribute two-thirds of local taxable property to the ninety-two signers, editor Roberts had taken the reasonable step of including valuable real estate and coal and iron properties, like the Sloss Furnace, that technically lay a few feet outside the actual city limits but that were crucial to the city's economic aspirations. *Inside* the city limits the ninety-two actually owned two-fifths of the real estate.

26. *Independent*, January 4, 1879.

27. *Independent*, December 22, 1877; *A New English Dictionary on Historical Principles* (Oxford, UK: Clarendon Press, 1988), vol. 5, pt. 2: 186. In 1898, Senator Furnifold Simmons (Democrat

from North Carolina), who served in the Senate from 1901 to 1931, also used the "incubus" metaphor. See Gilmore, *Gender and Jim Crow,* 85 and 94.

28. *Independent,* December 22, 1877.

29. *Independent,* August 18, 1877, November 2, 9, 1878; *Iron Age* October 30, 1878; DuBose, *Jefferson County and Birmingham,* 278, 290, 296–99, 534–35.

30. *Iron Age,* November 7, 1877, December 12, 1877, January 9, November 13, 20, 1878, November 30, 1882; J. P. Ross, "Notes on Birmingham Public Utilities," typescript, Birmingham Public Library, 1932, 1–9; DuBose, *Jefferson County and Birmingham,* 278, 290, 296–99, 534–35; *Birmingham City Directory, 1887; Independent,* August 11, 18. November 10, December 22, 1877, November 9, 23, 1878, February 1, 1879; *Advertiser,* January 26, 1879.

31. *Independent,* November 9, 1878.

32. *Iron Age,* December 12, 1877, November 13, 20, 1878, November 30, 1882; *Independent,* December 15, 1877, November 23, 1878, January 4, 25, February 8, 1879, November 27, December 11, 1880; DuBose, *Jefferson County and Birmingham,* 534; *Weekly Advertiser,* December 10, 1878.

33. *Independent,* November 27, December 4, 11, 1880. The seemingly neutral provision requiring "at large" election of aldermen was the first legally imposed restriction by the city of Birmingham on the effectiveness of the votes of African Americans. Such restrictions continued through the 1870s and 1880s but were largely ignored by C. Vann Woodward in his history of Jim Crow disfranchisement. Woodward discounted what he called "cursory histories" which found "that Negro disfranchisement followed quickly if not immediately upon the overthrow of Reconstruction." See *The Strange Career of Jim Crow,* 53–54.

34. *Independent,* October 19, 1878, December 4, 1880.

35. *Independent,* December 11, 1880.

36. US Census, 1880, Manuscript Population Schedules, Jefferson County, Alabama; Birmingham *City Directory,* 1883; *Negro American,* October 9, 1886; Jefferson County, "Concise Form . . . Taxes Due, 1884."

37. US Census, 1880, Manuscript Population Schedules, Jefferson County, Alabama; Birmingham *Pilot,* October 27, 1883; *Gazette,* January 29, 1887; US Congress, *Labor and Capital* 4: 402–5.

38. US Congress, *Labor and Capital* 4: 405.

39. *Independent,* November 27, December 4, 11, 1880.

40. *Independent,* January 4, 1879; *Advertiser,* January 26, 1879; *True Issue,* July 10, 1880.

41. *Independent,* December 11, 1880.

42. US Congress, *Labor and Capital* 4: 371.

43. *Iron Age,* November 23, 1882.

44. US Census, 1880, Manuscript Population Schedules, Jefferson County; US Congress, *Labor and Capital* 4: 369–70; *Iron Age,* November 25, December 2, 9, 1886, November 27, December 4, 1884.

45. Birmingham, Board of Education, *Annual Report,* 1887: 136; B. H. Hudson statement in the *Pilot,* March 22, 1884; Birmingham, Board of Education, *Annual Reports 1884, 1887;* Board of Education, "Minutes" 1: 38–39 (July 27, 1885), 130–31, and John H. Phillips, "Brief Report of the Present Condition of the Public Schools of the City," in "Minutes" 1: 184–85 (November 6, 1889). The ratios are based upon the several time series of black/white school ratios in Harris, "Stability and Change," 375–416.

46. *Pilot,* August 18, 25, September 1, 1883, February 23, April 5, June 21, 1884; *Gazette,* March 13, June 5, November 13, 1886, February 5, 1887, January 4, May 3, 1890, June 11, 1892, June 23, 1894; US Congress, *Labor and Capital* 4: 398. The first issue of the *Pilot* that has survived was August 18, 1883. See also November 3, 1883.

47. *New York Times,* June 9, 10, 1880.

48. *New York Times,* June 3, 5, 6–10, 1880.

49. *New York Times,* June 9, 10, 1880; H. Wayne Morgan, *From Hayes to McKinley: National Party Politics, 1877–1896* (Syracuse, NY: Syracuse University Press, 1969), 95.

50. *Gazette,* February 8, 1887, April 28, 1888.

51. *Pilot,* October 20, 1883.

52. *Weekly Pilot,* August 18, September 1, 1883, October 20 and 27, February 23, April 5, June 21, 1884; see also Thomason's testimony in US Congress, *Labor and Capital* 4: 396–99.

53. *Gazette,* February 10, September 22, 1883, March 1, 1884, January 5, 1885; *Pilot,* April 5, July 3, 1884.

54. *Iron Age,* April 16, 23, 1885; *Gazette,* July 11, August 8, 1885.

55. On the Greenback-Independent coalitions in Alabama, see Matthew Hild, *Greenbackers, Knights of Labor, and Populists: Farmer-Labor Insurgency in the Late-Nineteenth-Century South* (Athens: University of Georgia Press, 2007), 10–12, 31–35; Letwin, *The Challenge of Interracial Unionism,* 57–67; and Samuel L. Webb, *Two-Party Politics in the One-Party South: Alabama's Hill Country, 1874–1920* (Tuscaloosa: University of Alabama Press, 1997), 59–85. In discussing the collapse of the Greenback Labor Party in northern Alabama between 1882 and 1884, Hild makes only passing reference to African American politicians and voters, and no reference to them in Jefferson County (34–35). Daniel Letwin writes that in the coalfields "African Americans were central actors" in the GLP. But he does not detail the activities of these African American leaders, apart from the miner Willis J. Thomas, and was unable to provide information regarding Thomas's "origins" or background. Letwin also notes that, while "the mining district continued to vote for independents during the early 1880s, Greenback activity seems to have ceased." On the one hand, he finds that "interracial cooperation was a compelling imperative in the miners' challenge to the operators and to Bourbon rule." On the other hand, he observes that "interracialism had its limits" and that "the frequency with which Greenback leaders of both races stressed the importance of black-while collaboration highlighted the continuing significance of racial differences, just as it did a determination to overcome them." Letwin, *The Challenge of Interracial Unionism,* 66–67, 217–18n17.

56. *Pilot,* January 12, 1884.

57. *Pilot,* February 9, 1884.

58. *Iron Age,* March 27, 1884; *Pilot,* April 5, 1884.

59. *Iron Age,* March 27, April 10, 1884; *Pilot,* April 5, 1884.

60. *Pilot,* March 22, April 5, May 31, 1884; *Gazette,* April 19, 26, May 3, 24, 31; 1884.

61. *Pilot,* June 7, 14, 1884.

62. *Pilot,* June 7, July 5, 1884; *Gazette,* June 14, July 5, 1884.

63. *Pilot,* June 7, 14, 1884.

64. *Pilot,* June 21, 1884; *Iron Age,* June 26, 1884.

65. *Iron Age,* June 26, 1884.

66. *Iron Age,* July 10, 1884; *Pilot,* July 5, 26, August 2, 1884.

67. *Iron Age,* July 10, 17, 31, August 7, 1884, *Pilot,* July 5, 26, August 2, 1884.

68. *Iron Age,* July 10, 17, 1884; see also July 31, August 7, 1884; *Pilot,* July 5, 26, August 2, 1884.

69. *Pilot,* July 5, 26, August 2, 1884; *Iron Age,* July 10, 17, August 7, 1884, August 17, 1882; *Gazette,* August 9, 1884.

70. *Iron Age,* July 10, 17, August 7, 1884.

71. *Gazette,* August 30, 1884.

72. *Pilot,* June 14, July 5, 1884; see also June 7, August 2, 1884.

73. *Gazette,* September 6, 1884, July 11, 1885.

74. No issues of *Magic City* seem to have survived, and Welch's endorsement is found only in the *Iron Age,* November 27, 1884; US Congress, *Labor and Capital* 4: 379.

75. See chapter 5 of this book.

76. *Gazette,* January 10, 1885; see also April 28, 1883. The white *Iron Age* made no mention of the fire. The *Birmingham City Directory, 1883,* misspelled Fielding's name "Phelan."

77. *Gazette,* February 13, 1892, June 3, 1893; *Truth,* February 7, June 11, 1903, July 29, 1905, March 3, 1906, April 6, 1907, January 11, March 15, September 19, 1908; *Negro American,* October 29, 1887; *Gazette,* January 29, August 20, 27, 1887, June 1, 1889, February 1, 1890.

78. *Iron Age,* January 29, 1885.

79. *Pilot,* July 26, 1884; *Iron Age,* January 29, 1885.

80. *Iron Age,* November 27, 1884, January 29, 1885.

81. *Gazette,* July 26, October 18, 1884, January 5, February 7, November 7, 1885; *Iron Age,* November 27, 1884.

82. Talbert, *The Sons of Allen,* 130; Smith, *A History of the African Methodist Episcopal Church,* 72, 90; "Rev. Isaiah H. Welch, D.D." in Richings, *Album of Negro Educators.*

83. *Gazette,* September 11, 1886; *Negro American,* October 9, 1886.

84. *Negro American,* October 9,1886; *Iron Age,* November 25, 1886; *Gazette,* September 11 and November 27, 1886; *Negro American,* October 9, 1886.

85. *Iron Age,* December 9, 1886. On the election of 1886 in Birmingham, see McKiven, *Iron and Steel,* 78–79. McKiven is correct in observing that "Lane won the election with the support of white and black workingmen."

86. *Iron Age,* December 23, 1886.

87. *Gazette,* December 18, 1886, April 30, July 16, September 4, November 26, 1887, August 11, 1888, December 9, 1890, March 14, 1891, June 9, 1894; Penn, *The Afro-American Press and Its Editors,* 320; *Negro History Bulletin* 5 (January 1942): 92–93.

88. *Iron Age,* October 11, 1888. Also see chapter 1 of this book.

89. *Age-Herald,* March 10, 13, 14, December 22, 1889.

90. *Age-Herald,* March 10, 13, 14, December 22, 1889.

91. *Age-Herald,* March 8, 1889; November 22, 1890.

92. *Iron Age,* October 11, 1888; *Age-Herald,* March 26, December 3, 1889.

93. *Negro American,* December 24, 1887.

94. *Gazette,* November 19, 1887.

95. *Iron Age,* November 16, 1882; *Age-Herald,* January 13, April 4, 1891; and Harris, *Political Power in Birmingham,* 200. See also Stanley B. Greenberg, *Race and State in Capitalist Develop-*

ment: Comparative Perspectives (New Haven, CT: Yale University Press, 1980), 222. Regarding the 1891 vagrancy law, Greenberg writes: "As Carl Harris points out, businessmen helped create a public impression that Blacks were prone to idleness and crime and, at the same, attempted to elaborate the state and local government regulation of vagrancy."

96. US Congress, *Labor and Capital* 4: 326.

97. *News,* November 10, 12, 1888; *Independent,* December 10, 1881; *Iron Age,* January 11, February 1, 1883; *Age-Herald,* October 23, December 23, 1889, April 4, 1891; US Congress, *Labor and Capital* 4: 370. On the later development of the system, see Carl V. Harris, "Reforms in Government Control of Negroes in Birmingham, Alabama, 1890–1920," *Journal of Southern History* 38, no. 4 (November 1972): 567–600. On the corrupt uses of the criminal justice system, particularly at the Jefferson County level, see Curtin, *Black Prisoners,* 206–10.

98. *News,* November 10, 12, 1888; *Independent,* December 10, 1881; *Iron Age,* January 11, February 1, 1883; *Age-Herald,* October 23, December 23, 1889, April 4, 1891; US Congress, *Labor and Capital* 4: 370.

99. US Congress, *Labor and Capital* 4: 456; *Pilot,* August 18, 1883; *Iron Age,* November 22, 1883.

100. Reports by Dr. Jerome Cochrane, state health officer, and Dr. J. B. Gaston, president of the Alabama Board of Health, regarding the New Castle Prison near Pratt Mines, as seen at an inspection, March 10, 1882. Published in *Iron Age,* November 23, 1882; *Pilot,* August 25, 1883. See chapter 6 of this book on conditions in the convict stockade at the New Castle coal mines. See also Curtin, *Black Prisoners,* 73–78, 86–88, 130–31, and 198.

101. *Iron Age,* October 4, 25, December 20, 1883; *Age-Herald,* October 31, 1897; *Iron Age,* November 2, 14, 15, 1887.

102. *Pilot,* August 25, 1883.

9. THE POLITICAL REALM, 1888–1901: EXCLUDING BLACK VOTERS

1. *Gazette,* April 28, February 18, May 19, June 9, July 7, 1888.

2. *Gazette,* November 17, 1888; *Alabama Sentinel,* February 4, 18, 1888.

3. *News,* November 22, 1888; *Gazette,* November 17, 1888.

4. *News,* October 12, 25, November 2, 1888. In 1888 the *Age-Herald* was created through a merger of the daily *Herald* and the weekly *Iron Age.* Harris, *Political Power in Birmingham,* 296–97.

5. *News,* October 26, December 4, 1888; DuBose, *Jefferson County and Birmingham,* 407–8.

6. *News,* November 2, 9, 1888; *Age-Herald,* March 23, 1889. Quotation from Robert Warnock in *Age-Herald,* November 18, 1894.

7. *Age-Herald,* December 3, 1889; see also January 17, March 26, December 22, 1889.

8. *News,* November 9, 1888.

9. *News,* November 10, 12, 1888; *Age-Herald,* November 14, 1888.

10. *News,* November 15, 1888.

11. *Gazette,* February 18, May 19, June 9, July 7, November 17, 1888; *News,* November 24, 1888.

12. *News,* November 23, 26, 24, 28, 30, December 3, 1888.

13. *Gazette,* December 8, 1888.

14. *Alabama Sentinel,* December 8, 1888; *Age-Herald,* December 5, 1888.

15. *News,* November 16, December 4, 1888, *Age-Herald,* December 5, 1888.

16. This timetable is consistent in a general way with the one Morgan Kousser posits for the history of disfranchisement in the South at large, although Kousser focuses on state-level rather than local politics. In Kousser's view, the conclusive disfranchising constitutional conventions and constitutional amendments represented the culminating episodes of an extended process that involved a sustained effort by white Democrats to decrease political activity by African Americans. See J. Morgan Kousser, *Shaping of Southern Politics: Suffrage Restriction and the Establishment of the One-Party South, 1880–1910* (New Haven, CT: Yale University Press, 1974); and Kousser, "Progressivism—For Middle-Class Whites Only: North Carolina Education, 1880–1910," *Journal of Southern History* 46 (May 1980): 169–94. Also see the coda to this book.

17. *Age-Herald,* December 23, 1888.

18. *Age-Herald,* January 8, 1889.

19. *Age-Herald,* December 23, 1888; January 8, 1889.

20. Benjamin Harrison, "Inaugural Address, Monday March 4, 1889," www.presidency.ucsb .edu/documents/inaugural-address-41.

21. *News,* March 7, 8, 1889.

22. *News,* March 8, 1889.

23. *News,* March 16, 1889.

24. *News,* November 9, 12, December 7, 1888; March 27, 1889.

25. *Gazette,* February 2, 1889; *Age-Herald,* January 26, 1889; *New York Times,* December 19, 1888; Stanley P. Hirshson, *Farewell to the Bloody Shirt: Northern Republicans & the Southern Negro, 1877–1893* (Bloomington: Indiana University Press, 1962), 174–75.

26. *Gazette,* October 5, 1889; Hirshson, *Farewell to the Bloody Shirt,* 205–6.

27. *News,* October 2, 3, *Age-Herald,* October 5, 9, 1889.

28. *News,* October 2, 3, 7, 1889.

29. *Age-Herald,* October 5, 6, 7, 1889.

30. *News,* October 2, 3, 7, 8, 9, 1889; *Age-Herald,* October 8, 1889. By 1893, when the force of letter carriers had expanded to sixteen, five of them were Black. Birmingham *City Directory, 1890:* 30–31, *City Directory, 1891:* 572; *City Directory, 1893:* 690.

31. *Gazette,* February 27, April 30, June 11, 1892, June 3, 1893.

32. Hirshson, *Farewell to the Bloody Shirt,* 205–14; Vincent P. DeSantis, *Republicans Face the Southern Question: The New Departure Years, 1877–1897* (Baltimore: Johns Hopkins Press, 1959), 198–206.

33. *New York Times,* July 24, 1890; Hirshson, *Farewell to the Bloody Shirt,* 225–26.

34. *Gazette,* August 16, 1890.

35. *Gazette,* October 4, 1890.

36. Vernon L. Wharton, *The Negro in Mississippi, 1865–1890* (Chapel Hill: University of North Carolina Press, 1947), 199–215; Albert D. Kirwan, *Revolt of the Rednecks: Mississippi Politics, 1876–1925* (Lexington: University of Kentucky Press, 1951), 58–84.

37. *Gazette,* October 4, 1890; Hirshson, *Farewell to the Bloody Shirt,* 231–35; DeSantis, *Republicans Face the Southern Question,* 206–15.

38. On the organization of white workingmen within the Democratic Party in the early 1890s, see McKiven, *Iron and Steel,* 81–83.

NOTES TO PAGES 208–215

39. For analysis of the "Elements" and the election of 1894, see Harris, *Political Power in Birmingham*, 36, 60, 66–74; and McKiven, *Iron and Steel*, 83–88 and 187n28. In 1977, Harris saw city politics as less polarized along the class lines dividing whites than McKiven did in 1995, but both agree that, in McKiven's words, "white workers . . . remained in the Democratic Party and saw the reform ticket as not only somewhat antagonistic toward them but also a threat to white supremacy" (*Iron and Steel*, 187n28).

40. This discussion of the "two police forces" relies heavily on the excellent account in McKiven, *Iron and Steel*, 84–86.

41. *News*, September 2, 1890; *Age-Herald*, November 8, 21, 1890, February 25, March 26, 29, 30, 31, April 26, 1892, November 20, 1894. On the background and career of T. W. Walker, see Lynne B. Feldman, *A Sense of Place: Birmingham's Black Middle-Class Community, 1890–1930* (Tuscaloosa: University of Alabama Press, 1999), 82–84, 102–5. Feldman details Walker's career in business and organized religion but does not discuss his political interests.

42. Birmingham *Times*, September 12, 1894.

43. Quotation from McKiven, *Iron and Steel*, 86.

44. On Comer, Rhodes, and the formation of progressivism, see Hackney, *Populism to Progressivism*, 15, 124–25, and 127–33. For comparisons between the progressivism of Comer et al. and varieties elsewhere in the nation, see *Populism to Progressivism*, 311–31 and 329–32. For a critique of Comer's progressivism and an argument that the Alabama Populists were more deserving of being described as "progressive," see Webb, *Two-Party Politics*, 219–20.

45. Bigelow, "Birmingham," 208; *Negro American Press*, January 20, 1894; *Age-Herald*, November 20, December 2, 1894.

46. *Age-Herald*, November 13, 1894, *Independent*, November 15, 1894.

47. *Wide Awake*, November 17, 1894, qtd. in *Age-Herald*, November 20, 1894.

48. Birmingham *Times*, April 13, 1898, January 18, 1899; *Independent*, December 20, 1894.

49. *Age-Herald*, November 20, 1894.

50. *Age-Herald*, November 20, 1894.

51. *Age-Herald*, November 18, 24, 25, 28, 1894; *Independent*, November 22, 1894.

52. *Age-Herald*, November 27, December 1, 1894.

53. *Age-Herald*, December 5, 6, 1894; *Birmingham Times*, December 5, 12, 1894.

54. *Birmingham Times*, December 5, 1894.

55. *News*, December 5, 1894, qtd. in *Times*, December 12, 1894.

56. *Independent*, December 20, 1894.

57. *Times*, December 26, 1894.

58. See chapter 4 of this book.

59. *State-Herald*, November 15, 1896.

60. *Times*, April 29, 1896; *State-Herald*, November 15, 1896.

61. *Pilot*, September 15, November 3, 1883; *Negro American*, October 9, 1886; *Negro-American Press*, January 20, February 3, 24, May 5, 12, September 15, 1894; *News*, January 2, 1895; *Gazette*, February 8, 1890, May 14, 1892; Bigelow, "Birmingham," 215–16; Arthur Harold Parker, *A Dream That Came True* (Birmingham: Industrial High School, 1932–33), 26; Bond, *Negro Education in Alabama*, 169.

62. On Hudson's shareholding in the bank, see Feldman, *A Sense of Place*, 93.

63. For an excellent discussion of the career of Pettiford, see Feldman, *A Sense of Place*, 90–100. In 1894 Pettiford had reached out beyond the progressive business community, cooperating with Henry F. DeBardeleben during the coal strike to discourage the unionization of Black workers. See Feldman, *A Sense of Place*, 19.

64. *Gazette*, February 16, 1889; *News*, November 25, 1896.

65. *State-Herald*, November 18, 28, December 2, 1896; *News*, November 20, 25, December 1, 2, 1896.

66. On Birmingham city elections and politics from 1896 to 1921, see Harris, *Political Power in Birmingham*, 70–95.

67. Historian Daniel Letwin provides a discussion of the relationship between the labor movement in the coal fields and the political movements led by the Southern Farmers' Alliance and the Populist Party. He argues that the "public voice" of the miners was "suffused with populist sensibilities," and finds that in the 1894 election "most black miners" in Jefferson County "showed a Populist leaning comparable to that of white miners," despite "the Populists' ambivalent stance on the rights of African Americans." Letwin, *The Challenge of Interracial Unionism*, 95–116, quotations on 95 and 111.

68. For overviews of the complex politics of the disfranchisement movement in Alabama, see Hackney, *Populism to Progressivism*, 147–229; Perman, *Struggle for Mastery*, 173–94; Feldman, *The Disfranchisement Myth;* and McMillan, *Constitutional Development in Alabama*. The quotation of Booker T. Washington is from the *Advertiser*, December 17, 1898, cited in Hackney, *Populism to Progressivism*, 163.

69. *Times*, March 15, 1899; McMillan, *Constitutional Development in Alabama*, 257.

70. *Times*, April 19, 1899.

71. *Times*, April 19, January 11, 1899.

72. *News*, January 19, 1900.

73. *Age-Herald*, March 15, 20, 22, 1901.

74. *Age-Herald*, April 24, 26, 28, May 29, 1901; Bond, *Negro Education in Alabama*, 168–70; McMillan, *Constitutional Development in Alabama*, 263. For a discussion of Booker T. Washington's role, and the reception his petition received in the convention, see R. Volney Riser, *Defying Disfranchisement: Black Voting Rights Activism in the Jim Crow South, 1890–1908* (Baton Rouge: Louisiana State University Press, 2010), 115–17. On the activist protests that followed those of Washington, see Riser, *Defying Disfranchisement*, 117–21.

75. McMillan, *Constitutional Development in Alabama*, 263–82; Riser, *Defying Disfranchisement*, 121–24, which includes a description of some of Washington's behind-the-scenes lobbying with convention moderates.

76. *Age-Herald*, September 25, 26, 27, 1901; Riser, *Defying Disfranchisement*, 133–34.

77. *News*, April 17, 1900.

78. *Age-Herald*, November 13, 12, 1901.

79. Birmingham *Times*, November 22, 1901.

80. McMillan, *Constitutional Development in Alabama*, 350–52; Riser, *Defying Disfranchisement*, 136–37; Kousser, *Shaping of Southern Politics*, 165–71.

81. After their ratification defeat in 1901, some Black activists in Alabama went on to participate in constitutional challenges to disfranchisement. The multistate effort that resulted led to

three US Supreme Court cases, the first of which was *Giles v. Harris* (1903). Jackson W. Giles, a US Post Office worker who became president of the Colored Men's Suffrage Association of Alabama, brought the suit after being rebuffed in registering five thousand Black voters in Montgomery. In this case, the Supreme Court ruled that Giles's only recourse rested with Congress or the Alabama legislature. On the activism of Giles and other African Americans after 1901, see Riser, *Defying Disfranchisement*, esp. 1–9 and 138–254.

CODA: HISTORIANS AND THE INTERPLAY OF CLASS, RACE, AND CASTE

1. Woodward, *Origins of the New South*.

2. Woodward, *Strange Career of Jim Crow* (1955), 61–65.

3. Woodward, *Strange Career of Jim Crow*, 60–64, 78–82.

4. Woodward, "*Strange Career* Critics," 862; Rabinowitz, *Race Relations in the Urban South*.

5. Rabinowitz, *Race Relations in the Urban South*, 333–39.

6. Cell, *The Highest Stage of White Supremacy*, 14–20, 103–4, 169–70.

7. Woodward, "*Strange Career* Critics," 862–64.

8. Kousser, *Shaping of Southern Politics;* and "Progressivism—For Middle-Class Whites Only," 169–94.

9. Woodward, "*Strange Career* Critics," 862–64.

10. Kousser, *Shaping of Southern Politics*, 238, 247, 257–65; Cell, *The Highest Stage of White Supremacy*, 14, 20, 104, 136–42, 169–70.

11. Cell, *The Highest Stage of White Supremacy*, 131–70.

12. Woodward, "*Strange Career* Critics," 864.

13. This book reinforces the criticism by George Fredrickson of historians who "reduce race to epiphenomenal status, making it simply part of the superstructure that legitimizes the power of the ruling class," and follows Fredrickson's admonition to avoid holding only white elites responsible for intensifying racism. "A crucial task that remains in considering postbellum race relations," Fredrickson said, "is to account fully for the intense racism often manifested by less privileged whites." George Fredrickson, "The Historiography of Post-Emancipation Southern Race Relations: Retrospect and Prospect," chapter 10 in his *The Arrogance of Race*, 156 and 157. Fredrickson provided international context by suggesting the description of the post-emancipation South as a *Herrenvolk* society, "one in which people of color however numerous or acculturated they may be, are treated as permanent aliens or outsiders," and "a society in which political and social equality was prized by white males on the understanding that equal citizenship was the prerogative of the master race." Fredrickson, *White Supremacy*, xi–xii, and *The Comparative Imagination: On the History of Racism, Nationalism and Social Movements* (Berkeley: University of California Press, 1997), 107. See also *The Black Image in the White Mind*, 61–64.

14. W. E. B. Du Bois, *Dusk of Dawn: An Essay Toward an Autobiography of a Race Concept* (New York: Harcourt Brace, 1940), rpt. in *Du Bois's Writings*, 649.

15. Du Bois, *Dusk of Dawn*, 704.

16. Du Bois, *Black Reconstruction in America* (New York: Harcourt Brace, 1935), 694–95. Du Bois described the benefits for poorer whites of their membership in the dominant caste as "a sort of public and psychological wage." *Black Reconstruction in America*, 700–701.

17. Du Bois, *Dusk of Dawn*, 650–51.

18. John Dollard, *Caste and Class in a Southern Town* (1937; 3rd ed., New York: Doubleday Anchor Books, 1949). Dollard used social psychology to understand how whites enhanced their self-esteem by demanding protocols of deference from Blacks. During the 1930s, important anthropologists also studied the culture of race relations in the South through the lens of caste. See Allison Davis, Burleigh B. Gardner, and Mary R. Gardner, *Deep South: A Social Anthropological Study of Caste and Class* (Chicago: University of Chicago Press, 1941), and Hortense Powdermaker, *After Freedom: A Cultural Study in the Deep South* (Madison: University of Wisconsin, 1939).

19. Dollard, *Caste and Class in a Southern Town*, 61–63; W. Lloyd Warner, "American Caste and Class," *American Journal of Sociology* 42 (September 1936): 234–37.

20. David Levering Lewis, *W. E. B. Du Bois: The Fight for Equality and the American Century, 1919–1963* (New York: Henry Holt and Co., 2000), 444.

APPENDIX: SOCIAL PSYCHOLOGY, COLOR LINES, AND THE BLUMER MODEL

1. For the key works of Blumer, see "Race Prejudice as a Sense of Group-Position," 3–7; Blumer, "The Future of the Color Line," in J. C. McKinney and E. T. Thompson, eds., *The South in Continuity and Change* (Durham, NC: Duke University Press, 1965), 322–35.

2. Blumer's color line functioned like the interaction boundary cultural anthropologist Fredrik Barth defined in his "Introduction" to *Ethnic Groups and Boundaries: The Social Organization of Cultural Difference* (Bergen-Oslo: George Allen & Unwin, 1969), 10–15. In 1958 Blumer anticipated Barth by describing an in-group "sense of proprietary claim" to "the right to exclusive membership in given institutions such as schools, churches and recreational institutions" and about an in-group sense of proprietary "claim to certain areas of intimacy and privacy." Blumer, "Race Prejudice as a Sense of Group Position," 4.

3. Herbert Blumer, *Symbolic Interactionism: Perspective and Method* (Englewood Cliffs, NJ: Prentice-Hall, 1969), 3, 4, 10, 15–17, 49.

4. See Bobo, "Prejudice as Group Position," 445–72. One of the rare historians to have cited Blumer was George Fredrickson. See his "White Images of Black Slaves," 206–15, in which he suggests that "a widely held and publicly sanctioned stereotype, such as Sambo, can . . . be seen as a social and ideological 'norm,' reflecting what Herbert Blumer has called a 'sense of group position.'" Later in the essay, Fredrickson wrote: "As the work of Herbert Blumer has suggested, a relatively benign group stereotype is likely to be recast or reinterpreted when a dominant group perceives a genuine and immediate threat to its 'sense of position.' In such circumstances active racial hostility comes to the fore" (210 and 214).

5. See note 1, above. In figure 1, I have modified Blumer's model to include the public school in each color line, since the school necessarily incorporated social and political and economic functions. However, when southern whites thought of the public school in the context of race relations, they always regarded it as an extension of the family and consistently categorized it within the inner social color line.

6. See note 1, above. My summary discussion uses some of Lawrence Bobo's language in his powerful 1999 integration and elaboration of Blumer's group-position theory of prejudice. See Bobo, "Prejudice as Group Position," 449, 454–55.

7. See Barth, "Introduction," in Barth, ed., *Ethnic Groups and Boundaries*, 10–15; Marilynn B. Brewer and Donald T. Campbell, *Ethnocentrism and Intergroup Attitudes: East African Evidence* (New York: Wiley, 1976), 133–39; Richard D. Ashmore and Frances K. Del Boca, "Conceptual Approaches to Stereotypes and Stereotyping," in David L. Hamilton, ed., *Cognitive Processes in Stereotyping and Intergroup Behavior* (Hillsdale, NJ: Erlbaum, 1981), 1–35; and Thomas F. Pettigrew, "Extending the Stereotype Concept" in Hamilton, ed., *Cognitive Processes in Stereotyping and Intergroup Behavior*, 304–5. The word "stereotype" first entered the language of social thought in 1922 when Walter Lippmann defined it to mean "pictures in our heads" which shape and often distort our perceptions of groups of people. See Lippmann, *Public Opinion* (New York: Harcourt, Brace, Jovanovich, 1922), 1, 10, 55, 65, 72.

8. Some of Tajfel's experiments were called "minimal group experiments," referring to the fact that in the experiments groups were created based on very minimal criteria, so that between the in-groups and out-groups created there was no previous history, no instrumental factors, no competition for resources, and no other realistic conflict. Henri Tajfel, "Social Stereotypes and Social Groups," in Tajfel, *Human Groups and Social Categories: Studies in Social Psychology* (Cambridge, UK: Cambridge University Press, 1981), 145; Tajfel, "Cognitive Aspects of Prejudice," *Journal of Social Issues* 25 (1969): 80, 81, 91, 95–96; Tajfel, *Differentiation between Social Groups* (London: Academic Press, 1978), 10–11, 77–81; Tajfel and John C. Turner, "The Social Identity Theory of Intergroup Behavior," in S. Worchel and W. G. Austin, eds., *The Psychology of Intergroup Relations* (Chicago: Nelson-Hall, 1986), 6–24; Penelope J. Oakes et al., *Stereotyping and Social Reality* (Oxford, UK: Blackwell, 1994), 6–7, 90. See also Margaret Wetherell, *Identities, Groups, and Social Issues* (London: Sage, 1996), 194; Thomas F. Pettigrew, "Extending the Stereotype Concept," 312–13; Pettigrew, "Three Issues in Ethnicity: Boundaries, Deprivations, and Perceptions," in J. Milton Yinger and Stephen J. Cutler, eds., *Major Social Issues: A Multidisciplinary View* (New York: Free Press, 1978), 47; Ashmore and Del Boca, "Conceptual Approaches to Stereotypes and Stereotyping," 29; Mark Snyder and Peter Miene, "On the Functions of Stereotypes and Prejudice," in Mark P. Zanna and James M. Olson, eds., *The Psychology of Prejudice: The Ontario Symposium* (Hillsdale, NJ: Erlbaum, 1994), vol. 7: 33–54.

9. Tajfel, "Social Stereotypes and Social Groups," 148; David L. Hamilton and Tina K. Trolier, "Stereotypes and Stereotyping: An Overview of the Cognitive Approach," in John F. Dovidio and Samuel Gaertner, eds., *Prejudice, Discrimination, and Racism* (New York: Academic Press, 1986), 129; Wetherell, *Identities, Groups, and Social Issues*, 190–91; Michael A. Hogg and Dominic Abrams, *Social Identifications: A Social Psychology of Intergroup Relations and Group Processes* (London: Routledge, 1988), 20–21; P. F. Secord, W. Bevin, and B. Katz, "The Negro Stereotype and Perceptual Accentuation," *Journal of Abnormal and Social Psychology* 53 (1956): 78–83; and P. F. Secord, ""Stereotyping and Favorableness in the Perception of Negro Faces," *Journal of Abnormal and Social Psychology* 59 (1959): 309–15.

10. Pettigrew, "Three Issues in Ethnicity," 37–39; John Duckitt, *The Social Psychology of Prejudice* (Westport, CT: Praeger, 1992), 153–57; L. D. Ross, "The Intuitive Psychologist and His Shortcomings: Distortions is the Attribution Process," in L. Berkowitz, ed., *Advances in Experimental Social Psychology* (New York: Academic Press, 1977), vol. 10: 174–220.

11. Thomas F. Pettigrew, "The Ultimate Attribution Error: Extending Allport's Cognitive Analysis of Prejudice," *Personality and Social Psychology Bulletin* 5 (1979): 461–76; Pettigrew,

"Three Issues in Ethnicity," 37–44; Hamilton and Trolier, "Stereotypes and Stereotyping," 131–33; Duckitt, *Social Psychology of Prejudice,* 153–57.

12. See Snyder and Miene, "On the Functions of Stereotypes and Prejudice," 46–50.

13. Bobo, "Prejudice as Group Position," 445–72; Bobo, "Whites' Opposition to Busing: Symbolic Racism or Realistic Group Conflict?" *Journal of Personality and Social Psychology* 45 (1983): 1196–1210; Bobo, "Group Conflict, Prejudice, and the Paradox of Contemporary Racial Attitudes," in P. A. Katz and D. A. Taylor, eds., *Eliminating Racism: Profiles in Controversy* (New York: Plenum, 1988), 85–114.

14. Blumer, "Race Prejudice as a Sense of Group-Position," 3–6.

15. Regarding these experiments, see S. Alexander Haslam et al., "Stereotyping and Social Influence: The Mediation of Stereotype Applicability and Sharedness by the Views of In-Group and Out-Group Members," *British Journal of Social Psychology* 35 (1996): 369–97; Gretchen B. Sechrist and Charles Stangor, "Perceived Consensus Influences Intergroup Behavior and Stereotype Accessibility," *Journal of Personality and Social Psychology* 80 (2001): 645–54; Charles Stangor, Gretchen B. Sechrist, and John T. Jost, "Changing Racial Beliefs by Providing Consensus Information," *Personality and Social Psychology Bulletin* 27 (2000): 486–96.

16. S. Alexander Haslam et al., "The Group as a Basis for Emergent Stereotype Consensus," *European Review of Social Psychology* 8 (1998): 203–39; Micah S. Thompson, Charles M. Judd, and Bernadette Park, "The Consequences of Communicating Social Stereotypes," *Journal of Experimental Social Psychology* 36 (2000): 570–71, 595; Janet B. Rushcher, Elizabeth Yost Hammer, and Elliott D. Hammer, "Forming Shared Impressions through Conversation: An Adaptation of the Continuum Model," *Personality and Social Psychology Bulletin* 22 (1996): 705–20; Yoshihisa Kashima, "Maintaining Cultural Stereotypes in the Serial Reproduction Narratives," *Personality and Social Psychology Bulletin* 26 (2000): 594–604; S. Alexander Haslam, "Stereotyping and Social Influence: Foundations of Stereotype Consensus," in Russell Spears et al., *The Social Psychology of Stereotyping and Group Life* (Oxford, UK: Blackwell, 1997), 119–43; Naomi Ellemers and Ad van Knippenberg, "Stereotyping in Social Context," in Spears et al., *The Social Psychology of Stereotyping,* 229–30; Stephen Reicher, Nick Hopkins, and Susan Condor, "Stereotype Construction as a Strategy of Influence," in Spears et al., *The Social Psychology of Stereotyping,* 94–118.

17. Blumer, "Race Prejudice as a Sense of Group Position," 3–4.

18. Thomas C. Holt, "Marking: Race, Race-Making, and the Writing of History," *American Historical Review* 100 (February 1995): 7.

INDEX

Note: page numbers in *italics* refer to maps; those followed by "n" indicate endnotes.

CPSIA information can be obtained
at www.ICGtesting.com
Printed in the USA
LVHW101602010223
738413LV00003B/73